BELIEVING IN ACTION

Dedicated especially to the memory of
Jean Browne (Calcutta)
Kathleen O'Hanrahan (Zambia)
James O'Toole CSSp (Yemen)
Diarmuid Cashman (Tanzania)
Patrick O'Connor (Mozambique)
Dr Elizabeth O'Brien (Bangladesh)
Valerie Place (Somalia)
Peter Warren (Tanzania)

who died while serving overseas with Concern
in the fields indicated.

Believing in Action
The first thirty years of Concern 1968–1998

Tony Farmar

A. & A. Farmar

British Library cataloguing in Publication Data.
A CIP catalogue record for this book is available from the British Library.

Cover design by Alice Campbell.
Cover photograph by Pieternella Pieterse.
The photographs on pages 98–123 are from the Concern Archive, with the exception of those on pages 99–103 (top) which are courtesy John and Kay O'Loughlin Kennedy and p 112 which is courtesy Liam Burke.
Text edited, designed and set by A. & A. Farmar.
Printed and bound by ColourBooks.

ISBN 1-899047-81-6

First published in 2002
by
A. & A. Farmar
Beech House
78 Ranelagh Village
Dublin 6
Ireland
Tel: 353 1 496 3625
Fax: 353 1 497 0107
Email: afarmar@iol.ie
Web: farmarbooks.com

Contents

Preface   vi

Foreword *Séamus Heaney*   1

Prologue: Concern and the modern face of
humanitarian aid   4

1. Origins in Biafra   9
2. New countries, new roles   29
3. People to people   41
4. The field directors take charge   65
5. The end of the beginning   82

Scenes from thirty years   98

6. Famine returns to Ethiopia   124
7. After twenty years   144
8. Killing fields   163
9. Making a difference   183
10. A New Era   200

Epilogue   212

Appendixes

1. Concern's core values   214
2. Income and expenditure 1968–1998   216
3. Field directors 1972–2002   217
4. List of volunteers 1968–2001   219

Notes and references   232

Index   240

Preface

In the 1980s and 1990s Concern ran a mother and baby clinic in Kabele (local authority district) 37 of Addis Ababa, Ethiopia. This was one of the poorest parts of town, a violent, impoverished and ill-resourced place. The small bribes of cooking oil and grain that Concern provided to encourage women to bring their babies were very welcome. And if some of the oil was subsequently sold in the market, what did that matter?

One day a new mother came into the clinic, with a baby apparently suckling happily away. The baby was weighed and checked and treated, as usual, and the woman went happily off with her oil and wheat. She returned regularly for a few weeks. Then word seeped into the clinic that the baby was not hers at all, but belonged to a woman from a neighbouring Kabele.

The two women had fallen out, and by way of revenge, the real mother had spilled the beans. (This was no light matter—Marxist regimes do not take kindly to attempts to swindle the state.) Objectively Concern couldn't feel particularly cheated—the money after all was not given by the donors to benefit this Kabele or that, but the people as a whole. But official face had to be preserved, and the woman came no more to the clinic.

As well as illustrating the human conditions of Concern's work, this story casts light on this book. During the years the clinic was run hundreds of mothers and their babies were looked after. Sometimes these were happy, fat thriving babies—more often, because of the conditions in Kabele 37, they were listless, sick and hungry. The resources of western medicine could often restore some health, for the time being at least. But of all the women and babies treated the only one who survives for history is the fraudster who was so ill-advised as to fall out with her friend.

Ideally, the experience of the hundreds of expatriate and especially local workers and the thousands of beneficaries of their work should be at the core of the agency's history. We would like to know what the hundreds of people who were fed and looked after in camps and clinics, those who worked on engineering projects in the heat of Yemen or Bangladesh, or in urban rehabilitation projects in Ethiopia and Burundi thought about Concern. No doubt some records survive, and no doubt in theory it would be possible to decipher from Amharic, Khmer or Bengali the names, and to find them and to see how they fared. This might have been possible but unfortunately was not practical.

So this history has to see the world largely through Dublin eyes, and through Irish reports from the field. It is therefore primarily a view from the centre, where the organisation's workers held on course the troika of forces that make Concern work—donors, staff and beneficiaries. The centre was also the place where the future policy and plans of the organisation were evolved, by men and women passionately concerned to do the best for the beneficiaries with the donors' contributions. One result is that, as in conventional histories centred on kings and cabinets, there are more battles and debates in this account than ever affected the work of field volunteers or fundraisers.

The basic source I have relied on is the Concern archive, in which minutes of meetings of the council and other documents have been preserved. There are also evaluations and annual reports from the fields; interviews with key personnel; contemporary Concern publications—newsletters, fund-rasing information booklets and so on; and finally books and articles on general aid and humanitarian matters. Only the last have been referenced in detail. Other sources are mentioned in such a way that it is possible, with access to the archive, to discover the source of information or quotations.

Concern is particularly lucky in being able to include in its archive the cache of materials kept by John O'Loughlin Kennedy and his wife Kay who were so intimately involved in the establishment and early days of the agency. Without their careful preservation of materials the early chapters would have been thin indeed.

Particular thanks to Áine Fay and Imran Ansari in Bangladesh, Paul Sherlock and Ellen Pieterse in Ethiopia and Anne O'Mahony in Nairobi for their hospitality during field visits. In the Concern office Kevin Byrne, Eithne Healy and Lucy Deering were especially helpful. Finally, Jack Finucane and Tom Arnold were my 'minders' during the research and writing, first of all on trips to Ethiopia and Bangladesh respectively and then throughout the actual writing. I hope they remain as friends.

Tony Farmar
November 2002

Foreword

SÉAMUS HEANEY, PATRON

In the opening chapters of this vividly instructive book—at once a presentation of the history of Concern and an exploration of its developing philosophy and policies, a cross between a thriller and a position paper—Tony Farmar tells the story of the *Columcille*, a ship the organisation acquired in the early days of its operations. The name of this vessel would have reminded everyone in Ireland of a missionary who had found his calling as a result of a local war, one whose success had turned him from a visionary into an administrator, one whose commitments were beyond the sea but who remained answerable to ties, at once dynastic and affectionate, on the home ground. The purchasers of the craft were obviously interested in getting their hands on a facility, but in the process they had found themselves a symbol: much that was true of the 6th-century prince of Tirconnell has been true of Concern. Even the fact that the *Columcille* had to be got rid of later on had symbolic meaning, since it signalled the organisation's readiness to make new adjustments in new conditions in order tomove in pursuit of primary objectives.

From beginning to end, as the strategic review of 1998 made clear, the core objective has been the alleviation and ultimately the elimination of 'absolute poverty', a state in which people are 'at worst on the verge of death because of their inability to meet essential physical needs and at best struggling to supply themselves with food, clean water, shelter and health'. But this fundamental aim leads those who pursue it into regions that often lie equidistant from the Gap of Danger and the Slough of Despond. They and the poor they serve typically must negotiate conditions worsened by military and political crises, in contexts where human life, never mind human rights, count for little and where the normal regulating forces of shame and

[1]

civility have lost all effectiveness. What is astonishing is that this history of more than 30 years' first-hand experience in the compounds and the killing fields turns out to be such a bracing and hope-inducing read.

Concern stands as a magnificent answer to all the negative thoughts conjured up by the words Biafra, Bangladesh, Ethiopia, Sudan, Cambodia, Somalia, Rwanda, to all that is dismaying about the materialism of the developed word, all that causes our belief in the reality of disinterested effort and altruistic vision to falter. In the course of these pages the discouragement implicit in the names of those stricken countries is powerfully countered by the names that recur in the Concern story—above all the legendary names of its founders, but equally the names of those who have led and those who have volunteered, the 'trads' and the 'mods', the 'relief people' and the 'development people', those on the ground and those in the head office.

As Patron of Concern, I have been honoured to speak at several meetings of its sponsors and supporters. Like anyone faced with the evidence of so much unstinted giving of body and spirit, work that requires at one moment heroic courage and at another a gift for facing the humdrum, I am constantly at a loss for words that will match the valiancy of the effort. There is immense practicality about the jobs that Concern personnel do in the field, a readiness to combine state of the art methods with the primitive stand-bys: they will use the resources of the e-mail, for example, but they won't ever forget about the reliablity of the donkey. And yet this constant attention to doing good simply by getting things done, to providing bread rather than circuses, to getting into the refugee camps rather than seeking a place at the conference table, this can-do aspect of Concern should not mask from us the powerful idealism that underlies its operations.

In considering the work of aid organisations, we have become used to the language of management and accountancy, to monitoring efficiency levels and political implications, the exit strategies and the roll-on effects. Yet the idiom of the board room or the diplomatic communiqué or the post-colonial seminar is ultimately inadequate to cope with the dimensions of the overall thing. Like others vitally involved in the realities of a world where the disastrous is often more apparent than the delightful—people, for example, with religious or artistic interests—Concern has to keep delivering its own answer to the big question: to what end are we here on earth together? So it is no surprise that whenever I try to say something about the organisation, I invariably end up with a language that derives from the idioms of religion and poetry.

For a start, there's the famous line that W. H. Auden wrote in 1939 in the face of world war: 'We must love one another or die'. Even more appropriately, perhaps, there's the line as he revised it: 'We must love one another *and* die.' There's the old question and answer I learned in my catechism at primary school: 'Who is my neighbour? My neighbour is all mankind.' And there's Hugh MacDiarmid's definition of poetry: it is human existence come to life. Another useful statement about the purpose of literature applicable to Concern was made by the late Miroslav Holub, who compared the work of writers in the body politic to the work of the immunity system in the physical body. Like the immunity system, art work and aid work have a salutary purpose, they are evidence that we are here for good but no guarantee that good will always carry the day.

In future, anyone seeking to say something about the meaning or motives or achievements of Concern will find this book invaluable. It is as informative as it is inspirational. Tony Farmar has a gift for wise generalisation, a wonderful instinct for the telling detail or revealing statistic and a fair way of letting different personalities reveal themselves and the values they espouse. This is no dutiful, in-house paean by an organisation to its own virtues. It is a window on to the times we have lived through, often heartlifting, as often heartbreaking. A testimony to those who have chosen to live at that high level where they are bound to keep facing the challenge—clear, noble and exhausting—that W. B. Yeats formulated as follows: to hold in a single thought reality and justice.

Prologue: Concern and the modern face of humanitarian aid

4 March 2001: For ten days rebel incursions into Bujumbura, the capital of Burundi, have holed up Concern expatriate staff in their compound. Rebel troops, anxious to make their presence felt at international negotiations taking place in Arusha, Tanzania, now occupy perhaps a quarter of the city. Every night rockets and shells attack the presidential palace. Unfortunately, the Concern compound is not far away, and no one has great faith in the militia's accuracy. Four of the five expatriates have moved in their bedding and basic belongings. Emergency water supplies are set up, and evacuation plans made. Every day some of the two hundred local staff come in with a new crop of rumours—a few days ago it was said that piles of Kalashnikovs had been found in roadside ditches, waiting to be picked up by rebel soldiers passing themselves off as refugees. Some staff and their families have moved into the compound to be out of the zone occupied by the militia rebels.

Just outside Bujumbura the rebels are turning back trucks carrying food and other aid into the country. The government encourages the establishment of parties of local vigilantes. An 8 pm curfew is imposed, and the international community is given strict warnings not to talk to the press. Shellfire can be heard all night in the town. Nobody sleeps for more than four or five hours. The lives of Concern staff are at risk—perhaps the expatriates will have to be pulled out of the country.

This is a classic situation, where the needs and rights of an impoverished people are routinely, and often brutally, subordinated to military and political exigencies. The news breaks just as the agency's regional director, Jack Finucane, is on a scheduled visit to Ethiopia. He is now faced with a question that often occurs—has the time come when the programme is just too dangerous, when the gains are outweighed by the risks, when expatriate staff should be pulled out? The problem is complicated by the dense network of relationships created in modern humanitarian work—with the beneficiaries, who by definition need what Concern is providing; with the local staff, whose jobs and lives are at risk; with other NGOs (non-governmental organisations), who, if they choose to stay, may have to take on Concern's commitments; with the government, who will not be keen to be told publicly that their country is too dangerous to work in; and finally with the donors to the various projects, including the EU, UN agencies, any number of national and international agencies and, indeed, ordinary people up and down Ireland. All these interests have to be balanced against the responsibility to protect the staff.

Information about the situation changes hourly. It arrives by telephone and e-mail from head office in Dublin and from Bujumbura itself. As the crisis progresses, sometimes the staff are optimistic, sometimes less so. Auriol Miller, the acting country director, is new to the post, and is doing her best to see officials from the government and other NGOs to assess the situation. Most of the other aid agencies are pulling out and, as it happens, the government is quite understanding.

Burundi is a badly impoverished place, with a GDP of a mere $159 per head and an economy ground down by civil war and UN sanctions against its government. Its people do need whatever help the international community can provide, but there is no question of simply playing the Lady Bountiful. NGOs must obtain visas, licences and permissions from suspicious bureaucrats. Having identified specific areas of need, Concern had applied for permission to establish a programme to look after the health of some 70,000 people. This required two approvals, first from the Ministry of Cooperation and External Affairs, and then from the technical ministry, in this case the Ministry of Health. However, an increasing dislike of NGOs in Burundi (and in the Great Lakes region as a whole) had led to delays. Furthermore, the Tutsi officials were particularly unenthusiastic about Concern, knowing of its work with Hutus in neighbouring Rwanda.

The first hurdle, registration with the Ministry of Cooperation and External Affairs, had taken three months. Then officials in the Ministry of Health presented further obstacles. They claimed that Concern and the other NGOs were not really humanitarian, but had two secret reasons for coming to Burundi—to access local funds to maintain expatriate jobs, and to report on political, economic and human rights issues to their governments. Concern's wish to work in Hutu-dominated areas had not speeded the registration (another NGO looking to work in a predominantly Tutsi province, got approval in a few weeks).

Another typical feature was the multiplicity of NGOs in the area, and the consequent need for the government to control and monitor their activities. Concern had been the 43rd agency to be approved for work in the country. Each NGO had to be registered with the ministries, and registration could easily be withdrawn, as happened to Médicins sans Frontières (MSF) after a press release was rather too outspoken about the regroupement (forced villagisation) process. At last, after months of frustration, in February 1998 a convention had been signed with the Ministry of Health, and, subject to strict security precautions, Concern's various programmes were allowed to go ahead.

Now, in March 2001, Concern has five expatriate workers in Burundi, none, as it happens, Irish: three are from England—Auriol Miller, acting country director, Richard Hamilton, programme manager, Peter Sargent, finance and administration—and two are from France—Max Delville, logistician, and Laurent Hailait, food security. The programme is multi-faceted, and includes the equipping of nine health centres, a vaccination programme, supply of seeds and tools to 21,000 families, community self-help groups, the 'Young Shoulders' programme for families with dead or missing parents now headed by the eldest child, and work in the regroupement camps where 350,000 people had been forcibly moved from their villages as part of the government's scorched earth attack on the rebels. Total expenditure in 1999 was £1.6m, making it Concern's fifth most expensive programme.

This would not be the first time rebel activity had forced the agency to pull out of the troubled country. In 1994 and 1995 Concern had a programme of providing health and sanitation services to 30,000 Rwandan refugees in Kirundo (a province in the north of the country jutting into Rwanda). During that time two expatriate workers (working for other agencies) were killed. Racial attacks, killings and abuse continued; ambushes were commonplace. In August 1994 Mary Murphy, a Concern nurse, had the horrific experience of being caught under gunfire in a UNHCR house. While she tried to help a local colleague, who had been shot through the abdomen, more gunshots poured into the room. Lying on the floor she gripped his hand; then, as suddenly as it had started, the shooting stopped and a chilling silence replaced the previous deafening clamour. Would they shoot again, or perhaps throw in hand grenades? As they waited, her colleague quietly died, holding her hand. Later that day the Concern team formed a convoy with MSF and drove to Bujumbura. (A few months later Mary Murphy was back in Kirundo, where her work necessitated her driving past the house every day, forcing her mind back to that night and the dead colleague.) In 1995 Concern expatriates had retreated to Rwanda six times in six months before it was finally decided to hand over its operations to an African NGO called Intervention Humanitaire Africaine.

Now the staff are again at risk because of military activity. By the middle of the week Jack has made his decision, and advises the chief executive, David Begg, in Dublin that temporary withdrawal is the sensible course. David agrees. However, before the expatriates leave they ensure that seed stock is distributed before the rainy season. Local staff are told of the situation, and of the hope that it is only a temporary withdrawal. Then there are the computers and vans and land cruisers to be considered. In this case the Catholic network comes up trumps, for Jack is able to get the cars and computers stored in the papal nuncio's compound (the nuncio, Archbishop Michael Courtney, is an Irishman, and eager to help).

On the Saturday of the week of 10 March Jack and I wait for an hour or more in the heat of Nairobi airport to greet the Concern group as they step safely but somewhat shakily off the 17-seater plane that has just brought them from Bujumbura. The strain of the last few days is evident. There is a certain nervous hilarity, and a jittery sense of having come through something serious. Jack takes his little band to a local restaurant where they wind down over a few beers, organise home or local leave and tell over their war stories.

This time all is well; the military situation calms down, a few weeks later the immediate crisis is over, and the expatriates return to Burundi and resume their work.

This needs versus risks dilemma often occurs in Concern's activities—though it should be said that rarely are projects so dangerous. This highly interlinked world is a long way from the agency's origins, in a passionate Irish response to the images of the starving babies of Biafra.

1: Origins in Biafra

For all the achievements of the emerging development lobby,
no-one could pretend that '1 per cent of GNP' and 'fair trade'
evoked in the public mind the passionate concern that a
Biafran child could conjure.[1]*

Concern was founded in Dublin in 1968, as the channel for a passionate response by the Irish people to reports of a shocking famine in a far-away country—Nigeria. Leading that response was the Kennedy family, notably John O'Loughlin Kennedy, his wife Kay, and John's brother Fr Raymond, a Holy Ghost priest (their parents, sisters and in-laws, were also involved). When the Biafran war was over, the Kennedys and their colleagues discovered that the intense heat had forged an instrument for good in the world. This they were able to bring to many countries.

The Nigerian crisis, like so many of the situations that Concern was to work in over the subsequent decades, had its roots in the colonial inheritance. The astounding legacy of the 19th century was the way in which a few smallish European countries—notably Britain, France and Germany—had spread their power across the world. Africa, as big as the US, Europe, China and India combined, long remained the great truffle ground. As the American commentator John Gunther put it as late as the 1950s: 'Africa lies open like a vacuum, and is almost perfectly defenceless—the richest prize on earth.'[2]

The colonial enterprise had numerous motivating strands, some less disreputable than others. People argued that, following the parable of the talents, abundant natural riches should not be allowed to rot in the ground, but should be exploited for the benefit of all. Trade was good for everyone; the benefits of global trading would

*Notes and references start on page 232.

raise everyone's standard of living, from Africa to Asia. According to one historian: 'Many sincerely believed that [the] opening of China to the manufactured goods of the West would be as beneficial to the Chinese as it would be to the merchants themselves, and that it must, therefore, be forced upon them, poor ignorant creatures, even against their will.'³ If the rulers of any country sought to exclude their people from gaining these benefits, they were to be compelled. In the 1840s and 1850s, for instance, by brute force the British obliged the Chinese to allow them to trade in opium, and the Americans demanded at the point of guns that the Japanese open their ports to foreign trade. And if one should ask by what right this was done, the answer lay in the words of the great philosophical liberal John Stuart Mill, who wrote: 'Despotism is a legitimate mode of government in dealing with barbarians, provided the end be their improvement, and the means justified by actually effecting that end. Liberty, as a principle, has no application to any state of things anterior to the time when mankind have become capable of being improved by free and equal discussion.'⁴

Another important part of the rhetoric, and the motivation, of all this colonial activity was the West's 'civilising mission'—the famous White Man's Burden. In the 1850s the saintly explorer David Livingstone who 'discovered' Lake Nyasa and the Victoria Falls, had stressed the West's duty to bring the benefits of civilisation and Christianity to the people of Africa. People throughout Europe believed that Western Christians had a grave duty to spread to others not only the benefits of their superior truth, and hence enable the salvation of their immortal souls, but also the benefits of superior Western science and civilisation (medicine, hygiene, abolishing widow-burning, slavery, polygamy, juju etc.). In one respect at least, the missionaries were astonishingly successful. It is estimated that in 1900 there were about four million Christians in Africa out of a population of some 100 million; by 1980 there were 150 million Christians out of a total of 470 million people.

Nowhere did this missionary impulse become part of everyday life more than in 20th-century Ireland; from letters home and missionary publications such as the Holy Ghost's *Missionary Annals* (which were distributed in their tens of thousands) every parish knew in detail the conditions in this or that part of the wide-flung mission field. By 1965 there were over 7,000 Irish priests, brothers and nuns (and some laity) in Asia, Africa and South and Central America—at a time when there were 19,000 priests and nuns in Ireland itself. Among the best-known of the mission orders was the Congregation of the Holy Spirit (popularly known as the Holy Ghost Fathers). Through Raymond Kennedy, numerous members of the congregation were to become deeply involved in Concern.

The Irish province had been founded as an offshoot of a well-established French congregation. Three French Fathers came to Dublin in 1859 with a specific instruction to found schools and eventually to establish a stream of English-speaking missionaries to convert the British African colonies. Despite initial suspicion—old Maynooth hands did not readily forget the French Church's craven behaviour during the Revolution—their success can be gauged by the facts that a hundred years later the congregation ran several major Catholic secondary schools (Blackrock, Rockwell, St Mary's), John Charles McQuaid, Archbishop of Dublin, a member of the congregation, was the most influential churchman in the country, and there were over five hundred Irish Holy Ghost missionaries in the field. As many as half of these were based in eastern Nigeria. It was this intense presence that was to catapult certain members of the congregation into the world limelight.

At the end of the 1960s Nigeria, one of the biggest countries in sub-Saharan Africa was falling apart. In 1914 the British had clamped together the disparate kingdoms of the Muslim Fulani in the north of the country, the Yoruba state of Oyo south of the Niger, the kingdoms of Ife and Benin, whose artwork is world famous, in the centre and, to the east, the Igbo people, then usually referred to as Ibos. [5] From the founding of the federation there had been voices declaring the union to be impossible. Even before independence, the Yoruba leader Chief Obafemi Awolowo declared that 'West and East Nigeria are as different as Ireland and Germany, and the North is as different from either as China'. [6] Independence in 1960 did not make things easier. The very different political and economic styles of the three main regions caused constant friction. There were coups and ethnic massacres. One of the worst outbreaks occurred in 1966 (just as Ireland was celebrating the fiftieth anniversary of the Rising). Enraged by local rabble-rousers, northern Muslims attacked and massacred thousands of Igbo immigrant workers. As many as one and a half million refugees fled back to eastern Nigeria. They arrived in conditions that shocked and traumatised people. One Holy Ghost missionary later recalled working with the hacked and bleeding bodies of the survivors: 'My memories of autumn 1966 are of human suffering to excess—impoverished, dispossessed, dazed, sick, maimed, wounded, hurt beyond endurance'.[7]

This was only one incident in a long train of mutual distrust and, as the easterners saw it, victimisation of the Igbo people. By May 1967, the Igbo leaders finally announced that the time had come to split away from the federation, and they declared that the sovereign state of Biafra was open for business. Throughout Nigeria it had been Igbos who were technicians, mechanics, lawyers, academics, civil servants and officers. These now formed the backbone of Biafra. The rest of the federation, with more or less reluctance, declared that secession was not acceptable, and began to arm to force the Igbo back into the fold.

The sides were unevenly matched. Biafra contained only 14 million out of the country's total population of 55 million. On the other hand, the Biafrans had oil in the Rivers district, they had a unified and motivated command (including most of the officers of the Nigerian army), and they had been preparing for secession for a long time. Nine months before, for instance, the German-American gun-runner Hank Warton had crashed in French Cameroon with a load of weapons destined for Port Harcourt.

The first shots were fired in July 1967. Initially the federal government was inclined to regard the secession as a local policing matter, but that quickly changed when a detachment of the Biafran army was halted only 135 miles from the capital Lagos. This changed the federation's approach to that of total war.

As the fighting developed there was a shock to the complacency of the Holy Ghost Fathers, for the Ibo began to treat them with suspicion, as potential spies and saboteurs. There were cat-calls such as: 'You Irish priests will rule us no longer'. There were searches and threats. Reflecting many years later on the mission in Nigeria, Fr Kevin Doheny CSSp wrote critically of attitudes that may have led to this reaction: 'We condemned their juju instead of trying to Christianise it and baptise it. We even built Irish-style churches in a climate which called for greater ventilation and an African design. We did not master the Ibo language . . . we were perhaps sometimes too hard on their African clergy. There were even some incidents of open hostility, fostering animosity on occasion.'[8]

Gradually, however, the Irish priests demonstrated their commitment by staying with their parishioners even as they retreated into the Biafran enclave, by enduring the same bombings and discomforts and, more controversially, by a passionate (and practical) involvement with the Biafran situation. As *The Irish Times* put it: 'If skin pigment could be affected by will-power, many of the Irish in Biafra would have changed colour long ago to remove the last possible barrier to full identification with the people among whom some of them have lived and worked for over 25 years.'[9] The crisis saw a crucial change in the nature of the work that the individual priests did, and this was to inform the thinking of those later involved with Concern, such as the Finucane brothers, Aengus and Jack. As one historian put it: 'The Irish missionaries underwent a metamorphosis and from educators, managers and priests became aid workers. This was achieved with virtually no training. They directed the people from an area of a village when an attack made it necessary to do so. They helped set up feeding centres through which food could be distributed. A refugee camp could be found in almost every village school. They helped organise emergency hospitals. They helped the wounded after one of the frequent bombing attacks on the markets, and buried the dead.'[10]

Without outside diplomatic help, however, geography was against the break-away state. Over the next few months, the sheer weight of the 40 million people of the federation began to crush Biafra as the noose slowly tightened around it. In one of his stories Edgar Allen

Poe tells of a prisoner who realises with mounting horror that the walls and ceiling of his cell are steadily moving closer and closer, ultimately to crush him. Something like this was happening to Biafra. As the federal forces over-ran outlying area after area, the Ibo people, terrified by the memory of the massacres of 1966, fled into the heartland. Missionaries were faced with a dilemma—should they stay with their parishes or their parishioners? Most retreated with their people. Occasionally they were captured by Federal forces, who were often hostile. Many priests abandoned comfortable shirts and shorts in favour of white soutanes, to allay suspicions that they were mercenaries.

As the federal forces overran the normal food supply areas, more and more people chased less and less food. Hundreds of refugee camps were established, and starvation loomed. One missionary wrote: 'Last Sunday I found three orphans in one of the camps, about two, three and five years of age. They were very serious cases of malnutrition . . . I hadn't seen anything like it except in photographs of the concentrations camps in Germany.'[11]

In the parishes of rural Biafra Irish Holy Ghost priests were determined not to let their parishioners suffer, so they turned to the home country for help, stressing the fate of the innocent children. Famine was something that touched a special chord in Ireland—the word itself aroused an instant and sympathetic response. (The Dutch, who had more recent experience of famine in 1944–5, were equally responsive.)

Like all famines, this was a slow burning event which took a long time for the world to recognise. Only gradually did people in Europe with local knowledge and contacts begin to realise what was going on. One of the first off the mark was Raymond Kennedy. Born in 1926, educated in Blackrock College and ordained in the Gregorian University in Rome in 1954, Kennedy had been assigned to Owerri in 1955, so he knew Nigeria well. He happened to be out of the country at the time of the outbreak of war, but was in close contact with his confrères in Biafra. It was clear to him that things were going badly there. As early as September 1967 his brother Colm, an engineer with an interest in flying, had begun to talk about the possibility of establishing independent airlifts outside the control of the international industry, which was undoubtedly making a good thing out of Biafra's urgent needs for arms and supplies.

In December 1967 Raymond and his brother, John O'Loughlin Kennedy, arranged a press conference in the Shelbourne Hotel, Dublin, to raise awareness of the Biafran situation and to organise a Christmas mercy flight to be called 'Peace One'. However, both Church and government authorities were unenthusiastic, to say the least, about efforts to support Biafra. The hierarchy were vividly aware that although there were 700 Irish missionaries in Biafran-held territory, this was only a proportion of the 2,500 in Nigeria as a whole. His Holy Ghost superiors forbade Raymond Kennedy to address the press conference, and, in face of the hierarchy's disapproval, press coverage was weak. Some money was raised, however, and a ton of dried milk and some medical supplies were despatched.

Despite official discouragement, John O'Loughlin Kennedy and his wife Kay persevered. They had been much involved in Viatores Christi and other movements, and felt strongly that they had a duty to help. By tapping contacts, they formed a list of 'old coasters', or people with experience of Nigeria such as those associated with Viatores Christi, wives of those working in Biafra, missionaries, and teachers with Nigerian experience. These were invited to their home in Northumberland Road, Dublin. The meeting was addressed by two Nigerians who had been sent to Europe by the Archbishop of Onitsha to publicise the situation. Because many of their listeners knew intimately the places they described, their first-hand accounts of conditions inside the Biafran territory had a great impact. Without a clear idea of what was to be done, the group decided to call themselves 'Africa Concern', and to meet every Tuesday. It was, as the Kennedys put it, 'a Frank Duff kind of thinking, where the symbolic step had to be made when you didn't know what to do.'

They ran a jumble sale, and started a campaign of letters to the newspapers. Subscriptions started to roll in, and soon the house in Northumberland Road began to fill with volunteers, the very first being Tony Kelly of Aer Lingus. (The tradition of office volunteers persists—during the Somalia crisis over 40 volunteers worked long hours in the Dublin office.) A consignment of blankets, medical supplies, dried milk and the like, including contributions by Biafran students in Dublin, was despatched to Lisbon for onward shipment by Caritas Internationalis, the Catholic relief agency.

Independent of these efforts, in March 1968, the Supreme Knight of Colombanus, Vincent Grogan, initiated a quite separate appeal for the victims of the war among the Knights. In April they were able to send £1,200 (equivalent to over £12,000 in 2001) to Nigeria for the purchase of seedling yams and other necessities. In April, an interdenominational group, including the Knights, established the Nigeria/Biafra Refugee Fund. Together with Africa Concern they set up the Joint Biafra Famine Appeal. Many of the members of the Refugee Fund became long-serving members of Concern, notably Judge Kingsmill Moore (a senior Freemason) and Donal Nevin of the trade union movement. From the beginning there was a determined attempt to ensure that non-Dublin and non-Catholic voices were represented. Rev. Ivan Biggs, a Methodist minister, was the first secretary, and there were influential board members from North and South including headmistress Mary Guckian (Derry), Vivian Simpson MP (Belfast), and Val Jagoe who was chair for some years of the independent-minded Cork branch. Dubliner Sean Mc Cormack also served voluntarily as accounts supervisor for years.

In Biafra the noose tightened further. The capital Enugu had been over-run in October 1967, and now in May 1968 Port Harcourt, containing the country's last useable sea-port, the last proper airport, and also a huge stock of ammunition, was taken. As the federal army advanced, there were allegations of atrocities, and the atmosphere inside the enclave grew increasingly tense. The world response to the situation was stimulated by clever, often aggressive, PR and increasing exposure on television. The Biafran government employed the Swiss PR firm Markpress to issue horrifying pictures of children dying of marasmus and kwashiorkor.

The fall of the Port Harcourt area had meant that another million refugees flowed into the already stressed Ibo heartland. By July some 650 refugee camps had been established, holding perhaps 700,000 people. Outside the camps a further four million displaced persons hunted for food. Protestant and Catholic missionaries did heroic work. Frederick Forsyth had particular words of praise for the Holy Ghost Fathers and the Irish Holy Rosary Sisters: 'To have to see twenty tiny children brought in in an advanced state of kwashiorkor, to know that you have enough relief food to give ten a chance of living while the others are completely beyond hope; to have to face this sort of thing day in and day out; to age ten years in as many months under the strain; to be bombed and strafed, dirty, tired and hungry and to keep on working, requires the kind of courage that is not given to most men who wear a chestful of war ribbons.'[12]

The worst period in Biafra was in June, July and August 1968 when it is believed that up to 6,000 children were dying every week. As Fr Donal O'Sullivan reported to the superior-general of the Holy Ghosts: 'It is no longer the people in the refugee camps that suffer the most. People in their own homes whose number are swollen by refugee relatives from the North are now in a desperate condition awaiting the new harvest'.[13] The major killer was the protein deficiency disease kwashiorkor. Even at the best of times the protein content of the average east Nigerian diet was not more than minimal. In wartime, with the usual supplies of meat and other protein cut off, there was a disaster waiting to happen. Just-weaned children, the most vulnerable and heart-rending victims, were fed cassava and yam, with perhaps a little fish in the sauce.[14] This diet was not balanced enough.

Television, new to many Irish homes, brought these events excruciatingly close. The most dramatic coverage was that shown on 12 June 1968 on the BBC, at the height of the suffering. Day after day the message was hammered home by the media: 'Look, watch—these children are being slowly starved to death. And what are you doing about it?' Reinforcing the message, African leaders Félix Houphouet-Boigny of Ivory Coast and the elder statesman, Julius Nyerere of Tanzania, speculated that 100,000, or perhaps even 200,000, Biafran lives had been lost in ten months. Frantic, European Catholic and Protestant Church groups even considered hiring space for food on gun-running flights. Resisting that idea, they soon established their own ecumenical relief flight operation—called

Joint Church Aid.

The loss of Port Harcourt in May had meant that the Biafrans now had to establish makeshift airports if the flow of arms and aid was to continue. Best known of these was Uli, which over the next few months was to symbolise Biafra's struggle. Uli airport, codenamed Annabelle, was no more than a slightly widened strip of motorway in the bush converted into a military airport. About a mile long and 22 yards wide, it made, as one pilot commented 'a nice wide road, but a damn narrow runway'.[15] It was, of course, protected by anti-aircraft batteries, so that it would have been impossible to land safely without the secret landing codes. These codes were closely protected by the mercenary pilots whose main task was to feed the Biafrans' insatiable demand for arms and equipment. To muddy the waters, the mercenaries would often top up their cargo holds with relief supplies.

For the rest of the war Uli was to be Biafra's lifeline to the outside world. Through this strip in the jungle flowed arms, aid and journalists, often in the same planes. In fact the very first plane to land at Uli, on 22 May, carried a mixed cargo of military supplies and relief materials. Although strenuous efforts were later made by relief agencies to separate relief cargoes from arms, there was always a 'whiff of cordite' about the airport, which was primarily an instrument of Biafran government policy, and only secondarily a conduit for aid. Military and government flights always had priority over food and medicine. Despite this, over 5,000 relief-only flights were made between September 1968 and the end of the war in January 1970.

In June, the Catholic and Anglican Bishops of Owerri launched the Joint Biafra Famine Appeal at an emotional meeting in Dublin with the slogan S. O. S. (Send One Ship). A number of advertising people had already been helping the appeal, and they now decided to use all their skills to boost the campaign. Within a week of the bishops' appeal, letters had been posted to advertising managers in newspapers and magazines up and down the country, enclosing design and layout for 8 inch, double column advertisements. Such was the atmosphere of the time (and perhaps the very unusualness of the request) that the response was almost universal. Publication after

BIAFRA

SEND ONE SHIP

- **THOUSANDS ARE DYING AN AGONISING DEATH BY STARVATION**
- **THE REFUGEE POPULATION NUMBERS 4 MILLION PEOPLE**
- **INNOCENT CHILDREN, WEAKENED BY LACK OF FOOD, VULNERABLE TO THE DISEASES THAT GO HAND-IN-HAND WITH SUCH A DISASTER— DIE FIRST**

BISHOPS' APPEAL

Bishop Joseph B. Whelan and Bishop G. E. I. Cockin, the Catholic and Anglican Bishops respectively of Owerri Biafra appealed to the people of Ireland at a meeting in Dublin on Friday, 28th June, 1968— to send a shipload of relief supplies to the refugees in Biafra.

The Joint Biafra Famine Appeal Committee have undertaken to raise the necessary money—£100,000 within five weeks.

Please send something—anything—**now** to:

Joint Biafra Famine Appeal

C/o Bank of Ireland, College Green, Dublin 2.

This is the J. O'Loughlin Kennedy "Africa Concern" and Mr. Vincent Grogan, c/o Knights of St. Columbanus, Appeal Fund.

publication donated free space, and many backed up the donation with editorial comment. Sometimes advertisements were sponsored by commercial organisations. Poster sites, bus window bills, television and radio airtime were also procured, and many printers and design staff gave their skills free.

The response to this campaign was stunning. The Irish people had never been hit so effectively with such an appeal, and they responded with extraordinary enthusiasm. Small odd sums, such as the 34 shillings sent by a pensioner, or mites of money sent in by children who had given up sweets or film-going, were particularly affecting. The present-day equivalent of £130,000 came in the first week, and thereafter for the next 12 weeks money poured into Northumberland Road. For those inside Africa Concern the response was confirmation that this was in a sense God's work, whatever the hierarchy might feel. By the end of the first year the fund exceeded £326,300 (over £3 million in present values). Post came literally in sackloads, and the small volunteer staff struggled to cope. Despite working day and night the inexperienced workers were in danger of being overwhelmed. Looking round for someone to help, the Kennedys had the inspiration to approach Paddy McGrath of the Irish Hospitals Sweepstakes. He immediately lent the services of three of his employees on full pay for several months, on the sole condition that his generosity be kept secret, lest it stimulate other such demands. These women, experienced in the sweepstake's systems, immediately introduced proper accounting controls.

In July 1968 an advertising studio manager called Patrick Crane began a fund-raising tradition that has served Concern well. *Missionary Annals* described his response to the media coverage. 'In the sickly-sweet atmosphere of a Dublin flat a girl with slightly glazed eyes tossed back almost copper curls and smiled. Between flame-manicured fingers she produced what looked like a plug of tobacco, a cube no bigger than a baby's finger nail—marihuana. Patrick politely nodded refusal and, shaken by the great hunger for escape which compelled a pretty twenty-year old to resort to dangerous drugs, escaped himself to the refuge of his Synge Street bachelor apartments. Next evening, preparing a solitary steak tea, he was struck by a newspaper picture of a starving Biafran boy and with slow horror read that a chief symptom of his advanced malnutrition was that the "hair turns red as the pigment is drained from the skin". The sharp contrast between the red-haired white girl looking for "kicks" and the skeleton-framed black boy whose change of hair colouring denoted the nearness of death made Patrick ponder—and put away his steak and onions.' With Kay O'Loughlin Kennedy's help, he organised a 48-hour fast over a July weekend, using a child's coffin borrowed from Staffords the undertakers. As he sat day and night by the GPO, teams of volunteers with collecting tins poured £2,300 into the coffin (equivalent to some £25,000 in 2001).

Africa Concern was pushing at an open door, but continued to push hard. The text of advertisements was often crude. 'Will you kill this child?' asked one. 'He is caught in the living hell that is Biafra. He has had no food for a month, and his stomach is swollen and covered in sores. His little sister is already dead.'

More subtle was a neat exploitation of county pride. John O'Loughlin Kennedy was by training an economist, whose 'day job' was manager of the Economist Intelligence Unit, directed by Garret FitzGerald. He set subscription targets for each county in Ireland, and assiduously published the results, making sure that every local newspaper knew exactly how its county was doing. Cork—whose target had been set, said Corkmen, insultingly low—subscribed six times what had been expected. So great was the interest that in one issue The *Kerryman* carried seven items relating to Biafra. Local pride was very much at stake. Kay O' Loughlin Kennedy remembers a subscription from a man who had lived in Dublin for at least 30 years: 'This is to go down for the credit of Roscommon, mind', said he, 'not Dublin!' Most counties amply exceeded their quotas—the original target was £50,000 but £136,000 was received in three months. As well as cash from individuals, companies made subscriptions, both in cash and kind, typically dried milk, tinned meats, medicines and clothes.

The next question was: how could Concern deliver the aid to the starving in the besieged enclave of Biafra? This boiled down to two problems: how to get the bulk goods to somewhere near Biafra, and then, since the only way in and out of Biafra was by air, how to break down the cargo into airliftable ten-ton units and organise flights. In July, Africa Concern chartered the SS Korbach from England; with her came 600 tons of salt, courtesy of ICI. She picked up 750 tons of dried milk in Belfast and arrived in Dublin on 1 August where a further 700 tons of food supplies, cloth and medicines were loaded in great haste. By 24 August SS Korbach arrived at São Tomé, a Portuguese island just two flying hours from Uli, where Fr Tony

Byrne, an Irish Holy Ghost priest, working with Caritas Internationalis organised the Joint Church Aid relief flights into Biafra. Three nights later the first of the Irish supplies landed in Biafra. The speed of the Irish reaction was remarkable—the Korbach was only the fourth ship to land supplies for Biafra into São Tomé.

The supply route from Europe to São Tomé was satisfactory as far as it went, but each plane could only transport a mere ten tons. More was needed. At one point there was discussion of establishing a land corridor between the armies through which aid could pass. The Biafrans rejected the idea, partly on security grounds and partly because of fear that the food would be poisoned. As Kevin Doheny said to Frederick Forsyth: 'I cannot give a cup of milk I know has come from Nigeria to a small baby. However small the chance, it's too big.'[16] (This intense partisanship led Africa Concern to courses of action that caused some embarrassment to the Irish government. Basing its judgement on reports from its Lagos-based ambassador Paul Keating, ministers became privately convinced that Africa Concern and the Holy Ghost priests involved were closely implicated in gun-running.[17])

Between 10 and 15 flights a night flew into Uli; mostly from São Tomé, where Holy Ghost Fathers Tony Byrne and Billy Butler organised the flow. One night the flights were for the (Protestant) World Council of Churches, the next for Caritas Internationalis, the Catholic aid body. On Catholic nights the current parish priest of Uli (in succession Joe Prendergast, Aengus Finucane and Harry Mullin) became the ex-officio Caritas representative responsible for unloading the supplies into lorries. This was demanding, unrelenting work: in the pitch black of Uli airport, with an enemy bomber circling high overhead (out of reach of the anti-aircraft fire) and occasionally getting lucky with a direct bomb hit, the ten-ton planeloads had to be man-handled into lorries in the humid tropical night. It had to be done quickly, so that the plane could take off again, and with luck return with a further load. The lorries then travelled in convoy 12 miles to the Catholic mission at Ihioma where a great barn-like structure, originally intended for a new church, was the staging post. As natural social centres, schools and churches inside

Biafra became provision points. The importance of these parish networks, Catholic and Protestant, was such that they became the essential pre-condition to the successful delivery of aid in depth to Biafra. Other, later, disaster areas, notably Somalia, lacked such a pre-existing network, and aid was much less effective accordingly.[18]

But in a hungry world, looting was a constant risk: on one famous occasion, as the historians of the Joint Church Aid airlift report, 'a man jumped out of a car and held up the last lorry in a convoy at gunpoint. An indignant Fr Gus Finucane jumped out of a Peugeot 404 estate, threw himself at the bandit and embraced him in a 19-stone rugby tackle. The bandit's accomplices started their car and abandoned their friend' who was handed over to the authorities.[19] At Ihioma the parish priest (Mick Courtney and later Jack Finucane) organised the distribution to hundreds of villages across the country in a fleet of 97 heavy lorries.

By this time Joint Church Aid and other agencies had established an air-bridge from São Tomé to Uli averaging over 200 flights a month; the International Red Cross were flying in some 140 flights a month from Fernando Po. In February, to the irritation of the Joint Church Aid organisers, Africa Concern started its own service from Libreville in Gabon. In the first month of operation it organised 25 flights carrying 125 tons of salt, 72 tons of milk powder, 38 tons of noodles as well as rice, stockfish and meat. By the end of the war Africa Concern had organised 287 such flights (one every working day for 11 continuous months). This was an extraordinary feat of dedication and organisation from a small group in a small country thousands of miles away.

Then information reached Dublin that substantial amounts of food could be acquired along the West African coast, which would cut the need for the long trip across the Bay of Biscay. There was also the tantalising possibility that a ship of appropriate size might, with the tacit approval of the federal government, be able to make a river journey into the heart of Biafra. A single ship could carry the equivalent of several night flights. So the imaginative, but fateful, decision was made to purchase a freighter capable of trading along the coast. To enable the Joint Appeal to own a ship, it was incorporated, under the name of Africa Concern Ltd, and was formally constituted as a limited company on 29 July 1968. Its basic objectives, as detailed in the memorandum were: '(a) The provision of aid of every kind for the assistance and development of peoples in any part of the world and especially in Africa. (b) The soliciting and collection of donations of every description whether in money or in kind for any purpose or for or in connection with any object of the Company. (c) The operation of every kind of transport business by air, sea or land.'

All this happened at tremendous speed, driven by an overpowering sense of the Biafrans' need. By the middle of August Africa Concern had identified, purchased and refitted (with the help of a windfall from the Dutch charity Mensen in Nood[20]) a 600-ton ocean-going ship, renamed the *Columcille*. After refitting and loading in Dublin (including a troublesome delay for engine failure necessitating the flying into Ireland of specialist engineers from Holland) the *Columcille* landed its first cargo in São Tomé at the end of September 1968, a mere three months after the bishops' original appeal.

Money continued to flow into Africa Concern's office, though now at a less hectic pace. By the end of 12 months businesses had contributed £100,000 and individuals £225,000. Income during the war amounted in total to over £1 milliion, equivalent to over £12 million in 2001. (It was not until the Ethiopian famine of 1983/4—another television-led appeal—that equivalent levels of donations were to be attained.)

In May 1969 Raymond Kennedy, general manager of Africa Concern since the previous October, reported to the board that the *Columcille* had been loaned to the Nigerian Red Cross to operate on the federal side; as well as the airlift, there were Africa Concern medical teams in Nsukka and Ivory Coast and later another in Abidjan. A doctor and two nurses had been sent to Libreville to help look after children evacuated from Biafra. Also, as Kennedy wrote, 'our office acts as a central sorting office for mail in and out of Biafra. In addition we arrange the flights of missionary and other personnel connected with Ireland going from Europe to Biafra'. Thirteen Biafran students stranded in various European universities were being subsidised, and finally, 'we have undertaken to find a school in Ireland for Col Ojukwu's brother and Major-General Effiong's two daughters'. (It is difficult to see that the unswervingly pro-federal Irish government would have been keen on such help being given to the Biafran leader and his chief-of-staff or even that members of the public who gave money would see this as part of Africa Concern's remit.)

Of course all this activity, and especially the intimate involvement of missionaries, did not go unnoticed. In October 1968 the Nigerian Commissioner Chief Anthony Enahoro complained bitterly to the Irish government about the activities of Holy Ghost priests who, he claimed, were 'indistinguishable from rebel supporters'. He accused named priests of gun-running. In November, to the astonishment of both Africa Concern and Caritas, Raymond Kennedy was personally named in a Nigerian government press release as the organiser of Cuban and American mercenary groups destined for Biafra. This was, needless to say, indignantly denied.

There is no doubt that in order to establish the Africa Concern airlift Raymond Kennedy did associate with some colourful individuals, among them one described as 'a kicked-out White Father' who claimed a connection with German Caritas, and was suspected of wanting to add arms to the cargoes of food and medicine. The plane ultimately chartered by Africa Concern, it transpired, had been used for arms running. Although Concern was absolutely scrupulous, in the heated atmosphere of the time guilt by association was enough, even for the Irish government. Thus when Africa Concern chairman Vincent Grogan visited Lagos in November 1968 the Irish ambassador declined to meet him lest he give the group 'an official blessing'. The Irish government felt acutely the need not to upset the Nigerians, who generally regarded even UNICEF, the Red Cross and Caritas with suspicion. The fearsome Colonel Adekunle, nicknamed the Black Scorpion, bluntly declared: 'I want to see no Red Cross, no Caritas, no WCC, no Pope, no missionary, no United Nations delegation. I want to prevent even one Ibo having one piece to eat before their capitulation.'[21]

Irish official circles had very little experience or understanding of the kind of lobbying and activism that Africa Concern was involved with. There was a certain disdain of 'amateur' activism. Todd Andrews, one of the great and the good of the Republic, wrote in his autobiography: '"Concerned" citizens seemed to me to be divided into different categories. Some were idealists prepared to go to the scaffold to eliminate the injustices of society. Some were dissatisfied because their jobs did not give them the power and influence they felt capable of exercising on contemporary events. Some were parlour pinks enjoying the social cachet attached to radical chic in pubs and suburban drawing rooms.'[22] Immediately after the war the Irish ambassador to Nigeria was harsh in his judgement of the Holy Ghosts, one suspects with Africa Concern largely in mind. They were, he wrote, 'impertinent busybodies from abroad who involved themselves in the internal affairs of Nigeria and by their propaganda and comfort to the Biafrans unduly prolonged the war and caused great suffering to the Nigerian people'.[23]

The Irish government, the hierarchy and the Joint Church Aid organisers could not understand why Africa Concern did not simply flow its donations through the established channels. Joint Church Aid had established understandings with the federals in order to keep the channels open, including detailed lists of exactly what types of aid would be sent in. Raymond Kennedy preferred to announce in advance what wouldn't be sent (explicitly arms and military personnel) and respond to felt needs thereafter. Perhaps as a consequence, the cargoes sent by Africa Concern were extremely varied, often in response to specific requests. The 46 flights organised into Uli in November 1969, for instance, carried kerosene, salt, milk, fertiliser, candles, stationery, meat, maize, flour, rice, beans, agricultural equipment and several batches of 'personal parcels'—seeds for Fr Paddy O'Connor, whiskey, and even on one occasion a Christmas tree. Raymond Kennedy took the view that the Irish missionaries in Biafra would work better if they had a beer or two in the evenings, and so sent a consignment. The teetotal Protestants in the World Council did not approve. In fact, many in Joint Church Aid had serious reservations about Africa Concern's activities, fearing that the elaborately constructed relationships between Church groups and with the federal Nigerians would be put at risk.

There was some substance in this. Certainly the Kennedy brothers took a robust attitude to established ways and patterns. As Raymond wrote on one occasion: 'Our number one aim is to get more food and medicine into Biafra. We have nothing like enough money to do the job. Therefore we must collaborate with people who are not very nice, or whose motives are somewhat suspect, as long as they are not actually doing wrong.'[24] The air service used by Africa Concern, BIAS (Belgian International Air Services), certainly was involved in carrying arms into Biafra, as Raymond admitted. 'It does appear that some of the work done by BIAS is connected with arms. However, being a small organisation which cannot fund all its activities unaided, we are compelled to receive help from any quarter that is not too embarrassing.'[25]

Why *was* Africa Concern so insistent on ploughing its own furrow in this way? Perhaps part of the answer lies in the strong patriotic feeling that Ireland was at last (after generations first under the British thumb and then under the self-restricting 'ourselves alone' philosophy) making a difference on the world stage: the money donated had been Irish money, the aid was Irish, and it should, if possible, be given by Irish hands to the beneficiaries. There were also the strong personal relations between the senior Africa Concern people and the Irish missionaries. In the end Concern spent £600,000 raised by the Joint Biafra Famine Appeal and £400,000 from international sources.

By December 1968 the Joint Church Aid's airlift was well under way, having clocked up over 900 flights in four months. The situation inside Biafra began to ease a bit. Now a scheme was set up to evacuate children from the stricken area. UNICEF was against the plan, and others pointed out that for the cost of housing 1,000 children in a foreign country, 100,000 could have been supported in Biafra. Nonetheless, over a thousand children were flown out to Libreville in September 1968, although very little attempt had been made to provide receiving accommodation. Furthermore the children's inadequate ID stickers had peeled away in the heat. In 1969 Africa Concern, with the help of the Order of Malta, sent a medical

team to Abidjan, but they reported back that things were still cha-
otic: 'Doctors have been drifting in from France and America, sent
by various organisations that have no communication with each other
and this can lead to chaos utter and complete.'[26]

The civil war dragged on through 1969, with a prolonged stale-
mate between May and November. During this time Biafran fears
about genocide waned—there were now more Ibos living outside
the enclave than within, and no massacres had occurred. Not that
this feeling was necessarily reflected in the outside world: in Ireland
a stream of articles in publications such as *Missionary Annals* kept
the fear alive. For instance, Bishop Joseph Whelan CSSp, who left
Biafra to a hero's welcome in Dublin in January 1969, began publishing his graphically illustrated 1968 diaries a few months later, by
which time they no longer represented the current situation. But in
the end, as one historian put it, 'there was no "genocide", massacres
or gratuitous killings . . . but there was mass hunger and there were
concentrations of starving, sick and exhausted people, usually refugees caught a long way from home, some of whom died because aid
was too slow in reaching them.'[27]

After the war came to an end Western aid remained a vexed issue
for the Nigerian government. They were especially sour about the
role, as they saw it, that the missionary aid agencies had played in
prolonging the war. The missionaries still inside the Biafran enclave
were rounded up and held by the Nigerian army on charges of ille-
gal entry into the country; many, including Jack Finucane, had an
uncomfortable few days in prison before being expelled. At first sight
this must have seemed a sad ending—but in fact Biafra had provided the seedbed both for Concern and for numerous other world
aid agencies.

2: New countries, new roles

Aid work is essentially emotional. In the profession we may be more prone than others to the influence of emotions—why else would we take up such work? And if we are deeply committed to one set of people we will tend to develop a dislike for another. During disputes we, more than most people, quickly take sides, and in case of conflict we find it hard to be impartial.[1]

Long before the end of the Biafran war the board had declared its unwillingness to allow Africa Concern to be restricted to a single theatre. As the minutes of an early meeting (3 October 1968) recorded: 'It was resolved that the Joint Biafra Famine Appeal angle be allowed to peter out and that the Africa Concern Limited image be emphasised so as to allow for a continuing effort to help underdeveloped areas even when the immediate Nigeria/Biafra conflict is over.' There was a reasonably clear image of how this might be done: 'It was resolved that the sending or financing of specialist teams to help with relief work or rehabilitation or development of underprivileged countries was, in principle, an appropriate activity for Africa Concern.' The Kennedys and others were determined to continue the work begun in eastern Nigeria.

However, there were many soul-searchings to go through before the new course could be established, and these were not helped by the fact that there were strong-willed characters on all sides. The release from the tensions of the war period gave the members a chance to look round, and not everybody liked what they saw.

In those early days there were few models of aid agencies to follow—many of the now-familiar names owed their origins, as did Concern, to the Biafran crisis, and so were, like Concern, feeling their way into new roles. In Ireland there was the Irish Red Cross (established as late as 1939), but this had a very specific brief. Trócaire and Goal had yet to appear. Gorta had been set up in 1965 by the glamorous Minister for Agriculture, Charles Haughey, initiating a brief burst of general enthusiasm. Tins were rattled outside shops, bring and buy sales were organised and students in duffel coats had fun pushing sponsored prams up and down the country. Not to its advantage, Gorta had been established with an unwieldy board, intended in a rather literal-minded way to be representative of all walks of Irish life (not forgetting the Irish Ballroom Proprietors Association).[2]

Perhaps decline was inevitable. After the optimism of the 1960s, even very well-established British agencies were finding it difficult to sustain public enthusiasm for overseas aid. Some of the most idealistic fell into a kind of despair. In the light of the scale and emerging complexity of crises, it was argued, how could even the most generous of donors make more than an iota of difference? This was not a case of resigning oneself to cursing the darkness, but a 'realistic' assessment that what a small country such as Ireland could achieve was little, and just possibly might leave the recipients worse off in the long run. Inside Oxfam, an agency that could generate multiples of the sums Concern had access to, senior people were beginning to regard what even they could do as 'too tiny to be useful on any scale that mattered'. They urged the agency to devote its time to public enducation and political lobbying to 'sting the state into action'.[3]

As usual in Ireland, the attitude of the Catholic Church was an important element. For long the Church had tended to discourage lay initiatives in aid and mission work, regarding this as work appropriate for the specialised bodies within its own compass. In the past there had been bursts of lay activity, when current events seemed to force a reaction. Thus in 1870, amid scenes of enormous excitement in Dublin, an Irish ambulance corps was financed and established to make a brief and ineffectual expedition to France during the Franco-Prussian War. Again, in 1945 the Irish Red Cross set up a 100-bed hospital in the Normandy town of St Lô which had been completely flattened in the path of the D-Day invasion. In August 1945 the advance party (which included Samuel Beckett as translator and storesman) arrived in St Lô and began to erect the 25 linked huts that made up the hospital buildings. Among the early staff was Maurice Fitzgerald, whose grandfather had been awarded Red Cross medals for service in France with the Irish Ambulance Corps in 1870. Fitzgerald, who later became a senior UN official, forms a curious link between Concern and these early adventures, for he became a shareholder of Africa Concern, and was an active contributor to the debates about Concern's future in the 1970s.

In St Lô what particularly impressed the local population were the cleanliness and the 'bright rooms full of flowers' (as one French journalist put it) that the nurses brought. They were a marked contrast to the conditions in the still-ruined town, where the streets were lined with six-foot high piles of rubble, and the people lived still in shaky ruins and cellars. The cheerful discipline of the Irish nursing profession was long to be the mainstay of many of Concern's activities.

The Irish hospital in St Lô was very popular, not least because it provided medical services free. And therein lay a classic aid dilemma. For although there had never been any intention of establishing a permanent presence, insufficient thought had been given to what is now called the 'exit strategy'. Once the immediate crisis was over, how was the hospital to extract itself and still leave the people of St Lô better off? Fundraising appeals had simply said that the hospital would last about two years, or 'as long as the funds held out' (another aid dilemma—the duration and scale of programmes should relate to needs, not means).

At the end of the war income from the Irish Sweepstakes, which had been dedicated to the Irish Red Cross for the duration, reverted to hospital building in Ireland. Funds were consequently low. Furthermore, the French doctors began to resent the apparently endless disruption of the market for their services. They put pressure on the French Red Cross Society to get the Irish hospital out. Bad-tempered debates in the local council pitted the medical men against the townsfolk. Complicating the issue was a hare-brained scheme to move the whole hospital lock, stock and barrel to Warsaw (by then in the Soviet sphere of influence). This of course came to nothing, and the 50 or so Irish doctors and nurses returned to Ireland in December 1946. The hospital itself continued to function under French management for another ten years and remains a happy memory for the people of St Lô.[4]

The intense activity and excitement of the Biafran campaign had bound the members and volunteers of Africa Concern together. Biafra was, after all, on the international stage, and Concern, and Ireland, were there as a part of the action. This was intoxicating. The excitement of those hectic months, the constant travel, the bustle of volunteers, the parcels of post from Biafra to be redistributed across the world, daily press releases, the endless stream of small decisions to be taken, filled the horizon. Afterwards it was natural that questions would be asked, decisions coolly assessed, future directions explored. A rumbling debate began which occasionally became heated and personal.

In the meantime the circumstances of the people in eastern Nigeria did not miraculously improve with the ending of the war. Inside the former Biafra transport was poor and food supplies difficult to sustain. There were still many homeless refugees and as usual war had disrupted ordinary agriculture, so food aid was sorely needed. On the other hand, the Joint Church Aid programme had come to an abrupt end with the over-running of the enclave, and the federal government was hostile to the missionary and aid agencies. So for some months after January 1970 Africa Concern continued more or less surreptitious aid activity in the former secessionist area. Elsewhere there was naturally some unfinished business, in particular the orphans (who should never, according to some commentators, have been taken out of Biafra) still in Libreville, Gabon and Abidjan, Ivory Coast, where Concern representatives continued to look after them. (In the end 5,000 children were cared for and safely returned to Nigeria.) Students were still being supported throughout Europe.

Concern was not the only organisation that had to think hard about the future. The Holy Ghost Congregation was faced with a serious dilemma. The sudden return immediately after the Nigerian war of more than 200 men looking for work was extremely awkward. With no mission station remotely the extent of eastern Nigeria, there was enormous difficulty in placing them , especially as the impact of the Vatican Council was just then recasting the traditional missionary role. Many priests were thrown more of less on their own resources, finding parish work in the US and elsewhere. The provincialate was not therefore inclined to raise too many queries when Aengus Finucane and others, while retaining membership of the congregation, in fact committed themselves to Concern. For similar reasons, the leaders of the congregation were anxious if possible to mend fences with Nigeria. In early 1970 John O'Loughlin Kennedy, as executive director of Africa Concern, met Bishop Joseph Whelan who, in so many words, warned him and Africa Concern off Nigeria—Africa Concern was, to O'Loughlin Kennedy's astonishment, diplomatically told to find some less politically involved babies to feed.

In fact, a stream of new projects presented themselves to Africa Concern. 'Strange as it may seem,' commented one report, 'our efforts have been increased and become more varied since the war ended.' Raymond Kennedy and Vincent Grogan flew to West Africa in April 1970, and explored possible projects in Gabon, Ivory Coast and Equatorial Guinea. By June Concern's assets consisted of the *Columcille* (then on charter to UNICEF, with finance from the Irish government) and a net £79,400 in the kitty. A projects committee was established 'to make decisions on projects within our established field of action and organise the necessary research and assessment of larger unfamiliar projects'. These were mostly small: £1,231 for a Catholic mission homecraft centre in West Cameroon, £700 for a community scheme in the Gambia, £50 for the purchase of a bicycle for a catechist in Kenya, and £50 to help restock a poultry farm in former Biafra. A set of accounts dated October 1971 notes grants to countries as far apart as Paraguay and Ethiopia.

But a stream of such projects hardly satisfied the members' high ambition to help the world. Throughout 1971 and 1972 the organisation went through a very tough re-assessment of the way it was run and what it should be doing. One group, led by Maurice

Fitzgerald and backed by Michael Fingleton[5] (later chairman) and others, felt strongly that Africa Concern should be closed down, and a new organisation called variously Concern or World Concern established in its place. A main plank of these proposals was that the principal shareholders in Africa Concern, Vincent Grogan and John O'Loughlin Kennedy, should retain responsibility for its liabilities.

In February 1971 Fitzgerald, expounded in a memo to shareholders his vision of a 'secular, charitable, non-sectarian organisation to channel in the most effective way aid subscribed by the Irish people to the developing countries'. He was blunt about the reasons for his proposal: 'Africa Concern had become a household name in Ireland, had acquired the goodwill of most people and had gathered a first-class team of dedicated workers. With the cessation of hostilities, however, a completely new situation arose and I feel that no real effort was made to meet the new conditions. Our failure in this respect is only too apparent in the lack of financial support from the Irish public now prevailing.' (The newness of everyone to the rhythms of fund raising is evident. Experience since has shown over and over again that the public will always respond strongly to a vividly perceived crisis. Concern's income has consistently peaked on foot of crises—Bangladesh, Ethiopia in 1975 and 1984, Sudan, Somalia, Rwanda, etc. Typically it might take two or more years to push through projects financed by the money received during these periods.)

A principal problem was the embarrassing cost of the *Columcille*. Even idle in dock the ship was expensive to protect, maintain and insure. Some were for selling it, some for hiring it out, some for trying to trade with it. John O'Loughlin Kennedy's idea was that if appropriate charters could be found, the ship could trade, and the profits used to cover the overheads of the Concern office, thus ensuring that as much as possible of the public's donations actually got into the field. This vision was no doubt influenced by the very well-known St Vincent de Paul Society rule that every outside donation went directly to the needful, and that the members themselves paid all operating expenses by special collections. However, as he found out, finding appropriate charters was not easy, and in the meantime the ship was eating its head off. In early 1971, O'Loughlin Kennedy went to Lagos to explore options. (Conscious that the Nigerian government would hardly greet him with open arms he travelled on a seaman's visa, under the name of Seán Ó Cinnéide, a ploy the Irish ambassador did not think funny.) There was no luck in either selling the ship for a decent price or gaining charters, and the costs of keeping it in dock were alarming. The 1971 accounts showed that the net costs associated with the *Columcille* were £40,000 out of a total expenditure (field and non-field) of £199,000. At one time the idea of sailing the ship into international waters, opening the seacocks and simply letting it sink was seriously discussed.

At the AGM in April 1971 the discussion veered to the current situation in East Pakistan (now Bangladesh), which was attempting to break away from West Pakistan. Could the *Columcille* be brought to help in some way? Five months previously the country's central coastal area had been hit by one of the most devastating cyclones ever. At least 300,000 people were killed and thousands more made homeless. Concern had already accumulated money to help these people, but because of the presence of the hostile West Pakistan army, which was attempting to prevent the two wings of Pakistan from breaking apart, they had so far been unable to spend much. (In these early days of humanitarian agency activity a slightly helpless accumulation of money was not unusual. Raymond Kennedy reported that there was as much as £800,000 still in English banks originally collected for Biafra; the Irish hierarchy similarly had collected £280,000 for Pakistan but had as yet been unable to spend more than £20,000.)

There was some rather wild talk of organising a Biafran-style airlift, or perhaps trying to bring the *Columcille* surreptitiously into 'the port of Bengal'. With his usual trust in the flow of events, John O'Loughlin Kennedy proposed that 'we have to get the boat out there with its first load and when it is there buy more supplies locally—then a pattern will be established and then the money from bank accounts will flow in.' Because the conflict between East and West Pakistan was technically an internal one the Red Cross and other organisations could not become involved. Here Concern's reputation for independence was an asset. As it was said at the AGM in April, 'other organisations might not like to send aid direct, and we could be used as a front.'

Just as new funds for Pakistan began to flow in, Fitzgerald despatched memos in July and August 1971 to the shareholders stressing the need to reconstitute Africa Concern as a 'secular' organisation to channel aid to the Third World. He declared there were 'ethical questions' about continuing to finance the *Columcille* out of ordinary donations. 'Stories,' he declared, 'are circulating in certain business circles about the *Columcille*.' Another acrimonious meeting of shareholders, in November 1971, became mixed up with blunt criticisms of the Kennedy brothers' management style. This meeting was carefully tape-recorded. Much of the time was taken up with the *Columcille*, which was increasingly becoming an albatross around the organisation's neck. The meeting was very long and somewhat inconclusive, and ended in the early hours of the morning on a note of farce: 'Kingsmill Moore: That was my wife on the phone. She wants to know if this meeting is ever going to end?'

The official board minutes recorded that 'most of the disquiet generated amongst shareholders had arisen from misconceptions or misunderstandings based on unchecked hearsay. In particular it was shown that Africa Concern was not bankrupt, had never been bankrupt.' (These early minutes were all written by Kay O'Loughlin Kennedy who had not been trained in the dull and formal ways of a professional company secretary. They are vivid and often entertaining. In October 1972, for instance, it is recorded that 'in the course of the discussion that followed, the chairman left the meeting, making an unparliamentary comment.' Alas, the last phrase was scrubbed from the official record.)

The debate over Concern's new direction and its style of stewardship and management, rumbled on throughout 1972. The fundamental conflict was between the inspired enthusiast and the cool professional. The latter, embodied by Michael Fingleton, persistently sought more financial and operational planning and a more broadly-based management team. To a lesser extent it was also about personalities: the Kennedy brothers, John and Raymond, had all the creative verve of starters. But the executive committee also noted in a report in June 1973: 'Fr Kennedy does have immense talents for which we are grateful and quite determined not to lose, [however] we feel that a flair for administration and day-to-day personal [personnel?] handling are not his special line and are often the cause of unnecessary trouble to him and to us.'

There was also a religious issue. The demand for a 'secular' organisation was a constant refrain, implying that although Africa Concern was certainly interdenominational (as its letterhead proclaimed), it was still too clerical. Africa Concern had been founded in an intensely religious environment. Many of the leading characters were priests, mostly Catholic, but also Protestant; the chairman had been the Supreme Knight of the Knights of Columbanus; the core organisers, John and Kay O'Loughlin Kennedy, profoundly felt that the organisation's success was a sign that God blessed the work. For the thousands of volunteers working to raise funds, it was a chance to show a new post-Vatican II kind of practical Christianity.

One of the Holy Ghost priests intimately involved in the early years, Michael Doheny, who in the next few years did much to sustain the enthusiasm of new volunteers in the field, was in Calcutta acting for Concern—he was also acting as chaplain to Mother Teresa's nuns. He wrote in February 1972, making it clear what side he was on. 'The ideals of Concern as I see them have found a rare fulfilment here. Its whole concept and history is based on big thinking, daring decisions, adventurous action . . . if the moment comes when the virtues we aim at are respectability and caution or what they call "diplomacy" we are no longer the Concern I know and wish to serve . . . It seems to me there is no shortage of "prudent" people in the world, but a famine of creative courageous thinking.'

Unimpressed, on 10 May three shareholders (Maurice Fitzgerald, Michael Fingleton and Brendan Byrne) and three non-shareholders, including Fitzgerald's wife, wrote another strong letter repeating and adding to criticisms of the accounting stewardship. The letter was aggressive beyond the heat typically generated in voluntary organisations.

At the end Michael Doheny, just home from the subcontinent,

gave the view from the field, in his characteristic style. 'I came back ten days ago full of the glory of Concern . . . a few weeks ago we had Cardinal Conway in Calcutta and Mother Teresa had recommended to the Cardinal that he channel any available funds through Concern. I came home full of the joy of it and I see this letter. In God's name we are spending energy and worry on negative things, let's get together—let's back up our team in Bangladesh.' The meeting ended with a unanimous vote of confidence in the executive.

Not that that was the end of it. In July 1972, Raymond Kennedy, now acting as Concern's first field director in Bangladesh, sent an anguished letter home. He had received a cable noting 'some problems at board level please avoid further firm commitments until I see you' signed John O'Loughlin Kennedy. (This imminent visit to Bangladesh was another source of complaint by dissident board members.) Plagued by difficulties of communication as well as stress and discomfort in the field, Raymond Kennedy described his 'sickening sense of insecurity' as board members played what seemed to him to be Machiavellian games. Clearly the board, distracted by its internal dissension, was failing to take account of the special sensitivity of field personnel thousands of miles away from the central office. (The difference in outlook between head office and the field is a recurring theme throughout the 30 years of Concern's history.) It is typical, for instance, of the hypersensitivity isolation induces that although Bangladesh had hardly been discussed, Raymond Kennedy was inclined to take the May meeting personally: 'It is all too patently clear that some or other persons have no confidence in our operations in Bangladesh and, therefore by implication in my efforts to direct it.'

His feelings were hardly assuaged when he received in August a cable from Vincent Grogan, the chairman, stating 'Board assures you support for all approved projects subject to resources . . .'. The threat implicit in 'subject to resources' was not what someone dealing with the new Bangladesh government at the highest level wanted to hear. In September, as he was in the process of handing over the leadership of the Bangladesh operations to Aengus Finucane, his brother summoned him home immediately—'developing situation demands your attendance' as the cable put it. For Raymond Kennedy this was an unhappy closure to an extremely successful initiative; for Concern as a whole the operation in Bangladesh has continued to be one of its crown jewels.

To add to the general sense of stress, in August 1972 Concern had to move house. For the last three and a half years the AIB had let them use their premises at 45 Pembroke Road, rent free, on condition that when the bank needed the room they would vacate immediately. This now happened, and the organisation moved into new premises in 35 Lower Grand Canal Street. These were generously provided, rent-free, by Charlie Kenny of Clancourt Holdings. Two years later a long-term home was found by Michael Fingleton who negotiated with the Little Sisters of the Assumption a very favourable deal for their premises 35–7 Lower Camden Street, which was to be Concern's home for the next 23 years.

It was clear that the organisation could not survive in this quarrelsome manner, and eventually substantial changes were made. On 1 January 1973 a new company, limited by guarantee, called simply Concern, took over the shares and therefore the assets and liabilities of Africa Concern. [6] The articles established a Council of management as the basic governing body, elected by the members at an annual general meeting.

At this point, John O'Loughlin Kennedy offered his resignation on his appointment as director of An Taisce, a post he took up in March. His brother Raymond became executive director in his place, working with a seven-person executive committee, a subset of the Council. A new and experienced executive secretary, Alan Williams, replaced Rev. Ivan Biggs, and immediately set about professionalising the fundraising process. To everyone's relief, the *Columcille* was sold at last.

The squabbles just described had not prevented Concern undertaking its proper tasks. There were now nine full-time paid staff in the office not to mention part-timers and numerous volunteers. A great deal of the day-to-day work was in fact done by unpaid volunteers. In the field there were 65 volunteers, 43 of whom were based in

Bangladesh. Concern financed or assisted volunteers in seven other countries including Yemen (6), Peru (5), Jamaica (3) and Iran (3). Over half of the volunteers were medical—nurses (32), doctors (5) and a pharmacist. At home thought was being given to the division of responsibilities in the office: an education section, a section dealing with volunteers, with fundraising etc. A report on the accounts system suggested various measures for tightening up and regularising systems.

The boardroom contest that ended in this compromise had been between, as one might say, charisma and a business-modelled planning and control system. The real Irish contribution for the next thirty years was not to be money, though this was forthcoming in generous quantities, but people—the hundreds of idealistic young Irish volunteers who went to the Third World to make their contribution, and with them the thousands of local workers who made the work of these volunteers possible. Concern's task for a generation was to stimulate, direct and protect these volunteers, and to ensure as far as possible that they delivered to the people they tried to serve nearly as much as they learned themselves.

3: People to people

A band of men and women, enlightened though not radical,
humane, essentially prosperous, committed to humanising war,
but seeing no reason why they should not have fun in the
process . . . [and] individual delegates who took off for distant
war, in countries they knew nothing about, where languages
were spoken that they had never thought to learn, enduring
without complaint the most extreme privations only to return
to volunteer for more.[1]

When Africa Concern was founded in 1968 there were some 2.5
million refugees across the world, a quarter of whom were in Europe, victims of the Cold War.[2] Ten years later there were 10 million, a quarter now being in Africa. By 1988 there were 14 million,
of whom 6.8 million were in Asia. By 1998 the number of refugees
had gone down to 12 million, with the largest group still in Asia.
Most of these refugees squat in camps of various sorts. Because of
their association with emergency situations, these camps have been
for 30 years the centre for Concern's most stressful activities—in
India, Bangladesh, Cambodia, Somalia, Ethiopia, Sudan, Rwanda
and Sierra Leone.

Prison and refugee camps rival hand-held submachine guns and
high-rise flats as more or less brutal icons of the way the 20th century did its business. By nature temporary and makeshift, some camps
(such as those established to look after famine victims in north Ethiopia) are closed down once the immediate disaster is over, others (such
as those housing the Biharis in Bangladesh) carry on for decades. A
few, such as Dachau and Auschwitz, have even become permanent
shrines to the suffering of their inmates.

Although military camps had been established since time imme-
morial, the special 20th-century usage began during the 1895 Cuba

uprising against the Spanish colonial power. In an attempt to sup-press the rising the Spanish army corralled civilians and internally displaced refugees/prisoners into a series of so-called '*campos reconcentrados*'. They quickly achieved an unenviable reputation—thousands (perhaps as many as one-third of the internees) died.[3]

A few years later in South Africa, after two years of war the mighty British Empire had humiliatingly failed to defeat the Boers, and tempers were wearing thin. In 1901 the newly arrived General Kitchener decided to copy the Spanish tactic and sweep the veldt clean—burn the farms, loot the cattle and push the women and children into a series of camps along the railway lines. Conditions in these camps became (and remain) a scandal. More than 20,000 Boer civilians died in them.[4]

A new twist was put to the camp idea in Lenin's USSR with the publication of the *Decree on the Red Terror* in September 1918. As the Gulag's historian, Alexander Solzhenitsyn, wrote: 'Here is where the term—concentration camp—was discovered and immediately seized on and confirmed—one of the principal terms of the 20th century and it was to have a big international future! And this is when it was born—in August and September 1918 . . . here in 1918 it was for the first time applied to citizens of one's own country.'[5]

As if to demonstrate the universality of the form, the next out-break was during the 1930s in the USA, where 400,000 people left the dustbowl states, particularly Oklahoma, to go to California to seek work. The camps set up by the US government to accommo-date them had much in common with the later camps in Thailand and Rwanda in which Concern was to work. Although basically dreadful, they were at least a huge improvement on the squalor and fear of the makeshift road-side encampments previously in use. The 'Okies' as they were called, were despised and attacked by the native Californians—'Niggers and Okies upstairs' read a notice in a cin-ema in Bakersfield. Most famous of these camps was Weedpatch, where a family could pitch its tent for $1.25 a week and gain access to running water, sewage, garbage disposal. At the recreational hall there were dances and pie suppers, cake-walks, weddings and mov-ies.[6] A few years later the first of the German concentration camps were opened. Like the Russians it was claimed initially that the camps were for 'social re-education'—as the notorious phrase '*Arbeit Macht Frei*' on the gates of Dachau and Auschwitz signified—but this purpose was quickly lost. [7]

Enormous numbers of refugees created by the ending of the Second World War had been herded into camps prior to processing by the authorities, but the camp as an integral part of disaster relief really began in 1969 as the Biafran government struggled to accommodate thousands of starving refugees. A year later, when millions fled the marauding Pakistani army from what became Bangladesh in 1970, the natural reaction of the Indian government was to establish camps, and it was in Salt Lake, Calcutta, that Concern first became involved in camps as such.

Camps are places where the normal respects, customs and dignities of human life are easily discarded. The relationships of work to food, of age to substance, of wisdom to serenity are disrupted. Above all, the camp occupants have lost much of their human autonomy—they are in someone else's hands.

Camps are instant towns, characteristically squalid, overcrowded, makeshift and mean; as well as being under-supplied with basic necessities such as water, latrines, medicine. They might contain no more than a few hundred people or, as in the larger Rwandan camps, several hundred thousand. The classic problems are lack of adequate shelter, food shortages (for these ersatz towns are not placed on trade routes), sanitation, water, and of course the medical results of having so many sick and often hungry people crushed together. Here a journalist describes one of the refugee camps in Thailand: 'Thousands of small huts were crammed higgledy-piggledy together. Piles of melon skins, chicken bones, beer bottles, empty tin cans, plastic bags lay over the ground. A stream running through them, low because it was the dry season now, contained only a foul-smelling slick of sewage. A little girl squatting to defecate was at once covered in a cloud of flies—flies were like a film over the camp. There was no running water; when the tanks filled daily by the ICRC ran dry, early, young people bathed and washed their clothes in the dank stream. Arrogant young soldiers, some with ancient weapons, prowled around the camp overseeing food distribution, arresting newcomers, sometimes shooting those who tried to leave.'[8]

In the Concern camps in Wollo in northern Ethiopia, in the 1980s, the average population was some 7,000, but most people came, stayed a few days, recovered and were discharged with a month's supply of food. So this was a small town with the shifting population of an enormous hospital. A regular problem is the effect of these thousands on the local economy: in Sudan the locals violently objected to the presence of the camps, as the residents depleted their already-low wood supplies; in Goma the aid-supplied markets inside the camps were so good that people came for miles to shop, ruining the native stallholders. As one journalist put it: 'After having all essential living expenses covered by charity, camp residents were free to engage in commerce, and aid agencies frequently provided enticements—like agricultural supplies—to do so'.[9] The Rwandan camps in Zaire of the 1990s were extreme examples: 'The camps were cramped, smoky and smelly, but so were the homes many Rwandans had fled; and unlike most Rwandan villages, the main thoroughfares of the big camps were lined with well-stocked pharmacies, two-storey video bars powered by generators, libraries, churches, brothels, photo studios—you name it.'[10] To Dominic MacSorley, however, they were 'the worst, most violent, inhumane and repressive camps I have ever worked in.'

People in camps are usually held a step apart from their everyday world (which may indeed have been swept away by flood, overrun by soldiers, or dessicated by drought), so camps establish their own focus. Bruno Bettelheim, a survivor of Dachau and Buchenwald, recalls that when, some time before Pearl Harbour, Roosevelt made a major speech denouncing Hitler, this excited the new inmates, but those who had been in the camp for a few months were only interested in the rumour that one Gestapo officer would be replaced by another. The theme of dependence (in this case on the people organising food supplies) is echoed in the short verse by a victim of the Ethiopian famine of the mid-1980s:

> I have come to hate my mother
> I have come to hate my sister

These days
I only love the white woman.[11]

Camps typically have too many young men with nothing to do, too many children, too many vulnerable women. Inevitably in this Darwinian environment the violent and unscrupulous thrive—the worst case of this was the dominance of the *interhamwe* in the camps in Zaire, but as Solzhenitsyn records, the Russian camps could not have been run without the trusties; nor could Auschwitz have been so 'efficient' without the Jewish *kapos*.

Camp life is deeply dispiriting: as 'Johannes', an Ethiopian refugee in Sudan, told Deirdre Purcell in 1987: 'It is not a dignified way for a man to live. I have no dignity. My son will have no dignity.'[12] For Siegfried Strauss, veteran of the First World War trenches interned in Dachau in 1938, 'the most difficult thing [was] the stripping away of civilised behaviour and the confrontation with the naked will to survive. Because that is the moment of truth—how you cope, how you behave, not how others behave, though that is terrifying enough.'[13]

These insights are surely true of the thousands of occupants of all the camps that Concern has ever been involved with. Faced with human misery on such scales, it is one of the greatest challenges for aid workers to preserve this sense of the individual tragedy.

The part of the Indian subcontinent now known as Bangladesh was for generations the wealthiest part of India. The rich silts of its 700 rivers constantly refresh an astonishingly fertile soil. Not for nothing was the country known as 'golden Bengal'. Traditionally it was the first treasure invaders of the subcontinent sought to secure. In the 1840s the British historian Macaulay wrote: 'The Ganges, rushing through a hundred channels to the sea, has formed a vast plain of rich mould which even under the tropical sky, rivals the verdure of an English April. The rice fields yield an increase such as is elsewhere unknown. Spices, sugar, vegetable oils, are produced in marvellous exuberance.'[14] All this in a country only twice the size of Ireland, large amounts of whose territory is permanently under water.

Without industry or substantial cities, Bangladesh was for years the most densely populated and most rural country in Asia. The bulk of poor cultivators and landworkers, especially in East Bengal, are Muslims. They are dependent on a precarious natural balance: every year the rivers flood, pouring some 140,000 cubic metres of water a second through the country, depositing the rich silt that fertilises the heavily worked soil. Too much flooding and the rivers devastate the land and the silt is carried into the Bay of Bengal; too little and the essential two or three crops a year cannot be harvested. Six months after the flood, in the dry season, the flows reduce to a mere 7,000 cubic metres a second, and the shrinking rivers constitute immense sandy natural obstacles to transport.

The *char* people symbolise this delicate relationship. Every year during the floods the great rivers twist this way or that, flowing now in one part and now in another of their beds. In doing so they deposit large new sand and silt islands—*chars*. 'The river breaks this way and wanders that way: it is the river's game' say the people who live on these islands. (Geology hardly ties down the path of even the biggest rivers—until the 18th century the Ganges actually flowed west of Calcutta.) Sometimes a particular island can remain stable for decades—sometimes it is wiped out after a season. As the floods start in June the *char* people wait to see if their island home is going to be washed away. If it is they will have no more than a few hours to gather their livestock and meagre belongings and shift elsewhere. If they are lucky, they can enjoy the great fertility of the *char* for years together, growing a wide variety of crops. Some four million people live on the *chars* in this way and Concern has a number of programmes relating to them.

The second half of the 20th century was a period of extraordinary turmoil for the country that became Bangladesh. Increasing control over the ancient killers smallpox and malaria meant that population inexorably rose: in 1901 it was 29 million; by 1951 it was 45 million; by 1974 it was 71 million; now it is estimated at 125 million.

In 1945 it was clear that the British Raj was doomed. It was merely a matter of time—and the deadly question for all India was:

would the majority Hindus manage to maintain hegemony over the predominantly Muslim areas, or would a separate Muslim state be established? With all to play for, the communal situation rapidly worsened. In August 1946 pro-Pakistan activists in Calcutta called a general strike (*hartal*—a form of political action still common in Bangladesh). Goaded by extremists calling for a 'Day of Action' to achieve the Muslim state of Pakistan, Muslim workers went on the rampage and killed several thousand Hindus. The ground was ill-chosen, for majority Hindus retaliated in kind, so that by the end of a week there were more than 20,000 dead, most of whom were Muslim. As the British governor of the province reported 'midnight gangs come out in many quarters; there is some looting and arson and much stabbing. In some areas the streets are a shambles with corpses (grossly mutilated) and debris from looted shops'. With public services at a standstill, the army had to be paid extra to remove the thousands of rapidly-rotting corpses.[15] There were also violent outbreaks in Noakhali and Tippera in present-day Bangladesh. Gandhi himself travelled to Noakhali to preach peace.

In Bihar, maddened by what they were hearing of anti-Hindu riots in east Bengal, Hindus began to exact their revenge, eventually killing and wounding nearly 8,000 Muslims. Many Muslim Biharis fled to the safety of predominantly Muslim areas of east Bengal, beginning an emigration that was to see up to half a million Biharis arrive.

In the months leading up to the creation in 1948 of Pakistan, there were more horrible inter-communal attacks in the north-west, but Bengal a thousand miles to the east was hardly affected. But as the dust settled after partition, it quickly became clear that Jinnah and the other founding fathers of the Muslim League had given little thought to what was now East Pakistan. Their sympathies and interests were entirely with the West. There was a jolt, for instance, when Jinnah announced that the national language of Pakistan was to be Urdu—which was widely spoken in West Pakistan but hardly at all, except by the Biharis, in the East.

By 1970 it had become clear to most Bengalis that the joint state of East and West Pakistan was not a success. The casual attitude of the West was symbolised for Bengalis when two days after a devastating coastal cyclone which killed at least 250,000 people head of state General Yahya Khan spent a mere 24 hours in Dhaka. Infuriated, Sheikh Mujibur Rahman, head of the pro-independence Awami League, declared: 'We must rule ourselves. We will no longer suffer arbitrary rule by bureaucrats, capitalists and feudal interests of West Pakistan.'[16]

A general election was unexpectedly called in December 1970, Sheikh Mujibur Rahman's party won all but two of the 162 seats allocated to East Pakistan, giving them a clear majority of the 300 seats in the whole country, East and West. Ali Bhutto's Pakistan People's Party came a poor second with 81 seats. Sheikh Mujib, as he was known, set about fulfilling his pledges. Faced with the break-up of its hegemony, the West Pakistan military government reacted quickly and aggressively. The National Assembly was suspended, Sheikh Mujib was captured and imprisoned, and soldiers were poured into Bengal. Aided by pre-established hit lists, and by information from local informers, the army immediately started a brutal terror campaign, intended to club the Bengalis into submission. Students and intellectuals were the first victims—in one case the army used tanks to slaughter students in their university hostel.

By the end of the summer as many as 300,000 people were reported to have lost their lives, a number that climbed to perhaps a million by the end of the year. Throughout the country the army attacked towns and villages with flame-throwers and from gunboats, and raped and shot at will, targeting particularly the minority Hindu population. John Horgan described what he was told in *The Irish Times*: 'One well-corroborated story tells of the occasion when the troops separated about 2,000 men from their wives and children and attempted to machine-gun them to death. About 800 died in the fusillade; the others shammed death, hoping that the soldiers would go away. But the soldiers piled the bodies of the dead and the living like children building a house of matches, poured petrol over them and set them alight. Luckily it was dusk and some of the men managed to escape, with the petrol on their skins still alight, into the forest.'[17] Work in the fields came to a halt, threatening the country with famine. Young Bengalis organised themselves into bands of guerrillas and did their best to fight back.

The local informers were none other than the Biharis who had fled from Hindu attacks in the 1940s. Many of them had done well in East Pakistan, becoming doctors, small traders, and skilled workers on the railways and in the jute mills. But perhaps because few spoke Bengali, they never integrated. During the December election they exacerbated their unpopularity by siding with the West Pakistanis, and suffered attacks as a result. When the army came, stories began circulating about how Biharis, knowing intimately the people and the neighbourhoods, would betray this or that activist or denounce neighbours. Other tales told how gangs of them carried out their own murders.[18] Their activities during Bangladesh's war of independence were to earn them great and abiding hatred—immediately after the war many were viciously attacked, their homes and shops (some of which they had taken over from murdered Hindus) were looted. They quickly huddled for safety into refugee camps, which for some years they were too fearful to leave. To this day thousands of Biharis live in more or less squalid enclaves and camps.

During this 'campaign' of the Pakistan army, as many as ten million Bengalis fled across the border into India, and it was in the camps established for them that Concern became involved in the subcontinent for the first time. As before, Raymond Kennedy was the pioneer, flying into Calcutta as early as May 1971 to assess the situation. India had not been a missionary field for the Holy Ghosts since the 1880s, so the organisation lacked the intimate knowledge of the area that had so marked its activity in eastern Nigeria. He returned to Ireland at the beginning of June and immediately a Pakistani famine appeal was launched. Over £17,000 [£250,000 in 2001 terms] was received in a fortnight, which rose to nearly £70,000 by the end of August. 'Hunger Lunches' consisting of a bowl of soup and a roll were organised in staff canteens up and down the country.[19]

At the end of June a medical team (part financed by the Tom Dooley Fund and the *Irish Independent*) was on its way to its first assignment in the Garo hills in Assam, some 150 miles north of Dhaka. These first volunteers, the predecessors of so many, were: Dr

Joe Barnes (Dublin), Mary Byrnes (Dublin), Dolores Doyle (Dublin), Marguerite Lovett (Tipperary) Patrick O'Sullivan (Cork), Joy Searight (Leix) and Seán Staunton (Offaly). Despite the pressing needs of the quarter of a million refugees, this was a dangerous area, where Bengali freedom fighters were attacking the Pakistani army from tolerated bases inside Indian territory. By the end of July the Concern team was forced to retreat to Calcutta where more refugees in the Salt Lake camps awaited. For the next few months the small Concern team worked in the refugee hospital near Calcutta. It was here that Concern was exposed to a personal tragedy. Joan Helena Browne, a nurse from Kerry, arrived in India on 24 December and immediately went on night duty at the Caritas Refugee hospital in Salt Lake. Less than three weeks later however, Jean, as she was known, contracted cerebral malaria. She collapsed and died. Her body was flown back to Kerry. This, the first among a thankfully small number of expatriate deaths while on Concern duty, was a sobering reminder that for the volunteers there was potentially something more at stake than a hunger lunch.

In December the simmering row caused by the Indian toleration of Bengali guerrilla fighters finally burst into hot war. The much larger and better equipped Indian army poured into Bangladesh and crushed the demoralised West Pakistanis in only twelve days. The 'father of the country' Sheikh Mujib, released from his death sentence in West Pakistan, flew into Dhaka in January 1972 to become the country's first prime minister. Bangladesh, the scene of Concern's most extended efforts over 30 years, was born.

The first team of volunteers moved into Bangladesh in February 1972. The Salt Lake camp was closed, and Joan Barrett, Kate McKee, Kay Moriarty, Maura O'Loughlin and Kathleen O'Shea, under the direction of the field director, Raymond Kennedy, arrived in Dhaka. The first month was spent meeting people, establishing an office and working out where the Concern volunteers were to be disposed. In March, Concern received a formal letter of approval from the Bangladesh government to operate as a relief organisation. The letter, signed by Rab Chaudhury, the co-ordinator of External Assistance for Relief and Rehabilitation, who was long a good friend to

Concern, outlined a formidable series of projects amounting to an expenditure of £50,000.[20] The agency was not, of course, alone—in the early 1970s there were over a hundred foreign NGOs in Dhaka. Many of the agencies' staff had been in Biafra and regular Nigerian evenings were held to revisit that experience.

Most of the early work was medical, in particular supplementing the serious shortage of health professionals; the World Health Organisation estimated that there were no more than 600 fully trained nurses in Bangladesh, to serve a population of 75 million, and most of them gave up work on becoming married. At home in Ireland this work was promoted with the slogan in large letters: 'Send a pound to send a Nurse' and, much smaller, 'or a doctor, a teacher or an engineer.' In April 1972 the board was told that the Concern team consisted of seven nurses, a teacher, an engineer, and a 'general help'. Usually the nurses would be sent to a hospital or a clinic to help with, for instance, in-service nursing training, or six weeks stand-in duty as matron. A typical case was the clinic established in November 1972 at the invitation of Fr Joe Lehane, an American Holy Cross priest, by three Concern volunteers in Srimangal, in the east of the country near the Indian border. The three, Sr Elizabeth O'Brien, Susan Kinsella and Irene Casey, (a doctor and two nurses) opened the clinic doors at 8 am, and worked through until 3.30. They treated some 800 patients a week, carefully allocating special days to men, to women, to ante-natal and gynaecological work and so on. On the wall of the dispensary the local man-about the house had the carefully inscribed sign—'Farmecy'. The waiting room was a simple mat shelter, open at the sides, with long bamboo benches.

Susan Kinsella described one of their programmes: 'Fifty undernourished boys between eight and twelve years were selected for a three-month programme of CSM [corn. soya, maize] feeding. Blood charts and weight records are kept. You may wonder why "boys". The answer gives an insight into Muslim society here. You see girls are at home all day and pick up bits of food around the house, the boys on the other hand are out in the fields working all day and get nothing until they come home after a hard day, to a scanty evening meal. To these we add some post-polio cases and some mentally retarded. We insist that they earn their food by helping in the preparation and making paper bags for medicines. The result of this experiment will guide us for future programmes. But as we watch, their skeleton-like, sometimes horribly deformed, bodies fill out and take shape and we begin to notice the flood of life and energy that springs up within.'

Occasionally a particular case would stir the imagination. Irene Casey described one such to Michael Doheny: 'Two weeks ago on Sunday morning a girl of four years old was carried in by her mother. Her limbs were like spindles, her bones protruding. Her name was Rumida, A dirty rag covered her mouth. When I removed it the sight was so horrible that I almost passed out, The little mouth was one mass of pus. The cheeks and chin were red and raw, but apart from a tiny bit of skin under her nose her lips were completely gone and the gums exposed. Measles had led to a sore on the lips; this had been treated by a "local practitioner"—result infection—result this mess. Our first problem was feeding, no great problem for us by drip, but the parents had to be taught how to do it at home. (There is no hospital and it cost them 6 rupees for a rickshaw to come, which they can't afford every day.) Now they come every day (we subsidise the rickshaw); we are treating the skin hoping it will generate. A graft of course would be the answer. At present even to find a bit of skin to give an injection is a difficulty. Yet our lady is putting on weight and one can almost see the trace of a smile on her caricature of a face. How I long to see those lips restored.'

By mid-July Concern had begun to establish a dispensary in the Bihari city of Saidpur, in the north of Bangladesh. This is a railway town, where during the war of liberation thousands of Biharis fled to safety from the neighbouring districts. Even today, there are virtually no cars in the town, so the tight streets are full of rickshaws, ox-carts and cyclists and goats and hens and women carrying babies (a few in full *burkas*), dogs idling on the roadside, scratching themselves. There are shops, single small rooms open on one side with the proprietor facing out; the stock might be a small range of branded goods, or pills or homeopathic medicines (very popular) or fast food being cooked in a great wok or perhaps metalwork being done on the spot. The smells are warm and strong and persistent. The common mode of transport is the bicycle rickshaw, whose passenger is lifted above head height from the road, the rickshaw-wallah spinning his vehicle through the flat, slightly dung-smelling streets, circling round a tight corner, his bell clattering away and the wheel close to a grim looking open drain. Seeing a white face, people shout 'Hallo Brother'—and other things less polite.

During the war, the town was hopelessly overcrowded. One day, so many refugees crowded into a building that it simply collapsed, crushing the people on the ground floor. In September 1972 a nutritional survey pin-pointed the needs of infants whose mothers were too undernourished to lactate. A quick programme of bottle-feeding was established, which was later replaced by daily cooked meals for the mothers starting in the sixth month of pregnancy. The survey was carried out by Irwin Shorr from Rhode Island, USA, one of five Concern volunteers from the US at the time. He was one of the many for whom his nine-month stint in Bangladesh was a life-changing experience. He remained a great supporter. Elizabeth O'Brien, whom we have seen already in the clinic in Srimangal, was another.

In January 1973, Aengus Finucane, who had been deputy field director, was appointed field director when Raymond Kennedy became executive director in Dublin. There was now a team of 35 expatriate volunteers under Concern's care, of whom 25 were Irish; there were hundreds of local employees.

For the next 25 years expatriate volunteers were to be at the heart of Concern's work in Bangladesh and elsewhere. Aengus Finucane's key contribution at this stage was to establish a system of implementing projects using expatriate managers and local staff. The European staff gave a full range of logistic and human support to enable local staff to operate in very difficult circumstances. Over 1,600 young men and women, often immediately after completing training or a degree, spent two years in often difficult, even dangerous conditions. (As full a list as the Concern files hold makes up Appendix 4.) They were responding to a generous impulse, a call to service that was being felt by idealistic young people in many Western countries: those who were stimulated by the Kennedy rhetoric to join the Peace Corps, to do Voluntary Service Overseas, or to work for Gorta or Goal or any one of the numerous similar organisations in Canada, Germany, Holland, France and a host of other countries. The impulse can be made to seem naive, even patronising; it was certainly unselfish and brave. And sometimes it called for a special surge of courage: in 1977 for instance the newsletter reported how volunteer Liz Lane tied a rope around herself before plunging into a foaming flooded river to rescue three men trapped in an overturned land cruiser. Or the occasion in 1985 when public health nurse Mags Fitzpatrick found herself effectively alone in a mud hut on a remote hillside in Wollaita, Ethiopia, with a mother-to-be in full labour.

The volunteers believed in action—the New Testament injunction is, after all, to save the wounded traveller here, now; not to complete a three-volume study of the socio-economic conditions of those preying on travellers. Enough of them died overseas to worry parents. There was one death from militia action, and seven from other causes. The volunteers stayed (most of them) to the end of their term and made friends. It wasn't, of course, all one-way: most volunteers learned at least as much as they gave. They also signed up for a taste of foreign travel, a bit of adventure and a time away from the banality of life in Ireland. A camp in Thailand, a vagrants' home in Bangladesh, a medical centre in the Yemen, however squalid and hopeless and frustrating, seemed straightforward and useful by comparison with a local nine to five job, the troubles in the North, and the antics of the men in mohair suits. Every time you fed a hungry child, or sank a tubewell, or established a latrine in an urban slum, you could feel you had done *some* good. And no one could contradict you.

The physical and mental well-being of the volunteers was felt as a great responsibility by the early field directors. It was an important part of the Holy Ghost formation that a sick missionary not be a burden on the community he is hoping to serve and that there is therefore a duty to look after oneself. 'When visiting a remote parish house on the mission,' Aengus Finucane recalls, 'the Superior's first call was always to check that the bathroom, the kitchen and so on were satisfactory.' Although some agencies have taken the idealistic view that it is desirable that their volunteers live as the local people do, Concern provided well for its volunteers. Communal meals were regular and nourishing, bedrooms and other facilities as good as could be got.

For some of the volunteers this life had a deep and fashionable appeal. The hard work, the communal living, simple frugal entertainments (Scrabble, the inevitable guitars) made some Concern houses not far off the archetypal 1970s hippie commune. Communality was emphasised by the custom that anyone leaving should dispose of clothes—Anne Cummins, one of the early volunteers in Bangladesh, still remembers a particularly covetable shocking-pink dress that passed through two or three hands before coming to her. And it was not unusual to find that someone from up-country had crashed on your bed. For others it could be trying—for instance, all the volunteers on a station were expected to eat together every night, and questions would be asked of absentees.

With so many idealistic young people living closely together, from time to time intense attachments grew up. The first Concern couple to be married were Neil Keane (from Mayo) and Kate McKee (from Armagh) in 1974. Intimate relationships were occasionally struck up with local staff, indeed five expatriate women married Bangladeshis over the years, but the differences between the cultures were difficult to bridge. And of course there were less permanent liaisons. On one famous occasion Aengus Finucane circulated a memo insisting that volunteers 'sleep on their own pillows'. Married couples volunteering together were not uncommon, which was fine in theory, but meant that work had to be found in the same area for say, an engineer and a nurse; with suitable accommodation; this did, as Aengus Finucane put it, 'make things a little difficult at times'.

In a letter to Raymond Kennedy in the early years Aengus unburdened himself about his recent personnel troubles: volunteer A had foolishly taken sides in a local political matter so had to be quietly moved to another part of the country; B 'was a problem almost from the word go . . . created really bad tension . . . but [the others] had all agreed to make a special effort to . . . make a go of things (this is near to heroic in [this] situation).' Then there was C who was a fine worker, but just couldn't get on with the local people, to the point where staff from a partner-agency refused to work with her. And of course accommodation was always fraught—D refused to share a bedroom with anyone except E, and indeed when asked to move threatened to cut short the contract and go home.

Health was another regular worry for field directors, particularly since volunteers were inclined to be casual about anti-malarial prophylactics, assuming even after a few months that they had built up their own immunity. It was not a tropical disease, however, that killed Elizabeth O'Brien whom we have seen running the clinic in Srimangal. In 1974 she was found to be suffering from cancer. She refused to go back to the US for treatment, and after a long illness she died in the Concern house on 8 September 1974. She donated her eyes to the Dhaka eye bank. A month before she died she wrote a moving letter to the field director, Aengus Finucane, in which she tried to encapsulate what her time with Concern had meant to her.

> Dear Father Gus and all Concerned,
>
> I wonder if I could try to write this letter to reach down into my soul and express the mystery I have been grappling with these past weeks and days. But I must try. What have you done to me? What have you done to all the people you come in contact with?
>
> And that means the poor Bihari children in the camps and cities; the oppressed Muslim women; the international people who have to defend themselves at your round table; the executives of international agencies in Europe; old age pensioners in Ireland; sophisticates in California parishes; all kinds of people.
>
> You seem to crack the hard little shells that hold us in and say 'Come alive. Be happy. Not to worry' This is a wonderful gift and the mystery becomes a clear reality. It is the mystery of LOVE.
>
> I would like to take you like seeds and throw you to the four corners of the earth. It would make a Springtime of this old world and it so badly needs a Springtime. But, instead your circle of goodness will slowly widen and encompass many people.
>
> Thank you so much for making me a part of it.
>
> You really are
>
> > Believing in Action,
> >
> > > Hoping in Action,

Love in Action.
Each and every one I love you Concern
Liz
August 14 1972.

Much of the emphasis of the period was on the programme to help the thousands of slum-dwellers summarily evicted from Dhaka to make-shiftcamps in Demra and Mirpur. At this time, too, Concern's model of feeding programmes to combat malnutrition was fully developed. It involved volunteer nurses supervising a system of intensive feeding and basic health care for children who were malnourished, and it arose from Concern's work in food distribution to Biharis in Saidpur and Dhaka. These feeding programmes were crucial in establishing Concern's high reputation with international emergency organisations and the model was later successfully transferred to camps in Thailand, Ethiopia, Sudan and Somalia

The range of projects gradually expanded, with particular attention given to helping women in their central role in the family economy. The touchstones were 'respond to need', and 'serve the poorest of the poor'. 'Need' was interpreted liberally, and was certainly not limited to emergency relief. Mary Humphreys remembers, for instance, the war widows programme she was involved in before leaving Bangladesh for the Yemen. Work with the Maldah people (who, like the Biharis, had sided disastrously with the West Pakistan army during the war of liberation) concentrated on the Pirganj camp. For a year Concern ran a dispensary in the camp and also supplied a resettlement programme which provided housing, farm implements, seed and wells. Other activities in the Saidpur area included:

— a mother and child health programme
— a village health programme in Dinajpur, dispensary, provision of tube wells and latrines to encourage hygiene
— training in needlecraft and basket-making for 800 women
— a special programme for the destitute older people
— a central dispensary in Rangpur, dealing with over 350 cases a day ranging from TB to malnutrition

In Mymensingh there were
— a building programme of schools and a maternity wing to the local hospital
— a substantial women's training programme financed by Bread for the World.

A large number of primary schools were run especially for the Bihari population around Chittagong, and Concern also provided staff and equipment for an eye hospital.

In Khulna there were four Bihari schools, a women's training centre and a handcrafts centre. There was also a programme to help the shanty-town dwellers who had been evicted by the government in January 1975 and forced to relocate. A similar programme operated outside Dhaka.

In 1975 a controversial project began which some believe to be the finest thing that Concern has ever done in the country. It started on a dreary Sunday in mid-year, in the sultry heat of Bengal. Two volunteers, Sheelagh O'Leary and Dorothy Devlin, were killing time when their driver Jule approached: 'he wanted to show us something', as Dorothy wrote later. 'Jule drove at his usual reckless pace along endless inadequate roads until we finally arrived. I realised that Jule, himself a poor Bengali, feared our reaction to what he was showing us, and anticipated the horror which would consume us over the next few hours. In front of us loomed a huge house, what in happier times would have been a handsome mansion. Now, in spite of the crushing heat, the dampness of both house and yard conjured up an intense chill. The smell was constant and cloying—human yet foul in its intensity. There were endless rooms, varying only in size. None of the rooms seemed to have any purpose other than to contain people. There were people everywhere. There were men, women and children crammed in a scene of complete disorder in every available space. People were lying, sitting or just standing around. There didn't appear to be any family groups, the strongest emotion that seemed to creep amongst these people was isolation. The silence was crushing; these people seemed to have lost the will and ability to converse, or to smile, all sense of joy had left them. One could sense a complete inertia. I felt unwelcome, and intrusive as if somehow these people retained an awareness of the inhospitable horror they were forced to endure, resulting in feelings of angry helpless shame. I felt we were treading on people's souls. I remember desperately seeking the facilities required for daily survival. I sought sanitation facilities, food storage and preparation facilities and I sought medical facilities. There were simply no facilities of any kind. I tried to find some form of authority to whom we could refer— there was no authority. These people needed care—from the utter silence their needs were screaming in continuous shrieks. These people needed a supply of clean water and they needed food. They needed their insect-infested wounds dressed. They needed treatment for their fevers and intestinal disorders. They needed treatment for their oozing, infected eyes. Many desperately needed skilled and kindly care for their hopelessly emaciated bodies.'

Later Dorothy and Sheelagh learned that these people were detained in so-called 'vagrants' homes' under the Vagrancy Laws (established by the British during the 1943 famine), by which anyone found with no fixed abode and no visible means of support could be detained indefinitely. In effect it was mostly women, widowed perhaps, or victims of rape rejected by their families, or mentally ill, or just extremely poor and reduced to begging and prostitution, who were incarcerated in these homes. Under the law the magistrates simply committed them to the homes and then left them until they could prove 'rehabilitation'. Some might be there as long as ten years. Small children stayed with their mothers, larger ones were put into separate homes.

The grossly underfunded Department of Social Welfare was responsible for running the homes. Staff were paid little and were poorly trained. To supplement their wages and to allow the women to accumulate enough to bribe someone to let them out, officials facilitated women leaving the home at night to prostitute themselves. To many in Concern these 'homes' were eerily like the workhouses that had weighed so heavily on the poor in Ireland in the 19th century.

The two volunteers were stunned and shocked by what Jule had shown them. They at once reported to Aengus Finucane, who quickly took the opportunity to see for himself the inadequate and even inhuman living conditions of these, the 'poorest of the poor'. The immediate impulse was to cry out loud and in public about this scandal. But, he argued, that would have done little for the people concerned. To be allowed to deliver any improvement in their conditions required that the department trust Concern not to embarrass them. A deal was struck. Concern would be allowed into the homes but on strict conditions: there was to be no photography, only personnel directly involved were allowed visit; funds were not to be sought from third parties; above all there was to be no publicity. (The rigour with which the department attempted to hide these homes from the public incidentally provides a measure of Jule's courage in taking Dorothy and Sheelagh to see them on that Sunday afternoon.)

Inside Concern this programme became hugely controversial. Some could not stomach what they saw as the shoring up of an intolerable situation created by a careless government. It is, said advocates of this line, our first duty to keep our own hands clean, and reveal to the world what is happening, in the expectation that public pressure will improve things. Two volunteers felt so strongly on the issue that they actually resigned from Concern over this programme. Others, the majority, took the line that Concern's work is for the poorest of the poor, and they are the most likely victims of political conditions the government would like to conceal. As Aengus Finucane commented: 'If a clean human rights record was made an essential criterion for receiving aid, there would be a very short recipient list.'[22]

The difficult decision to work inside such conditions, regardless of the doubtful political situation and the trenchantly expressed opposition of aid colleagues, has been made by Concern on several notable occasions, as we shall see, notably in Ethiopia and Rwanda. Concern continues to work in the vagrants' homes, providing the same loving care that it has done for more than 25 years. Work now focuses on the fate of the 7,000 or so sex workers who were thrown out onto the streets when, under pressure from the mullahs and from human rights groups, the government closed the brothels.

Runaway boys are also a problem—the police pick them up from the streets and lock them into a cage in the homes, ostensibly waiting for their parents to collect them. But so little are the homes known of, so harsh are their own home conditions, that few parents actually do come.

Some of the Concern atmosphere of the day can be captured from Michael Doheny's description of a hospital visit on Christmas Day 1972. The hospital was the Sher-e-Bangla orthopaedic hospital in Dhaka, which was largely filled with wounded Freedom Fighters. Among the Concern volunteers working in this hospital were two Indian nurses, from Kerala, including the redoubtable Sister Theodora who was quickly appointed assistant matron of the hospital. 'It would have been difficult to match our Concern volunteers in smiling geniality and in the vivaciousnes which only joy-in-giving brings,' wrote Michael Doheny. 'The vivid reds and blues of their sarees contrasted with the dull brown brickwork of the hospital wards and the grey blankets of the disabled freedom fighters. We had gone from bed to bed, handed out gifts with a smile, a handshake and a greeting. The joy in the faces of those young men with their stumps of arms or bits of legs was worth coming from afar to witness and yet all was polite and almost formal in our relationship.'

'Suddenly someone (I think it was the towering Fr Aengus) said: "give them an Irish dance." Monica [Chambers, from County Clare] began to hum "The Rakes of Mallow". In a trice we were on the floor (yours truly in the midst) doing the Walls of Limerick or the Bridge of Athlone (it did not matter which). Then the miracle happened. It was like a thunder clap. We had broken through to those boys. We were one with them. Those who could move gathered round, those in bed suddenly came alive. A legless boy of about eighteen turns his tin plate upside down to make a drum and with his spoon begins to make time. "Link arms, swing it" comes the command and we are one swirling mass of humanity . . . Fr Aengus shouts: "A song!" Ethna Caffrey starts us off with a Bengali love song "*Eto Din Pore*" which wins their hearts. The strains of "Silent Night" from our volunteers is answered by "*Amar Sonar Bangla*" (Oh My Golden Bengal)—this is their song of freedom. As they sang those words of Rabindranath Tagore to a slow haunting melody, my mind flowed with it down the rivers of Bangladesh following those marching men, the fighters for freedom as they battle their way to Dhaka and freedom. There was none of us who was not moved. I saw an old man in a bed close by, the tears brimming in his eyes. Maybe he had lost a son, or had a daughter dishonoured. Our Concern volunteers responded with *"Amhrán na bhFiann"*. We were united in spirit and two nations were as one.'

Michael Doheny himself was a very important influence in the development of Concern. We have seen his enthusiastic support for the Kennedys at board meetings. In early 1972 he was working for CORR (Christian Organisation for Relief and Rehabilitation) as well as acting as a chaplain to Mother Teresa's children's home. Before that he had been in California encouraging the US organisation Concern for Bangladesh (later Concern/USA). With his leg-o'-mutton side-whiskers and his Nehru cap with a shamrock embroidered on the side, he had something of the medieval saintly wanderer about him. His newsletters are full of stories, largely true, and a kind of jolly piety that one associates with scout leaders. Yet it was a piety and a cheerful hopefulness, a conviction of the rightness of Concern's activities, that inspired and buoyed up many of the volunteers in dark and stressful moments. You could never quite pin him down—now here, now there, writing, inspiring especially new volunteers, exploring new areas of activity and making numerous influential films about Concern's activities. His special skill with these films was to bring stark images of poverty and soft images of volunteers into common and vivid focus. They were shown at fundraising evenings all over Ireland and were very successful. The tradition he started of regularly filming and photographing Concern's overseas workers and activities contributed greatly to a sense of ownership of Concern's overseas work among the fast growing grassroots support in Ireland of the 1970s.

In the years that followed many professionals were to volunteer their time and expertise in continuing this tradition. Most prominent among them were Michael Lally of RTE and his film crew colleagues, Brendan Frawley, Cyril Ryan and Michael Lee. Among journalists, Deirdre Purcell, Vincent Browne and Charlie Bird contributed much to present Concern's activities. Photographer Liam Burke made several overseas trips to help publicise Concern's work. Liam, Noel Gavin, Pat Langan and Karen Davies built up the organisation's photographic records through the 1980s and early 1990s.

There were now (1973) 35 expatriate volunteers in Bangladesh, including six from England, five from the USA, three from India and one from France, and inevitably the role of the field director was due to change. The first change was in the garnering of finance from outside sources. Aengus Finucane was particularly good at this, cajoling, charming and harassing the agencies into supporting his numerous programmes. In October 1973 he reported to Raymond Kennedy that he was receiving aid from IRC, Bread for the World, CORR, the Pro Nuncio, a Baptist Mission, and the German dioceses of Cologne and Rotenburg and further applications were being considered by CAFOD, Trócaire and Oxfam. He also maintained close contacts with agencies in Bangladesh such as the Bangladesh Red Cross and BRAC. In 1973 he established a series of St Patrick's Day reunions, which were both great parties and great excuses to entertain all sorts of people. At the very first Aengus Finucane presented a sprig of shamrock to Sheikh Mujib.

Clearly, once a field director could organise the finance, the relationship between head office and the field was going to change. By 1973 this was already happening, for when new projects for Bangladesh were proposed by head office to Trócaire and Secours Catholique Aengus Finucane protested, and eventually wrote bluntly to the executive director, Raymond Kennedy: 'I am not accepting responsibility for the implementation of projects which are not approved from here.'

Aengus Finucane was, at this time, a strong advocate of the independence of country directors. As he wrote: 'If we become more longterm there is a need for a lot of re-orientation and a much clearer working out of roles and procedures. It would put the whole organisation on a different footing for administration at home and here, for volunteers, for funding for accountability. Many things in all sectors are too haphazard at the present and can only pass because we are in a quasi-permanent state of crisis . . . I am not saying that I have lost faith in the organisation but I think the time has come when it is necessary and when, perhaps for the first time, we can afford and must consider more businesslike approaches. Going into long term development projects with big funding will of necessity make us a less personal organisation. Government money, and Trócaire money and big development money from other organisation necessarily curb individualism and impose more rigid procedures.'

4: The field directors take charge

*In my strong opinion, and I speak with the authority of
involvement in overseas aid for more than 25 years, the poverty
and suffering resulting from an emergency is almost all man-
made and therefore political. Wars and civil disturbances,
refugee situations, the denial of human rights and the poverty
that causes the deaths of unknown millions of children
throughout what is termed the Third World are the results of
political decisions and political mismanagement. In this
situation the North is rarely blameless.[1]*

Ethiopia is two places. Firstly it is an ancient country that can trace
its continuous political existence for more than 2,000 years (far longer
therefore than any European state); an empire straddling the Red
Sea that 4,000 years ago was trading with Egypt in highly sophisticated products such as spices, incense and myrrh; the home of ancient wonders such as the rock-hewn churches of Lalibela, the cas-
tles of Gondar and Axum, and the walled town of Harar; the only
African country that was never colonised. A country with a subtle
tradition of written poetry characterised by 'wax and gold', where
the outer wax (the plain meaning of the words) hides and yet reveals
the gold beneath. This Ethiopia is the oldest Christian country in
Africa, where devout Copts fast for nearly half the days of the year
(their Lent lasts two months during which no meat or dairy products are allowed) and there are monasteries in remote parts that have
been dedicated to Christ for more than 1,500 years.[2]

Then, secondly, there is the Ethiopia of famine—characterised
by television images of emaciated men, women and children marching miles from their drought-stricken villages to the doubtful haven
of a relief camp. So powerful indeed have these images been that it is
difficult to think of the other, older Ethiopia at all.

Geographically Ethiopia is also (broadly) two places—the highlands to the north, a continuous plateau over 2,500 metres above sea-level (Lugnaquilla, the highest peak of the Wicklow mountains, reaches just over 1,000 metres) and the lowlands in the south, stretching to the Rift Valley. The highland plateau is incised with plunging deep valleys and, as evidence of the progressive Sahel drought, the scars of old, dried rivers. This is the historic part of Ethiopia, where the bulk of the population lives. Unfortunately, it is the very part that has been worst affected by the desertification process and the associated failures of rainfall. The south of the country has quite a different climate, with malaria, tse-tse fly and a different vegetation.

The British broadcaster Jonathan Dimbleby went to Ethiopia in 1973 (not his first visit) to explore the extraordinary churches of Lalibela, in the northern highlands, 400 miles north of Addis Ababa. There are 11 of them, carved from the living rock. These 800-year-old Christian monuments are now a UNESCO World Heritage site. The most famous is the church dedicated to St George, Bet Giorgis; to create this thousands of workmen first excavated a pit 25 metres square and 13 metres deep, leaving in the middle a 13 metre high pillar, 12 metres square. Out of this pillar they chiselled from the living rock the perfect cruciform church, complete with a three-step supporting platform.

While he was in Wollo, Dimbleby learned something else. A great famine was brewing in the bleak northern mountains. Because of the remoteness of the area, the poor communications and the almost feudal nature of Haile Selassie's government, little had been heard about the effect of a prolonged drought in Wollo. In some areas there had been no rain for seven years. The looming crisis had, however, been identified by Kevin Doheny, who had been in Ethiopia since 1972. He had established the Christian Relief Association, later the Christian Relief and Development Association. (CRDA eventually boasted a membership of 105 Churches and NGOs, not including the Orthodox Church.) As chairman of the relief fund, Kevin Doheny was closely in touch with the worsening situation. Every week reports from the field by himself and others came to the office. Thus, on 25 June 1973, he wrote: '800 famine victims are in camp in Makele and more arriving every day. They get two meals of *injeera* and *wet* per day. Gross overcrowding . . . many TB cases . . . skin sores resultant from lack of water. All are malnourished . . . last week five children died.' So when he met Jonathan Dimbleby he was in a strong position to brief him and to point him in the direction of the worst areas.[3]

Ethiopian scholars identify various stages in the experience of famine. The first is the warning phase, when the price of foodstuffs rises, when peasants start to sell first family possessions, then tools and finally cattle. The next is the stage of crisis, where food is quite lacking—illness, migration or death are the consequence. Then the NGOs and local agencies step in, and food begins to be made available. Finally there is the stage of survivor guilt.[4] Dimbleby stumbled on the 1974 famine just as the crisis stage was deepening. The television programme he made, *Ethiopia—the Unknown Famine*, which was broadcast in June, awoke the conscience of the world.

One of the reasons for the slow filtering of information about the famine was the near-feudal governance of the country. Ras Tafari, known as Haile Selassie, who claimed to descend through 237 generations from Solomon and Sheba, was in his 80s; he had been the most powerful man in the country since 1917. His extraordinarily diverse country was the size of France and Spain together, with 25 million people divided over 80 ethnic groups, each with its own language and culture. Even the largest groups, the Amhara and the Oromo, were each scarcely a quarter of the whole. To hold the country together Haile Selassie used feudal deference (as late as the 1950s, it was customary, coming near the emperor in his Rolls Royce, for other drivers to leap out of their cars and prostrate themselves). During his reign he had initiated various liberal reforms—he founded banks, hospitals and printing presses; he abolished the slave trade, the use of stocks, and the custom of chopping off the hands of men accused of theft. With policies of divide and rule, he did hold on to power, but at the expense of becoming less and less effective. Not least was this seen in the fact that the feudal landowning system meant that great areas of royal, church and landowner estates were undercultivated while people starved.

The famine had started after the rains had failed for three years in succession. The first affected were a number of relatively 'unimportant' groups, such as nomadic pastoralists, small tenants and landowners, farm servants and labourers, craftsmen and beggars.[5] It was hardly for the King of Kings to concern himself with these, so he concentrated on his plans to create a massive dam to harvest the energies of the Blue Nile.

The international attention caused by Dimbleby's film stimulated internal unrest, and throughout 1974 the shadowy Derg, a group of Marxist military officers, initiated a creeping coup. Loudly protesting loyalty at every step, the Derg imprisoned, one by one, the emperor's ministers and advisors. The ageing emperor, like a frog in gradually heating water, did nothing. Every day the Derg ordered new arrests, and, it was thought, new killings. Outside the barracks the wives of the imprisoned generals and ministers queued with baskets of food to hand in for their loved ones—one of them, Tiruwork Asfaw, who later ran a Concern medical clinic in the city, attended thus every day for years before being told 'you needn't come any more'—which was all the information she was given as to her husband's fate.

During this period, the soldiers moved slowly, uncertain how the public would take the deposition of the emperor. Eventually, so much anger was generated by the contrast between the $100 million he was supposed to have siphoned into Swiss bank accounts and the poverty of the people that they made their last move. The 83-year-old Haile Selassie was driven away from the palace in September 1974 (to his disgust, in a small Volkswagen), to spend the remaining year of his life in imprisonment.[6] Now the 100 or more military delegates that made up the Derg would have to take direct responsibility for one of the poorest and least developed countries in the world.

Raymond Kennedy visited the drought-affected regions of Ethiopia in May 1973 on his way back from a visit to the Yemen where, as we shall see (Chapter 5), things were not going well for Concern. Then Kevin Doheny wrote requesting Concern's help. In a report to the board Raymond Kennedy wrote: 'Ethiopia is a country of 25 million people, with a literacy rate of less than 20 per cent. The general standard of living is very very low. The provinces of Wollo and Tigray have suffered drought for 3–7 years. The death rate stands at 600 per week. Kevin Doheny requests the services of three nurses, four civil engineers, a Pitman shorthand teacher and an English teacher.'

The board accepted this proposal, and a special appeal was launched. The first volunteer, nurse-midwife Dolores Crudge, flew from the Yemen to Ethiopia to start work in Wollo on 11 October 1973, just as a UNDP report highlighted the problems in Wollo and Tigray. The appeal, as was frankly admitted, was hugely helped by Jonathan Dimbleby's programme on the famine and also a programme on Radió Éireann by Liam Nolan. (To Raymond Kennedy's vigorously expressed annoyance, Nolan passed on some of the money raised to the Jonathan Dimbleby Fund rather than sending it all to Concern.)

By early 1974 there were two doctors and six nurses in Ethiopia working for the Catholic secretariat; more nurses, and engineers for water and road works were being recruited. However, too little thought had gone into the management of the team. A field director, Brian Pearce, was appointed, but on arrival he was co-opted to work for Kevin Doheny's committee in Addis Ababa, where his contribution was very highly valued.

In February, 1974, volunteer Paddy Fahey reported on his visit to Kobbo (200 miles north of Addis Ababa in Wollo Province): 'this team has been living under horrible conditions'. Neither the work nor the accommodation was satisfactory. It was unclear whether Concern or CRC, the co-funders, had the authority to spend money to improve living conditions, and the nurses 'have found a great lack of definition in the work available to them, and have to find useful work for themselves.' There was also tension between staff in Kobbo and Addis Ababa. Morale got worse, and in March one of the doctors came home early.

Concern had fallen into a common error: that of concentrating on providing resources (in this case, people) but giving too little attention to how those resources were to be deployed, supported and controlled. In Biafra this had not been necessary, because the parish network—priests and buildings—provided a ready-made distribution system and the people to operate it. All Concern had to do was to provide food. Given this experience, Concern can perhaps be excused for not immediately identifying the importance of the management role in aid.

Drawing on its own experience of innumerable emergency operations, UNHCR uses the term 'capacity' for this management and control role, and pinpoints the lack of such capacity as a crucial failing—'if capacity is weak then the emergency response is likely to be weak, even if resources are adequate.'[7] The impulse to give is admirable, but becomes little more than self-indulgence if no attention is given to how the gift relates to the proposed beneficiary. Writing about the Cambodian refugee crisis in 1979, the journalist William Shawcross noted various outlandish donations: 'an American group called La Lèche League offered to send a 747 filled with lactating mothers to suckle abandoned Khmer babies . . . Food for the Hungry came to the border with a large stock of woollen underpants . . . Enfants sans Frontières sent a consignment of foam mattresses—it is difficult to imagine anything more disgusting in a rainsodden refugee camp . . . 500 Japanese youths came to Thailand and spent four days instructing refugee children on the harmonica and *joie de vivre*.'[8]

In May the board invited Jack Finucane, then in Bangladesh as assistant field director, to Dublin to discuss the possibility of his becoming the new field director. He agreed, but only on condition that the field director should have the 'controlling of volunteers, transfers, repatriation if necessary, requests for personnel, purchasing etc.' The development of the field director model greatly reduced the number of lone volunteers assigned VSO-style to this or that hospital in Ghana, Zambia, Nigeria, Iran, Jamaica or Chile (to name such destinations from the executive director's report of 1 May 1974).

The new concept of field director implied a commitment to the development of a particular country well beyond the initial crisis. At a rather difficult meeting between Concern and the newly founded

Trócaire in April 1974, Bishop Casey did his best to keep Concern in the 'emergency' box. 'Trócaire,' he said rather grandly, 'does not propose to collect for emergency programmes, as that was the proper preserve of Concern.' Aengus Finucane retorted that emergency programmes inevitably led to development, and that in practice Concern had more of the latter than the former. The fact was that Trócaire, with the backing of the hierarchy, had enormous pulling power; its Lenten programme was already denting Concern's ability to carry out its commitments. Its very existence constituted a long-perceived threat. Indeed, Vincent Grogan and Raymond Kennedy had gone to Maynooth to plead that the hierarchy back Concern rather than establish another organisation. Unfortunately, Africa Concern's independence of action during the Nigerian civil war had not endeared it to the hierarchy, as we have seen, and the approach came to nothing.

Concern did have a strength in being able to react quickly to obvious human needs, unhampered by bureaucracy or indeed political 'niceness'. At the April 1974 meeting Bishop Casey described the procedure for arranging funding by Trócaire of projects in southeast Asia (including Bangladesh): 'monies to be spent on development work should be requested through the national secretariats or bodies with which Trócaire is associated, which in turn will submit them to the Asian committee, which will allocate the money.' Direct approaches from the field were discouraged. The minutes record that Fr Finucane 'pointed out the inconveniences' involved in this policy, as no doubt he did.

It should not be thought, however, that fundraising in Ireland had become insignificant. The executive secretary, Alan Williams, recruited in June 1973, brought a newly professional approach, addressing in particular the on-going problem of how to maintain the flow of funds when there was no special crisis to catch the public imagination. Unfortunately, he and Raymond Kennedy did not agree as to the role and scope of the job, and there was a sharp flurry of solicitors' letters, before work was resumed.

In 1974/5 over £500,000 was raised of which £37,000 was spent on administration, mostly on salaries for the 13 full-time paid staff and £53,000 on publicity and fundraising. With a little dip into accumulated resources, this allowed Concern to spend £475,000 on relief and development. It was a year of great growth in the organisation, in which the number of volunteers in the field doubled to 120. Income and expenditure rose commensurately: in the previous 12 months (1973/4) the expenditure had been £250,000 of which 25 per cent was spent on administration, fundraising and publicity work. Gathering these large sums required considerable organisation. In the past there had been the three 'hardy annuals' of the Concern fundraising year: the Christmas Fast, the Lenten Fast and the Harvest of Hope (in October). By the mid-1970s two of these had fallen away for different reasons, leaving the Christmas Fast as the one, big, regular event of the year. Because of Trócaire's Lenten campaign, Concern had eventually withdrawn from fundraising at that time. The Harvest of Hope was a sponsored harvesting of rose-hips from the hedgerows, with an idea of using them as a source of vitamin C. After a year or two however, this too faded away, when the rose-hips proved increasingly difficult to sell. Spring and summer became the lean months as far as fundraising was concerned. However, these activities were typically supplemented by special campaigns, often focused on Michael Doheny's films shown to factory groups, schools, churches and colleges; follow-up of individual media efforts, especially in the *Irish Independent*; leaflet mailings to previous subscribers, and various school collections.

In January 1975, Alan Williams reported that group fundraising events were becoming popular: 'the events take many forms e.g. dances, variety concerts, special church services, coffee mornings, sponsored swims, bicycle rides, walks, raffles or just plain "booze-ups"'. However, allied with this was an 'ever more pressing demand from active groups for projects to support. There is a demonstrated need for identification with some specific and well defined project within the Third World, and a reluctance to raise funds for the vaguely defined overall concept of "Concern".'[9]

The 1975 Christmas campaign raised over £66,300, nearly double the previous year's result. There were two reasons for this success: firstly a greatly increased network of local organisers—62 in all outside Dublin, and 20 in the Dublin area; and secondly, a new showing of the two-hour BBC documentary on world poverty *Five Minutes to Midnight* on RTÉ in early December, together with an associated article in the *RTÉ Guide* and follow-up advertising. The 48-hour fast was widely advertised on radio, which stimulated the recruitment of fasters, collectors and carol singers. Fast centres were set up throughout Dublin from Ballymun to Bray and as far out as Lucan. The biggest contribution, not surprisingly, came from the Grafton Street/Georges Street centre, which contributed £2,453 out of some £13,000 (actually, this was a relatively disappointing result from the Dublin area—26 per cent of the population should give more than 20 per cent of the total receipts).

Despite the freezing cold, almost all the centres had at least two people doing a continuous 48-hour fast, in some cases as many as eight fasted. Special caravans were supplied for the fasters' use, and a cheerful collegiality between fasters and collectors kept spirits high. In Greenhills College over 50 of the pupils fasted and a further 70 were involved in collecting over a wide area in cars driven by parents and teachers. (The new idea of sponsorship per hour fasted added to the Greenhills total, though as the organisers noted soberly, 'it takes some time to gather sponsorship money in'.) Headquarters in Camden Street maintained constant contact with each of the centres, making sure that the money donated was looked after, and that each centre had sufficient tins, stickers, posters etc.

In Ethiopia, the destination of quite a lot of this money, Jack Finucane took up his post in July 1974. This was something of a baptism of fire, as he wrote in his second report to Raymond Kennedy (15 August 1974). 'The past three weeks,' he wrote, 'have been the most difficult of my life.' The volunteers took the opportunity to unleash all the frustrations of the previous months on his head, and it was uncomfortable. The key perception that he passed on to Raymond was that the post of field director was the most important in the establishment of a new field and, most specifically, that it was a full-time job. Concern and the volunteers had, in his opinion, suffered as a result of the loss of Brian Pearce's expertise following his secondment to CRC.

In true Holy Ghost fashion, Jack spent the first weeks sorting out better accommodation at each site in the field. In Makalle, for instance, where there were five volunteers, he closed the gloomy 14-room house—nicknamed 'Colditz'—and rented two much smaller but more suitable houses. In Adigrat he did the same, getting rid of the previous house, which offered no privacy, and to which up to a dozen beggars swarmed every time someone opened the front door. As he wrote to Raymond Kennedy: 'You may think I have gone into the real estate business. I believe in good housing for volunteers, it helps the work so much. This is based on my experience in Bangladesh and Biafra. Personally I cannot stand dirt, and some of our houses were impossible to keep clean.'

By the time he arrived, as was reported in a booklet called *Concern in Ethiopia* published in August 1974, 'the famine situation had greatly improved in the highland region . . . relief grain had alleviated misery. Most of the shelters had closed and the short-term rehabilitation programme had distributed loans for seed and plough oxen. Both rainy seasons were adequate in this region in 1974 although pests, especially army worm, destroyed some of the harvest. This does not mean that the northern highlands are out of danger . . .' But though there was much to do, worsening social, political and security issues increasingly made Concern's work in Ethiopia impossible.

The Marxist revolution which had overthrown Haile Selassie was a constant source of social disruption: all urban and rural land was taken into public ownership, and an elaborate administrative structure of urban and rural councils linked every person directly to the state/party command structure. The old feudal structure was destroyed, and the land was distributed via peasant associations which quickly gained a reputation for being quarrelsome and corrupt. In October 1974, in Maoist Cultural Revolution style, the government announced that the educated few should pay back some of the benefits they had received from the taxes of the poor. All high school and university students, and their teachers, some 60,000 in all, were assigned to teaching programmes in the country to spend a year educating the rural poor. The programme was extended a year later. Unfortunately, the reluctant high school pupils and undergraduates were given no orientation and there was little local leadership or drive, so the main effect of the programme was to withdraw scarce skilled labour from the economy.

With Haile Selassie's unifying hand removed, the ethnic diversity of the country was quickly expressed in armed struggle. The Eritrean nationalists, who had been fighting for independence from Ethiopia since the 1960s, were now joined by the Tigray People's Liberation Front and the Oromo Liberation Front, not to mention the Ethiopian People's Revolutionary Party, who were aggressively critical of the military government. In 1976 tens of thousands of EPRP members were imprisoned, tortured and killed. Inside the Derg itself power struggle was constant, with two heads of state being killed before Colonel Mengistu established himself.

Despite the difficulties implicit in living in such revolutionary times, Jack Finucane was determined that Concern should contribute what it could, at least for as long as worsening safety conditions allowed. In mid-1975 there were 26 volunteers still in the country. They operated as far north as Asmara in what is now Eritrea, through Axum, the ancient heartland of Ethiopia, down to Chencha, 800 miles south towards the Kenyan Rift Valley. Perhaps the work that most catches the imagination was that supporting the fistula programme run by Dr Reginald Hamlin and his wife Dr Katherine Nicholson Hamlin. The Hamlin clinic cared for women suffering from this most distressing wound—an abnormal opening between the bowel and the vagina caused by prolonged labour in childbirth, or infected abcesses, perhaps aggravated by carrying heavy loads (women were often expected to carry enormous piles of fuel-wood). The fistula renders the woman continuously incontinent with consequences described by Jack Finucane: 'This makes her grossly infected, foul smelling and a virtual social outcast. Nobody can bear to be beside her for more than a few minutes because of the smell. Her husband leaves her and her family does not want her . . . at the Hamlin clinic these woman are housed in a special hostel, their infection cured; they are mentally rehabilitated, their continence is re-established and finally with new clothes, a little money and their confidence restored, they return to their families.' Over 16 years the

Hamlins had perfected a technique for the very difficult operation to repair fistulas, but now their programme was put under threat. The rural education programme had closed the university and they were suddenly without staff. Luckily Concern had a doctor/nurse-midwife team—the Corristines—who had already spent a year in the drastically over-stretched Adwa hospital and rural health programme. The couple moved to Addis Ababa in September 1975 where their services were made available to the Hamlin clinic.

However, in a report sent in February 1976, Jack stuck a note of pessimism. 'Because of political disturbances in the country,' he wrote, ' it is difficult for a volunteer organisation to operate. In the past year Concern has been forced to evacuate from six projects in Tigray, two in Eritrea and one project in Bale Province. One year ago we had ten Concern houses and 21 volunteers working in the north. Today we have one Concern house and four volunteers (two of whom are waiting re-assignments). Ethiopia has always been a difficult country to operate in, but such upheavals as I have mentioned make it almost impossible.' He went on to list the nine projects from which Concern had withdrawn in the previous 12 months, in all but two cases for political reasons.

A year later, February 1977, Council was told that the situation had worsened still further, and Raymond Kennedy expressed his fears about the welfare of personnel there. This was Concern's first encounter with sustained rebel-initiated insecurity and the first signal that expatriate volunteers were especially vulnerable. It was decided not to send any more personnel, and that those who were still at their posts would be offered the possibility of repatriation. Then Council directed that Jack Finucane be asked to run down the programme as quickly as possible. A month later Raymond Kennedy reported that there were then only three volunteers in Ethiopia, one of whom had opted to stay on indefinitely for personal reasons. Jack Finucane returned to Dublin in May, bringing with him numerous files and office records. Quite soon he was appointed field director in Bangladesh, in place of his brother Aengus who had taken a study sabbatical in Swansea.

By the mid-1970s Concern had established three major fields—

Bangladesh, Ethiopia and Yemen—each with several staff and a field director. There were also 20 or so volunteers in other fields (typically attached to hospitals run by other NGOs) including Peru, Israel, Sierra Leone, Nigeria and Kenya.

Concern first sent volunteers to the Yemen Arab Republic (north Yemen) in 1973, when midwife Suzanne Scally, from Ranelagh in Dublin, joined an international team in a hospital in Turbah near Hodeidah. Conditions in Yemen, were demanding, not least of the problems being a constant shortage of water. Michael Doheny reported that on his first visit to the mountainous Al Turbah regions in the extreme south of the country he was greeted with: 'You've come on the right day—we have water, and you can have a shower.' Three days previously they had had water only for drinking and cooking, but luckily it had rained. Lack of water in the district meant that skin diseases were prevalant: use of infected water brought parasites and diseases such as gastroenteritis, dysentery and cholera. Suzanne devoted much of her time to basic water hygiene.

In ancient times Yemen had been a rich and fertile country, home to the legendary Queen of Sheba, who came to Solomon, as the Bible says, 'with a very great train, with camels that bare spices, and with very much gold, and precious stones' (1 Kings 10:2). But despite its position on the Red Sea, world history had not been kind to Yemen, and by the time Concern arrived it had become one of the least developed countries in the world. Although fertile, too much of its agriculture was devoted to growing the mild narcotic *qat*, which increasingly replaced the exportable coffee for which the port of Mocha is famous. A coup in 1962 was followed by a seven-and-a-half-year civil war prolonged by the intervention on opposite sides of Egypt and Saudi Arabia. Even after the civil war petered out, there was dangerously little sense of a modern unified state—the tribal leaders (*shaykhs*) from the highlands were both armed and notoriously independent. In March 1974, for instance, Michael Doheny reported 'today was a lively day in Sana'a. 7,000 armed rebels arrived from a place only 34 miles from Sana'a to pledge their allegiance to Yemen for the first time. They took over and sang their war song, etc.'

During the 1970s two successive presidents were assassinated, and a rumbling dispute with South Yemen kept both countries on high alert. Although a series of local development associations had been set up, coordinated to a degree by the Confederation of Yemeni Development Associations (CYDA) the country suffered badly from a lack of skilled manpower and an administrative system completely dependent on a network of personal and tribal loyalties.

Raymond Kennedy visited Yemen in May 1973, on his way to Ethiopia. The Concern team was gradually built up so that by February 1974 there were seven members: two nurses in Turbah and five other staff in a new hospital in Hodeidah. This project alas, to which several Concern nurses were allocated, was a classic case of how things can go wrong, with the best will in the world. It started badly. The volunteers had been rushed out under the impression that the hospital was ready, but it was not, and they kicked their heels for three months in quite uncomfortable conditions. In an angry report echoing the volunteers' feelings, dated April 1974, the field director, Fr Michael Brosnan CSSp, criticised the Concern administration and the ultimate funders, the US Catholic Relief Service. 'CRS must take the blame.' he wrote, 'Concern must take the blame. It was an abuse of [the volunteers'] generosity.'

Summing up, Brosnan wrote: 'The dissatisfied and unhappy atmosphere around the place is going to be very discouraging for new volunteers coming.' In fact, he believed the whole hospital was ill-conceived, being out of scale with local need. 'The hospital at Hodeidah is out of place, a mistake from the start.' The Yemenis themselves looked on the hospital as a last resort, so they tended to bring patients in when it was far too late to do anything, and then felt aggrieved when no miracle was achieved. The local governor was of course extremely keen on such a prestigious project in his area, but this keenness was reflected more in elaborate illuminations of the hospital than actually paying the staff—'the hospital is one big farce for the political purposes of the Governor. CRS and the volunteers are pawns on the chessboard.'

Mike Brosnan left Concern at the end of 1975 to be succeeded by Fr Jimmy O'Toole who tragically died of a heart attack a few months later, having been scalded by excessive hot water in a shower. (Before going out to Yemen, Jimmy O'Toole had served as secretary of Concern, in 1983 and 1984.) Mary Humphreys, a safe pair of hands, was sent out to hold the fort.

Mary had originally been recruited from UCD to work as head-mistress in eastern Nigeria by Michael Doheny in 1962. Returning to Dublin just as the civil war was brewing, she became an active member of the 'old coasters' group that formed the early nucleus of the Joint Biafra Appeal fund. After working in Africa Concern's head office for some time she was posted to Bangladesh in 1972 where she started a women's career training institute devoted to the skills training (secretarial skills, handcrafts etc.) of women widowed by the war with Pakistan. After six months the institute was handed over to a Bengali counterpart.

To send a woman to the Yemen was brave, but not foolish. As she put it: 'You'd think that being a woman would have been a disadvantage, but to the contrary, since Yemeni men were used to looking after women, when I went in to see a Minister, his first reaction was to want to help me, and at the same time he would see me as no threat.' Her particular focus was to develop Jimmy O'Toole's work with rural development via the CYDA, moving away from the largely urban medical focus of activity heretofore. So when she made her report at the end of her posting in late 1975 she was able to report that 'our greatest concentration is in rural development', where five of the 15 volunteers were active, all coordinated by very close contacts with CYDA. A new field director, Séamus Connolly, went out in late 1975 and Mary began her long career in head office, but Concern was not to be in the Yemen for much longer. In May 1981, Paul Crowe, successor to Séamus Connolly, wound up the operation, and the organisation has not returned since.

Back in Dublin, as Mary returned, Council was facing consider-able difficulties. Despite increased professionalism in fundraising, and a large increase in numbers of volunteers financed, the income had not risen in real terms since 1973, and was not to do so for a few years. Various devices had been explored: John O'Loughlin Kennedy proposed a plan whereby businesses would sponsor volunteers, per-haps from their own staff; another scheme, which was put in hand in 1973, was to import handcrafts from Concern operations in Bang-ladesh and Ethiopia, thus making some money and at the same time providing a market for the goods. The old company Africa Concern Ltd (which had originally been established as a trading company to manage the *Columcille*) was the vehicle. Essie Harrington took on the management, and Concern Handcrafts was formally launched in 1974, with the idea of emulating the great success Oxfam had had with its shops.

At first sales were from head office, with a great sign across the front announcing the fact (a member of Council proposed that the sign be removed, on the grounds, among others, that it spoiled the Georgian facade). A shop was opened in April 1975 and a year later Essie Harrington reported that £19,000 worth of goods had been sold, not to mention various special sales in Cork, Drogheda, Gal-way and Limerick. A couple of years later the turnover had reached a respectable £40,000 a year, but the expenses were always just too much, so that by December 1982 cumulated losses (which in effect were guaranteed by Concern itself) amounted to £36,000. Because of difficulties in the main supply countries of Ethiopia and Bangla-desh—consignments were often delayed for weeks before being flown out of the country—the regularity of supply that such a commercial venture needs could not be maintained. Certainly it was impossible to enter into any wholesale deals. In the end, the handcrafts venture was wound up in 1983.

Although by 1977 Concern was a substantial organisation, with over 100 expatriate volunteers, not to mention many times that number of local staff, it was still feeling its way organisationally. On the non-executive side, so-called members (increased from 300 to 500 in 1977), typically ex-volunteers, members of local associations and so on, elected the Council (35 strong) at the annual general meeting. Members were equivalent to shareholders, and provided a guarantee for the company, limited to £5 each. One third of the Council retired every year. The Council was in practice made up largely of returned volunteers. Its key role was to ensure that the money subscribed by donors was put to appropriate use. It also decided on the appointment and remuneration of the chief executive, approved the annual budgets and the opening and closing of country fields. A subset of the Council were designated officers, including a chairman, a secretary and six others. These were the inner governing body.

The chief executive reported to the Council. Reporting to him were various home employees (notably those involved in fundraising, personnel and finance, and the field or country directors in charge of the volunteers and local staff in the countries). Exactly how these elements—Council, home and field staff—were to relate to each other was to take some working out as the business and operational environments grew increasingly complex.

Spurring the contention was, naturally, money. In the absence of specific crises, cash income was slow. In the 1970s there was certainly no sign of achieving the extraordinary income raised in 1968 and 1969. These were the years of the first OPEC use of the oil price weapon, when inflation peaked, in 1975, at just over 20 per cent per annum. So, confusingly, cash income was rising steadily, from £460,000 in 1973/4 to £683,000 in 1976/7, but in real terms a quite different picture emerged. In fact, in real terms income remained static between 1973 and 1979. Like most organisations at the time Concern struggled to understand the implications of this. Constant insidious increases in costs meant that commitments more than kept up with income.

The steady increase in commitments meant that there was a constant need to examine budgets, and pressure was put on field directors, notably in Bangladesh which represented the lion's share of development expenditure, to cut back. Given the ambitions and the personalities involved, this inevitably led to conflict.

5: The end of the beginning

Commenting on the unfortunate atmosphere at last Novem-
ber's Convention, Mr Dónal Ó Murchú made a plea that we
remember Concern's slogan 'Love in Action.' [1]

The last act of the creative but stormy Kennedy era of Concern was played out in 1976–8. The year 1976 started cheerfully enough, with executive director Raymond Kennedy outlining to Council his work plan for the first six months. Highlight of the plan was an intention to increase the number of volunteers in the field to 150; a new field director, in Sierra Leone, was to be appointed, with an expectation of 15 volunteers reporting to her. To finance this an increased effort was to be made to attract EEC and Irish government co-funding of projects.

Immediately after the Biafran war Africa Concern had spent much time and money on numerous small projects. This was still going on in 1976. There was a random aspect to these projects, which were typically proposed by missionaries in the field. In April, for instance, the projects committee recommended 16 projects involving the ex-penditure of some £32,000. The projects ranged from £75 granted to a hospital in Paraguay for the purchase of a medical microscope and £150 for a pilot irrigation scheme in Kenya, to the building of a girls' school in Ghana (£2,500). The two largest amounts were for £8,000 (teachers' salaries for a school in Sierra Leone) and £6,500 for a domestic science block in an agricultural college in Tanzania. In August, the projects committee authorised the expenditure of £75 for an artificial limb for a child in India. The annual budget for such small projects in 1976 was originally £62,000, but had been scaled back during the year to £43,000. As well as these small projects there were volunteers wholly or partly funded by Concern, particu-larly in Botswana, Tanzania, Zambia and Kenya who, in the old style, did not have the organisational support of a field director. One-third of Concern's development expenditure went on small projects and individual volunteers.

Other expansions envisaged included establishing a permanent office with an organiser in the US; Michael Doheny had been energetically exploring this for some time, and through the Irish-American network had obtained endorsement from Senator Edward Kennedy and various congressmen for the enterprise. Offices were also being established in Northern Ireland and in England.

To handle the extra head office work Raymond Kennedy proposed an increase in full-time head office staff, and some payment to the more experienced overseas personnel beyond the missionary-level subsistence provided heretofore. He was conscious that this was a significant shift from the former policy of relying solely on voluntary work, so he requested Council's opinion on the expected tension between fulltime and voluntary workers. He also highlighted in his report another tension 'which has been very useful to us' namely the employment of religious personnel to work with lay people. At this time most of the field directors were, as it happened, priests. He did not spell out exactly what the source of tension is, but he suggested that 'the time has come when we should have some consensus on this'. No doubt the gradual secularisation of Irish society was being felt inside Concern as elsewhere, and the special respect previously allowed to the clergy could no longer be taken for granted. The report closed with the pious impression that 'there is a continual growth in understanding and unity of purpose in the organisation, thank God'.

Sadly, this was only partly true, for personality divergences were still strongly present. In a letter to head office, Séamus Connolly, Mary Humphreys' successor in Yemen, noted how frustrating this could be. In April he and his fellow field directors were brought back to Dublin to discuss the situation, but the meeting was not a success. 'There was,' he wrote with unhappy frankness, 'no real communication between the important administrative people at home and in the field. I think communication was impossible because of the depth of personal mistrust dating to earlier days . . . every effort of communication is branded as being for or against someone or something. Personally I now consider it hopeless to make any criticism, positive or negative, without being immediately identified with one side or the other.'

As well as the after-swell of previous storms, there were one or two threatening clouds on the horizon. Specifically, there was the recurrent problem of fundraising in the absence of high-profile disasters. As we have seen, income in real terms stagnated throughout the 1970s. This was partly a function of competition. There were now three main Third World organisations in Ireland—Trócaire, Gorta and Concern—actively seeking the public's funds; but there were also Oxfam, the Church of Ireland Bishops' Appeal, the Irish Red Cross Society and smaller one-man outfits such as Aid from Ireland, as well as fundraising by individual religious orders. From time to time there were newpaper reports of charities whose non-field expenditure might reach as much as two-thirds of the total.[2] At the time Fr Jack O'Brien, the executive secretary of the umbrella body the Irish Missionary Union, declared that 'anything over 20 per cent of the gross income of any fundraising organisation' spent on administration would be too high.[3] Although this figure has been occasionally exceeded, Concern's *average* over the last thirty years has been half this limit.

With the weight of the Hierarchy behind it, Trócaire had hit the ground running in 1973, and immediately presented a serious challenge to Concern's fundraising ability. Its first Lenten Campaign raised £489,400, much more than Concern's annual expenditure. Over the next five years Trócaire was to raise a total of £4.6 million as against Concern's £2.9 million. Only after 1980 did Concern's income from donations begin to match that of Trócaire.[4]

A different challenge came in 1974 with the founding by the Department of Foreign Affairs of the Agency for Personal Service Overseas (APSO). Given Concern's dominant position in sending volunteers into the field, it was easy for a partisan eye to see this as yet another vote of no confidence in Concern by the powers that be. In February 1976 Dennis Tindill, secretary of APSO, went on a fact-finding trip around Africa. His report, relying on the dominant theory of development of the time, stressed the African need for 'skilled as opposed to unskilled' volunteers. Specifically he identi-fied the requirement for 'middle and upper echelon personnel—administrators, accountants, people with management experience'. He did not attempt to suggest how Ireland would be able to provide such personnel. Tindill concluded that APSO should not finance projects which do nothing more than 'tinker with the system, no matter how cheap, traditional or easy these may be to organise.'

This was seen, and was perhaps intended, as a direct criticism of Concern. John O'Loughlin Kennedy wrote a strong letter to Bill Jackson, then head of APSO, rejecting the apparent sneer about the qualifications of Concern volunteers, who were not the lovable ama-teurs as portrayed, but trained professionals. More fundamentally, he very acutely pointed out that anyone going out to the Third World expecting that their presence would change the system was heading rapidly for a nervous breakdown. That way madness lay.[5]

A month later Raymond Kennedy joined the fray with a letter distributed to all APSO council members, in which he complained that Concern's share of Irish government funds was dropping, while at the same time APSO 'keeps increasing its expenditure on staff and administration'. Bill Jackson responded defensively but robustly, rejecting the 'considerably personalised' criticisms by Concern of APSO executives, and bluntly noting that while at staff level things were fine, 'rapport at chief executive level' between the two organi-sations was not good. It was to take some time before this bridge was thoroughly mended.

It was not only Concern that had economic problems in these years. Ireland had entered the Common Market in a jubilant, buoy-ant mood, stimulated by 15 years of strong economic growth, by the heady 1960s and by a new self-confidence. There were high ex-pectations that the new partnership, with the very solid underpinning of the Common Agricultural Policy, would drive the economy to further heights. On the other hand, Irish manufacturing industry was clearly going to need considerable modernisation to enable it to compete internationally. The oil price rises were to cause serious problems for energy deficient countries such as Ireland. It seemed to some that the boom that had started in 1958 was about to deliver a hard landing; people began to worry about rising costs and lowering standards of living. The Irish government responded by uncoupling current expenditure from current income, thus enabling budget deficits. These were to be funded by foreign borrowing. In 1977 the new Fianna Fáil government was to compound the problems by a 'boom and bloom' attempt to buy a way out of the problem. Borrowings went up again, public expenditure and inflation followed, to be given a further boost when the second oil price rise came in 1979.

Socially, these were intermediate years; the country was digesting the relative wealth created since 1958, and the social changes brought by it and television, the tinsel herald of the new. Changes were occurring, but slowly. One of the more momentous changes was the surge in home ownership—by the mid-1970s for the very first time as many as half the houses in Dublin were owner-occupied. To pay for this, more women were joining the job market. (Just at this time the legal system expressed its confidence in female abilities by at last allowing women to become jurors.) All sorts of social welfare payments came on stream—including to unmarried mothers, who would no longer be hidden away in Magdalen laundries as had happened to previous generations. The 1971 census announced a radical shift to the country's self-image—it was the first time more people worked in industry than in agriculture. This was mainly due to the continued reduction in the numbers employed in agriculture, a fact which put constant pressure on unemployment rates. By the end of the decade Irish unemployment was one of the highest in the EEC.

Politically, people were much more interested in the economy and social questions than the problems in the North, but occasionally the Troubles there spilled south; most notably in the horrific bombings in Monaghan and Dublin in 1974. In February 1976 a bomb damaged the Shelbourne Hotel, and in July the British Ambassador was assassinated. Mary Guckian, headmistress of the Holy Child Infants' School in Derry and one of Africa Concern's earliest board members, wrote to Kay O'Loughlin Kennedy in a black mood

Table 5.1 *Expenditure May 1975–June 1976*

Development	£ooos	£ooos
Bangladesh	164	
Ethiopia	59	
Yemen	36	
Other volunteers	91	
Small projects	43	
Total development		393 *(78%)*
Promotion		
Development education	16	
Fundraising	62	
Total promotion		78 *(16%)*
Total administration		32 *(6%)*
Total expenditure		503 *(100%)*

following the bombing of the family shop. 'You have no idea of the demoralisation that has taken place here,' thanks to the Provisional IRA, 'evil, hard-faced men, who have made their money'. Disillusioningly, she continued: 'I don't think much of the Cardinal, priests or politicians who have only complicated things more. And it's not over, in fact the worst could still be coming.'

The scale of Concern's financial problem was clearly exposed by the 12-month accounts produced in June 1976. Receipts during the year were £486,000, expenditure £503,000. Crucially, accumulated reserves, the safety net for the continuing financing of projects and people in the field, had dropped from 18 per cent of expenditure — itself an historically low figure—to a mere 4 per cent. This implied a very dangerous level of reliance on the success of immediate fundraising efforts. Some years later a formal decision was made that at least three months' worth of expenditure should be held in reserve, to ensure the continued support of activity in the fields.

Initially this idea was resisted in Council, on the grounds that the donors wanted their money to be spent immediately in the field, not held prudently in Dublin.

As the balance of power between head office and field directors shifted, more attention was paid to managing the relationship. The field directors flew back to Dublin for a series of meetings in which they shared their experiences both among themselves and with the workers on the home front. Unfortunately, these meetings had the effect of increasing rather than reducing the distance between the field and head office. A further meeting in November 1976 was even less successful. No minutes were taken, but the tone can be judged by Council member Dónal Ó Murchú's comments at a Council meeting the following February. He noted the 'unfortunate atmosphere' and, with a reference to Concern's slogan, declared that the meeting 'had fallen far short of expressing Love in Action'.

A crunch meeting of the executive committee (established to enable Council to keep a tight eye on administrative matters) in October 1976 was told that the deficit against budget stood at £60,000, and that to meet current commitments Concern would need £250,000 income over the next three months. However, 'our recent past intake has been miserable [which] makes the proposed targets seem impractical.' The very survival of Concern itself was silently on the agenda.

With income running some 30 per cent below budget, there would have to be cuts. Staff salaries were reviewed, and a new, lower, wages scale adopted. This quickly led to staff shortages. Crucially field directors were asked not to draw down any money, even if budgeted, without specific approval in advance from the Dublin office. That ever-sensitive indicator, the ratio of non-field to total expenditure, rose to 39 per cent in the 1977/78 accounts (see Appendix 2).

As the largest user of money the Bangladesh budget naturally attracted the spotlight. After only a few years of independence, Bangladesh was an extremely needy country and the field director, Aengus Finucane, never had any trouble finding new projects. He had good contacts with other agencies and with funding sources so he was usually able to finance new ideas. As a result, head office supplied less than a third of his total budget. Nevertheless, the £164,000 that Concern did send to Bangladesh represented a third of the agency's total expenditure. Because of the multiplicity of funding sources, there was some confusion in Dublin as to which projects they were financing and which were financed from elsewhere. This was mirrored by a similar confusion in Dhaka. In October an accountant was sent to help sort things out, but failed to bring order.

In February 1977, Raymond Kennedy again referred to 'the recurrent financial crises in Bangladesh'. The problem was compounded further by worries as to Aengus Finucane's state of health at the time. His sickness had already caused delay in drawing down promised funds from a German agency.

A specific cause for head office fury was the fact that Bangladesh had unexpectedly drawn down £40,000 all at once. Part of the reason for this was a sudden crisis that had blown up in Burma, where ethnic conflict between the Muslim Rohingyas and the majority Buddhist population on the Burma/Bangladesh border had led to 125,000 refugees fleeing into Bangladesh—a country with meagre resources and a hungry population of its own to feed. This ethnic problem was to recur periodically over the next 20 years, and is still not solved. Aengus Finucane reported back to Dublin stories of rape, brutality and murder by the Burmese army, and the totally inadequate provision of shelter, food and medicines in the official camps.

For the next few months more or less bad-tempered letters passed to and fro between Dublin and Dhaka. A muddle on the part of the Bank of America had confused various accounts, but budgeting was less than transparent, and this was compounded by a complete lack of mutual confidence. In May the assistant field director in charge of administration and accounts resigned, fulminating to Aengus Finucane (who circulated the letter to Council) that 'I have simply no confidence in the competence of the [head office] accounts department to handle even the simplest of business transactions.'

Bangladesh was, of course, only part of the larger problem, and by May 1977 the executive director, Raymond Kennedy, had had enough. To the stunned shock of the staff he resigned. Many of the senior staff signed an open letter to the Council deploring his departure. For years he had been identified as the driving force within Concern, as the creative impetus. Only a few months previously Council had discussed the idea of offering him a five-year contract, so his resignation was all the more unexpected.

Pat Fryer, who was chairman of the executive committee, put in words something of that shock and the feeling of debt owed to Raymond Kennedy. 'Speaking personally his resignation came as a great shock and I received it with profound sorrow . . . he has been completely dedicated to the work of Concern—he literally thought, worked and lived Concern for these past nine years, has been the main architect and builder of the organisation and it is largely due to him that Concern enjoys the reputation it does, not only in Ireland but internationally . . . I think it a tragedy that so many of those working in Concern both in the field and on the Council at home have found it easier to concentrate on his shortcomings than on his positive qualities. Over the years his achievements have been outstanding . . . I believe that it will only be in the months ahead that we shall fully realise the loss we have sustained.'

Many of the staff agreed, and over the next few months a number resigned. These included Rosary Morley, the overseas coordinator, Bernie Coyle, the education officer, Mary Coyne, the book-keeper and Eileen Reynolds, the receptionist. Michael Holahan, the accountant, was also planning to withdraw. Monsignor Bruce Kent, the English priest who had come to fame through his anti-nuclear protests, also resigned from Council.

Council had quickly to appoint a temporary executive director to ensure continuity. Given the executive committee's comment, already recorded, that day-to-day administration was not Raymond Kennedy's forte, it seems odd that they should have plumped for Michael Doheny, who, as he himself admitted, knew little of business administration. On the other hand, he was nearly as well known to the public and the aid world as Raymond Kennedy himself. He held the post between June and September 1977, during which time his principal success was to tap his enormous range of contacts for financial support and to smooth relationships with other Irish agencies whose feathers had been ruffled.

In the meantime, Council had set about recruiting a new executive director. Out of 30 applicants the choice fell finally on 49-year-old Alex Tarbett, who had been on the governing body of Africa Concern and then Concern since the very earliest days. His lack of field experience, however, was a handicap. He was well-known in the business world having been, until recently, managing director of Jefferson Smurfit's book publishing activities. Before that he had studied for the priesthood, reaching his final year in Maynooth; he had then worked in educational and religious publishing, including considerable time spent on catechetical and liturgical books in West Africa. He insisted on being paid a salary of £4,000, considerably less than Concern was prepared to offer. (This was roughly what a 24-year-old executive officer in the civil service was earning at the time.) He explained that his other business interests, notably the chairmanship of Brunswick Press, a substantial and long established printing house in south Dublin, and his consultancy with British Airways, would make up the rest.

In his first report to the Council Alex Tarbett laid down the dimensions of the financial and emotional problem as he saw it. As the accounts for the year to June 1977 were to show, there was a deficit of £78,000 for the year. Total income was nearly £700,000, but virtually all non-donation income was earmarked to specific projects. Relations with the field directors and in head office were still prickly, and despite Michael Doheny's efforts some fence-mending needed to be done in Ireland with bodies such as the Department of External Affairs and Trócaire. Over the next few months Tarbett made a point of visiting the various field activities to see for himself, and this laid the foundation for better information flow and improved relations generally.

However, the Council was still troubled by 'hurlers on the ditch and dramatic critics', as Alex Tarbett complained in his report of December 1977, and the organisation was by no means out of the woods. His solution was to cut the budget by at least 25 per cent, and announce that no further projects, other than co-funded, could be initiated. Despite the resignations, the organisation simply could not afford to recruit. He also bluntly signalled a new no-nonsense approach: 'I intend to run the Concern office with a rigorous business discipline and I will have no hesitation in dismissing any member of staff who displays an emotional or personal ambition to the detriment of Concern. I hope that both the Council and the Executive Committee would behave in a more business-like manner and try to help Concern solve its present problems.'

By December Tarbett had begun to size up the problems. He proposed a drastic cut-down of the small projects, including those where individual volunteers were sent out to join non-Concern projects, and the expensive office in Camden Street was to be re-valued with a view to selling all or part of it.

It was a long tough run, but by August 1978 the executive director's report noted that 'the battle for financial survival seems to be taking a turn for the better'. Reserves had a much healthier look, and in 1979 income in real terms overtook that of 1973 for the first time. The following year income in real terms at last reached almost the level achieved 11 years before in the glory days of the Biafran campaign. Among the promising sources of income was a single donation of $82,000 from the builder Ted Foley in the US via Bishop William Johnson of Orange, California, a contract initiated by Raymond Kennedy. A major new field, Tanzania, with a complete focus on development, had been opened, and the policy of not replacing single volunteers in places such as Sierra Leone was reaffirmed. Alex Tarbett's controversial interview with *Business and Finance*, in which he apparently suggested that the volunteers might do something to help Irish business abroad, was forgotten. There was even time to think how the organisation might celebrate its tenth birthday.

Not that all was sweetness and light on the Council—there was the constant presence of 'rather unfair and destructive criticism' and the difficulty of making Concern's voice heard in Ireland when 'one knows that in the wings there are a number of Council members who are waiting to criticise any step forward'—as Alex Tarbett put it in his report of November 1978. Since most of the staff and Council were, and are, returned volunteers, they each *know*, from personal experience, how things should be done. All feel it their duty to make their views known. The end of active participation in Concern by the Kennedys was finally signalled at the AGM held in January 1979 when John O'Loughlin Kennedy decided not to stand for election to the Council. The minutes recorded a cool exchange, in which the chairman, Michael Fingleton, 'expressed disappointment and thanked Mr Kennedy for the outstanding work he did as a Council member over the years. Voting then took place.'

By the following year, Alex Tarbett had brought Concern back to an even keel. As Council reported to the AGM, the financial position was satisfactory, the three main areas of operation, Bangladesh, Yemen and Tanzania (where programmes had started in the late 1970s) were continuing to progress, and a new field, Thailand, had just been opened. There were now 33 volunteers in Bangladesh under the leadership of field director Jack Finucane; Tanzania had 12 volunteers led by Philip O'Brien and the expanding Yemen field had 15 under Fintan Farrelly. Aengus Finucane was field director in Thailand, with 16 volunteers. Despite frequent resolutions that the practice should stop, there were ten volunteers seconded to other organisations in Kenya, Malawi, Sierra Leone and Nigeria. The possibility of opening a field in Lesotho-Botswana was being actively explored, although this was overtaken in 1980/81 by the need to respond to a dreadful famine among the Karamajong in Uganda. Here 23 volunteers (including future chairman P. J. Howell) under Aengus Finucane and his deputy, Ciúnas Bunworth, struggled to help the people in a famine dismissed by the government with the memorably cynical line—'the Karamajong were always skinny'.

A distinctive Concern philosophy was emerging with regard to emergencies and rehabilitation—if not to development work. The key was the use of highly motivated volunteers in emergency and relief situations. (It was, incidentally, the only Irish agency to use volunteers in these situations.) Against those who derided such efforts as being at best drops in the ocean and at worst the blunderings of well-meaning amateurs, Concern argued that the presence of volunteers was essential to ensure that a reasonable proportion of aid got to those most in need. Bluntly admitting that all aid was vulner-

able to theft and diversion into the hands of the adequately-nour-
ished and well-armed, Concern believed that the only way to mini-
mise this and to ensure that the aid went to those in most need was
to be on the spot. 'Distributing food in a dignified setting to those
who most need it has become the hallmark of Concern's initial emergency responses.'[7]

Halfway through 1981 Alex Tarbett decided to resign, as he said,
to pursue his business career. He was thought by everyone to have
done a great job—and to all appearances he had, although it was felt
that he had begun to run out of steam at the end. At the simplest
financial level income had gone from £683,000 in 1976/7 to
£2,289,000 in 1980/1.

All in all, Concern was a much more stable and businesslike
operation than it had ever been. Completely unaware of what was
lurking in the accounts, Council chairman Michael Fingleton as-
cribed 'a lot of the success and stability of the organisation to the
considerable efforts of Alex Tarbett in his capacity as effective leader
of Concern . . . No matter what problems arose or what arguments
there were Alex Tarbett never took them personally and never held
grudges. In an organisation like Concern this was a great asset.' (The
older members of Council no doubt particularly appreciated this
thrust.) The chairman went on to say that it had been decided to
acknowledge Tarbett at a formal dinner in his honour to which all
members of Concern and particular friends of Concern would be
invited. In conclusion, the chairman once again 'thanked Mr Tarbett
for all his dedication and work.'

A new chief executive was needed, and after a quick recruitment
process the Council offered the job to Aengus Finucane. This was
not uncontroversial in itself. There were still rumblings of old fac-
tion wars, for the new chief executive was seen very much as a party
man.

Very soon after taking office, on 1 September, Aengus Finucane
went on a trip to the field, leaving the ordinary business of administration to carry on as usual; the Christmas Fast was being set up in
towns and cities up and down Ireland. The organisation was delighted when the UNHCR was awarded the Nobel Peace Prize, and

the Commissioner had gone out of his way to mention Concern as one of the partner agencies, especially in Thailand. In the Christmas newsletter the president of Blackrock College, Fr Aidan Lehane CSSp, movingly described his visit to the settlement at Demra in Bangladesh, where the government had dumped 25,000 Dhaka shantytown dwellers miles into the country. Concern had organised accommodation, clinics, latrines, schools and work opportunities for thousands of these people. Another page of the newsletter showed deputy chief executive David O'Morchoe presenting Alex Tarbett with a handsome set of cut-glass decanters on behalf of the staff.

There was, however, a hidden reef ahead. When Alex Tarbett had taken on the job of chief executive a few years before, he and everyone else knew exactly how bad the financial situation was. But in September 1981 there was a secret in the accounts that threatened to destroy completely Concern's credibility with the public and with donors. It started in November 1981 when the auditors reported that cheques that had been paid by the Cork branch could not be traced in Dublin. At the same time the Bishop of Orange was asking for a receipt for his donations. It quickly became clear that Alex Tarbett had been, to say the least, casual in the disposition of Concern funds. The full extent of the problem was to be revealed over the next few months. The auditors' report pinpointed overly-trusting systems inside Concern. This weak systems control inside Concern was echoed in the bank, which broke its mandate (and all normal banking rules) by allowing funds to be transferred on a single signature and into accounts other than that of the payee. This was to cost them dearly, for they had to repay the money that had been misappropriated.

Over the following months Michael Fingleton painstakingly identified step by step exactly what had happened and was able to present a complete dossier to the police, which eventually formed the basis of a successful prosecution. When the issue finally came to court, in July 1983, there were 29 charges altogether, for a total of £360,000. Of these only ten were persevered with, to spare the jury and as counsel put it, 'so as not to oppress the defendant'. The trial lasted only a few days, for Tarbett's defence was not vigorous, and Judge

John Gleeson noted how he had 'comported himself as a person of gentle disposition throughout the trial'. Distinguished clerics, including Cardinal Tomás Ó Fiaich, acted as character witnesses. The jury took just over an hour to find him guilty on all ten counts. In sentencing him the judge hinted at the motivation, commenting that Tarbett 'had seen himself as a philanthropic sir Bountiful, who had locked himself in a world of make-believe'. He was sentenced to three years' penal servitude.

The shock to the Concern community, to those hundreds who had fasted, rattled tins, or dropped envelopes in doors was immense.[8] A stain, a taint, threatened the whole fundraising enterprise.

For insiders the blow was severe and is remembered to this day.[9] The only consolation was that at least they had a new chief executive firmly in place—a priest with a public reputation for his work in the field. If the revelations had come out while Alex Tarbett was still in charge it is difficult to see how Concern could have survived. To sustain the faith, Aengus Finucane first had to bring the staff with him: just before the news broke, he explained in detail what had happened and explained how difficult the months between the first charge and the trial would be. For some, such as Paddy Maguinness, later deputy chief executive, this was a defining moment of commitment. Throughout 1982 and 1983 Aengus Finucane devoted himself to a vigorous campaign across the country to make sure that the vital local committees still believed in the cause. In the absence of detailed information, Alex Tarbett's many friends (not least among the clergy) assumed, in the Irish way, that he was innocent and that in some unfathomable way the organisation was grinding down the individual. While Aengus Finucane travelled the country, chairman Michael Fingleton devoted himself to the task of forcing the bank to repay the money. He was so successful that Concern was able very quickly to announce that the bank had already repaid £200,000 of the missing funds and the public was asssured that the rest would be recovered. After some shadow-boxing the bank behaved well and the money was paid.

In so far as there was any benefit from this sad affair, it served as a major wake-up call in terms of strict money control. So when the very large donations arrived a few years later on foot of the famine in Ethiopia in 1984, matters were extremely tightly managed. Since then Concern's accounts have been won category prizes in the Leinster Society of Chartered Accountants annual awards in 1988, 1989, 1991, 1996, 1998, 1999 and 2001.

In Concern's hour of need the great and good rallied round. The Christmas Fast of 1983 was joined by Pat Kenny, Éamonn Andrews, Siobhán McKenna, Maureen Potter, Donncha Ó Dulaing, Ciarán Fitzgerald and, from the US, Martin Sheen and MASH's Mike Farrell. In the summer the newsletter had proudly reported that Martin Sheen had given to Concern USA his $100,000 fee for his part in Richard Attenborough's film *Gandhi*—Attenborough himself was one of the celebrities announced as fasting for Concern.[10] The popular priest Fr Michael Cleary (later to achieve a different celebrity) joined Council as a gesture of solidarity. The autumn issue of the newsletter, published soon after the trial, reported events in Dublin (a concert at the National Concert Hall), Belfast and Cork, and in Kildare, Lucan, Tullamore, Kilcullen, Dundalk, Ballycastle, Naas, Birr, Newbridge, Loughrea, Newry and numerous other places. The final vindication of all this work came in 1984, when the news of the appalling new Ethiopian famine broke, and income from donations and fundraising events jumped to £5.6 million—from £1.2 million in 1983. A bad time over, Concern could now devote itself to its proper work.

Scenes from thirty years

The inaugural meeting of Africa Concern, 28 June 1968, Ely Hall Dublin (left to right) Bishop George Cockin, Anglican Bishop of Owerri, John O'Loughlin Kennedy (first executive director), Bishop Joseph Whelan, CSSp, Catholic Bishop of Owerri, Eastern Nigeria.

Rev. Ivan Biggs handing over a cheque for £2,000 on behalf of the Methodist Church Relief Fund to Kay O'Loughlin Kennedy, secretary of Africa Concern Ltd, watched by Fr Raymond Kennedy.

Fr Dave Regan supervising an Africa Concern feeding centre in Sao Tomé.

The Concern Team at 45 Pembroke Road, Dublin (left to right at back) Mary Humphreys, Catherine Modebe, Carmel Dinan, Fr Raymond Kennedy, Kay O'Loughlin Kennedy, John O'Loughlin Kennedy, (left to right, second row) Fr Jimmy O'Toole, Pearl Keaveny, Kitty Hanratty, Hilda Garland, Fouzia Bensoudan, Susan Stranb, (front, kneeling) Maurice Fitzgerald.

John O' Loughlin Kennedy (executive director Africa Concern), speaks at the launch of the Columcille. *Bishop Birch blessed the ship before it sailed for Sao Tomé (Dublin 1968).*

The Columcille *sailing from Dublin to Sao Tomé on 6 September 1968.*

Mike Farrell, star of MASH, *receiving a cheque for Concern from actor Martin Sheen who donated his earnings of $100,000 from the film* Gandhi *to Concern US.*

Directors of Africa Concern, autumn 1969. (left to right) Kay O'Loughlin Kennedy, Vivian Simpson MP, John O'Loughlin Kennedy, Judge J.C. Kingsmill-Moore, Val Jagoe and Sean MacCormack.

At the AGM of Africa Concern held at 45 Pembroke Road, Dublin, 14 March 1970 (left to right) John O'Loughlin Kennedy, Judge T. C. Kingsmill Moore (deputy chairman), Mary Guckian (director) and Vivian Simpson, MP (director).

Squatter families on the railway tracks outside Dhaka, Bangladesh, 1973.

St Patrick's Day 1973: Fr Aengus Finucane, field director in Bangladesh, presents shamrock to President Sheik Mujib Rahman; with Fr Michael Doheny and Ethna Caffrey.

(Left) Brian Pearce, Concern Representative, Ethiopia 1973, with a colleague.

Irwin Shorr supervising Concern Nutrition Unit, Saidpur, Bangladesh, 1973.

Mary Humphreys at a presentation at the Women's Training Institute, Bangladesh, 1973.

Dr Elizabeth O'Brien (USA) who died on 8 September 1974 while serving in Bangladesh.

Papal Nuncio Archbishop Edward Cassidy on a visit to Concern staff in Dhaka, Bangladesh 1975.

Pat Kenny of RTÉ collecting for Concern on the first day of the 1978 Christmas Fast in O'Connell Street, Dublin.

(Left to right) Seán Kelleher, chairman, Bord Bainne Staff Third World Committee, Hugh Byrne, overseas director, Concern, Arthur Prendergast, Bord Bainne Staff Third World Committee and Michael Fingleton, chairman of Concern, at a reception to announce Bord Bainne staff sponsorship of a Vagrants' Home in Dhaka, Bangladesh.

*Dermot Bradshaw, hon. secretary, Bill Jackson, chief executive APSO,
Michael Fingleton, chairman, and Alex Tarbett, chief executive, at the
premier of 'Karamoja Calls*

*(Left) Paddy Maguinness,
Northern Ireland organ-
izer, and Chris Patten,
British Minister for
Overseas Development, at
the opening of the Concern
Northern Ireland offices in
Belfast.
(Below) Taoiseach Garret
Fitzgerald and Sr
Stanislaus Kennedy, with
Aengus Finucane and
Concern volunteers, help
promote the Christmas
Fast.*

Bertie Ahern, TD, Lord Mayor of Dublin, helping launch the Concern Christmas Fast, 1986.

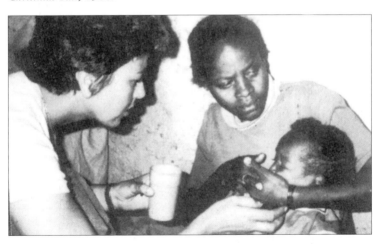

Claire Chamberlain supervising at a Concern feeding centre, Ethiopia .

Bob Geldolf, founder of Band Aid.

(Left to right) Vincent Browne, Deirdre Purcell and Pat Langan, the team behind the 1984 book Ethiopia—The Dark Hunger *with Fr Aengus Finucane.*

Harbo Refugee Camp, Ethiopia, 1984, after the Israeli tents had arrived.

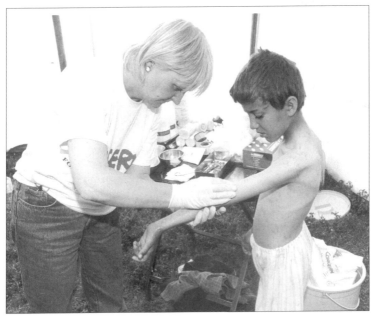

Terina Kelly vaccinating a young boy.

'He's not heavy, he's my brother' (Photographer Liam Burke)

Fr Ciaran Kitching, Concern field director, Thailand 1981.

The Concern team in Sudan, 1987.

Fr Jack Finucane, President Patrick Hillery, Fr Aengus Finucane, Seán Calleary TD and Peter Kierans, Concern chairperson, at the launch of the SOS appeal to send a ship to Ethiopia, November 1989.

On the Thai Border 1992, Dominic MacSorley, Fr Aengus Finucane and Angela O'Neill.

President Mary Robinson visits Concern staff in Baidoa, Somalia, 1992.

President Mary Robinson, and Phena O'Boyle (chairperson 1984–7) on assignment in Somalia 1992, with local volunteers.

Mike McDonagh and Valerie Place.

Mary Cronin, Somalia, 1992.

Anne O'Mahony, at a Concern feeding centre, Somalia, 1992.

Mags Fitzpatrick in Cherte camp, Wollo.

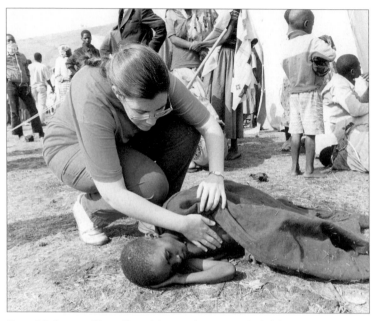

Lynn Mulrooney (from Canada) attends a very sick child in Tanzania.

Paddy Maguinness and Noel Molony, in Zaire 1994

Toireas Ní Bhriain, Sudan, 1993

Mother Teresa of Calcutta and one of her nuns meet Concern staff in Ethiopia (left to right): Ita Ward, Terry Asfaw, Nollaig O'Mahony, Kay Walsh, Frances McAllister, Marion McKeown and Eileen Quinn.

Gus McIntyre in a Somali school, 1993.

Áine Fay, Terry Asfaw and Asfaw Wasfihun, Ethiopia, outside a clinic in Addis Ababa financed by the people of Derry.

President Julius Nyerere (centre) with Eamon Brehony, Tanzania, 1987

Áine Fay with Siddeque Rahnan and Md. Mobin, Bangladesh, 2000.

Presidential candidates Adi Roche and Mary McAleese with David Begg at the launch of the Fast 1997.

US Secretary of State Madeleine Albright visits a camp in Rwanda, 1998, accompanied by Anne O'Mahony and other Concern workers.

Concern strategic planning meeting, Kimmage, 1990s.

Paul Sherlock, David Begg and Noel Wardick in Ethiopia.

6: Famine returns to Ethiopia

Dawn, and as the sun breaks through the piercing chill of night on the plain outside Korem, it lights up a biblical famine, now, in the 20th century. This place, say workers here, is the closest thing to hell on earth. Thousands of wasted people are coming here for help. Many find only death. They flood in every day from villages hundred of miles away, felled by hunger, driven beyond the point of desperation. Death is all around. A child or an adult dies every 20 minutes. Korem, an insignificant town, has become a place of grief.[1]

Drought and famine, never far away, returned to Ethiopia in 1982. So Concern returned to that benighted country, struggling as it was between aspiration and inheritance. Mengistu's revolutionary government was struggling to hold together the Abyssinian empire which was larger and much more diverse than a combination of Germany, the UK, Italy, Hungary and Albania. For nearly 60 years, from 1916 to 1974, Haile Selassie had managed to keep this ramshackle creation of his 19th-century predecessors together, but the Derg found things more difficult.

This was partly because of their ambitious plans to create a new Marxist nation—complete with collective farms and enforced 'villagisation' of pastoral peasants—and partly because of the Sahel drought which was forcing so many of the people into destitution. Over 90 per cent of the people were (and still are) dependent on rain-fed agriculture (little fertiliser is used) in a country subject to plagues of insect pests and continuing soil erosion. Then there was the war with Somalia to the east, a typical Cold War proxy fight financed by the US and the USSR. We have seen how Concern had to retreat in the face of Somali incursions into the Ogaden desert region in 1977.

As central control weakened various armed ethnic liberation groups sprang up. The Derg had inherited from Haile Selassie the long-running Eritrean separatist movement, which itself split on ideological grounds between the Eritrean Liberation Front and the Eritrean People's Liberation Front. It was the EPLF which was finally to celebrate de facto independence for Eritrea in 1991. Two other ethnically-based independence movements regularly created impossible conditions for aid workers. The Tigray People's Liberation Front had strong connections with Sudan, and sought independence for the Tigray region. Concern was to have a violent encounter with their ambitions.

In October 1982 field director Fintan Farrelly visited the town of Korem in the Wollo district, and was appalled to discover as many as 28,000 famine refugees in a makeshift camp outside the town. Here there was 'a dark, dirty building like a cowbarn, where there were between 60 and 70 people who were crawling in lice and lying in their own diarrhoea. Six of the children there were dying. Most of the families had bags of wheat but were too debilitated to prepare and eat it. One young girl of ten was found dead leaning against a sack of grain'.[2]

The Red Cross and Save the Children Fund already had teams in Korem, but there was clearly much to do, so Fintan and assistant director Moira Conroy immediately offered Concern's assistance to the local team responsible for health in the area. One by one the people were gently washed and disinfected and helped to feed themselves. A large hospital tent was set up, and by the following day the people in the barn at least had started taking an interest in life again and were helping to get the children to eat. Volunteer Anne McLoughlin, who had been working in the Concern office in Addis Ababa, came up to help, and Terina Kelly, a nurse who had worked with Concern in Bangladesh and Tanzania, joined the team a few days later. The plan was that Terina would take over from Moira after a few days, and run Concern's medical centre in the camp. But this was not to be. On 21 April, after only a few days in Korem, she and Anne were kidnapped by guerrillas of the Tigray People's Liberation Front, the start of an ordeal that lasted seven weeks.

As well as the two Concern nurses the guerrillas captured several local and expatriate workers from Save the Children Fund as well as two local priests and a number of nuns. For seven long weeks they straggled by mule and landrover 1,200 miles towards Khartoum. Travelling mostly at night, for fear of the Ethiopian army, the prisoners slept in crude huts infested with rats, scorpions and snakes and were constantly surrounded by heavily armed guerrillas. All they had to drink was heavily tainted water, and were vividly aware that every sip brought them nearer disease. When they were lucky they got bread, eggs and honey—otherwise just bread, or perhaps *injeera* and the highly spiced *wet*. At first there was also paralysing fear— death, or perhaps rape, or both; but after the first few hours it became clear that the guerrillas did not intend to harm them. They were to be released, once every ounce of publicity had been extracted for the cause. And so it was. Anne and Terina flew home to Dublin on 11 June to an emotional welcome (the air traffic controllers temporarily lifted a strike to let their plane through).

Around this time Jack Finucane replaced Fintan Farrelly as country director and a new office and compound with plenty of living space and a warehouse were established in Addis Ababa, on the edge of a bustling market; the site had formally been a combined café, restroom and brothel attached to the market, and now the local *kabele* let it to Concern rent-free on condition it was refurbished and returned on demand. Concern has been there ever since. The warehouse was the size of a moderate parish church, capable of storing hundreds of sacks of grain.

Famine was a frequent, almost endemic occurrence in many parts of the country. Even in good years peasants had to endure 'hungry months' between harvests. As a result, only especially widespread deprivations, such as in 1889–92, 1956 and 1974 were worthy of special remark.[3] But there had been a material worsening of conditions over the last generation. The general situation in the Sahel was well known; even 1,000 kilometres away in Addis Ababa, it was noticeable that rainfall in the northern uplands was failing regularly. In scarcely any years since 1970 had the rainfall reached the average of the 1954–70 period; in the 1980s one year succeeded another with less rain, reaching a low in 1984 itself. Poor, erratic, rainfall meant bad harvests, which in turn meant that, to keep up, yet more back-breaking work had to be done in the fields by undernourished men and women. Tools and animals had to be sold to buy food, which made the field-work even more demanding. As the vicious spiral went on, undernourishment meant that the whole family was vulnerable to disease. Infection in the family always carried away the babies and young children first.

Famine is never a random catastrophe, nor is it independent of political events. It is no coincidence that some of the areas worst affected by this famine were the ones in which the Ethiopian army was struggling with the Eritrean and Tigrayan liberation movements. There was also, it should be noted, famine in Wollaita, where rebellion was not a problem. Nor is famine a sudden event—it always throws a long menacing shadow before it. A deadly process takes place, as peasants and those with least resources sell what little they have—first their crops at crisis sale rates, then animals, then seeds, then finally household goods and treasured heirlooms. In each case the prices for these articles drop dramatically as the demand is overwhelmed by supply. An Ethiopian oral poet noted:

> I am the coming Famine
> But I am still in the marketplace—
> I have yet to enter your home.[4]

One peasant woman from the Lalibela area (where the rock-hewn churches are) described the long progress: 'We sold our belongings over several years; we hardly had any crops for three years; there was no rain; no point in sowing.'[5]

The remorseless loss of the people's ability to feed themselves was reported again and again by national and other agencies. In 1982 the official Relief and Rehabilitation Commission (founded after the 1970s famine to monitor potential famine conditions) declared that 5.5 million people faced food shortages; in 1983 a joint UN appeal called for relief assistance for one million people in the 13 worst affected areas. The rains failed again in 1983, which for anyone in the know meant that 1984 would be bad. The *Washington Post* quoted the head of the RRC as saying that 'unless there was enough international assistance thousands of people would stream out of the mountains seeking food. It will take years to rehabilitate them.'[6] The short spring rains failed in 1984, and the RRC again appealed for international help. In May, Jack Finucane told the *New York Times* about the threat of famine, but could not get them interested in the story.

Unfortunately, the government in Addis had other things than famine on their mind—in 1984 they were astounded to discover that the population, which had been reported as 31 million in 1981, was now 45 million. Some 10 million people, nearly a quarter of the population, had simply been overlooked in previous counts. Not only that, but the Derg were absorbed by the preparations for the tenth anniversary of the Revolution—to prevent any distraction from these celebrations foreign aid workers were not permitted to leave Addis in August and September, and the civil servants of the RCC spent time practising marching drill.

For most Irish people the Ethiopian famine started in October 1984, with two films made by Mohamed Amin, with a commentary by Michael Buerk, shown on BBC television news. In his autobiography Bob Geldof described how they affected him. 'The pictures were of people who were so shrunken by starvation that they looked like beings from another planet. Their arms and legs were as thin as sticks, their bodies spindly. Swollen veins and huge blankly staring eyes protruded from their shrivelled heads. The camera wandered amidst them like a mesmerised observer, occasionally dwelling on one person so that he looked directly at me, sitting in my comfortable room surrounded by the fripperies of modern living which we were pleased to regard as necessities. Their eyes looked into mine. There was an emaciated woman too weak to do anything but limply hold her dying child. There was a skeletal man holding out a bundle wrapped in sacking so that it could be counted; it looked like a tightly wrapped package of old sticks, but was the dessicated body of his child. And there were children, their bodies fragile and vulnerable as premature babies, but with the consciousness of what was happening to them gleaming dully from their eyes. All around was the murmur of death, like a hoarse whisper, or the buzzing of flies.'[7]

The impact on the public was immediate. Money poured into aid agencies, and Geldof's Band Aid began its extraordinary rocketing career. By August 1985 Band Aid/Live Aid had raised over $110 million, and subsidiary projects such as Fashion Aid, Sport Aid, School Aid and Action École were continuing to raise money. The Irish people once again lived up to their image of generosity, donating many times more per head than the British or Americans.[8] By September 1985 Band Aid had established a regular liaison committee with numerous agencies including CAFOD, War on Want, Oxfam, Save the Children and CARE. Concern, represented by Aengus Finucane and Ciúnas Bunworth, was the only Irish agency. The funds generated by Band Aid were eventually to help finance many a Concern programme. Even the UN system reacted, by hurriedly appointing a special coordinator of relief programmes, a retired UNDP career officer called Kurt Jannson, who had recently undertaken a similar role in Kampuchea.

Despite all the RRC's reports, supported as we have seen by UN agencies, little had happened until the television programmes in October—it is even now a matter of controversy as to why the international community was so slow to act. Perhaps it is no more than an extraordinary proof of an awkward fact of life for aid agencies. They can only act if they have money, and this must come directly or indirectly from the people's pockets. Unfortunately, the kind of knowledge produced in the RRC's early warning reports or in UN reports is not enough to stimulate action. As Bruno Bettelheim put it: 'We react with deep feeling to what we see and can feel in ourselves, to what is immediately before our eyes, or what we can understand from personal experience. We have not yet learned to deal with the experience of the total mass state. We simply cannot think in terms of millions—at least most of us cannot—but only in terms of the individual.'[9] The continuing question for all humanitarian agencies, professionally conscious of so much need in the world, is how to tread the line identified by Bettelheim: 'A few screams evoke in us deep anxiety and a desire to help. Hours of screaming without end lead us only to wish that the screamer would shut up.' The

Amin-Buerk programmes, which were ultimately shown on over 400 television channels throughout the world with an estimated audience of 470 million, intensely personalised the fate of the Ethiopians, and led to an extraordinary outpouring of support.

At first, the Marxist revolutionary government of Ethiopia, while being obliged to recognise facts, did not particularly relish having to take aid from the West, nor the implication that ten years after the Revolution it was unable to feed its own people. Agency workers experienced difficulties with work permits, with import licences and other bureaucratic hassle. Concious of international media image, customs officers looked with intense suspicion on video tapes, with the result that even so essential a boost to Concern's morale as a recording of the triumphant Irish Triple Crown victory over England at Lansdowne Road had to be smuggled in.

Immediately restrictions on internal travel were lifted after the tenth anniversary celebrations, Aengus and Jack Finucane, with Moira Conroy (deputy country director) went north to Wollo, and saw the streams of people on the road, 'tramping who knows where'. Thousands of people from Wollo, Tigray and north Shewa had left their villages in the hills and gathered in the towns. There they camped together in nearby fields, scraping pits in the earth, or piling stones for protection. They generally had no blankets or coverings, and very poor clothing. With nothing else to look forward to, they stayed in the hopes that somehow the local authorities would be able to look after them. Very often they were suffering from extreme malnutrition and for many it was already too late. In the event almost a million people would die before the next summer rains. The stricken people of Wollo lay in front of the Concern car in an effort to get the expatriates to buy the pitiful last goods they had—perhaps some tribal jewellery, hundreds of years old. (Soon opportunistic speculators would drive up from Addis to buy the precious objects at distress sale prices. Within days the jewellery and other artefacts were seen on sale in the smart antique shops of the capital for many hundreds of times what had been paid for them.[10])

The Concern exploratory team went back to Addis and quickly got permission from the RRC to provide assistance. Initially they started to work in an International Red Cross camp, but inter-agency rivalries made this difficult, so in October they set up their own camp.[11] The site chosen was a field just outside Harbu town, 365 kilometres north of Addis Ababa. A thousand or more people were already gathered there in squalor and hopelessness. With minimum equipment Concern workers started to do what they could.

Normally, the agency's work is done away from the public eye, in hot and remote border camps, in slums among the poorest of the poor, in villages far from the tourist trail. Few journalists or camera crews document latrines, street children or village micro-credit meetings. But in the case of Harbu camp we have two vivid eyewitness reports, from a Dublin journalist, Deirdre Purcell, and a Derry doctor, Raymond McClean, who both visited the camp in its early days. Deirdre Purcell left Dublin with a group of Irish journalists on 31 October. After a briefing in Addis she went north with Pat Langan, an *Irish Times* photographer, and arrived in Harbu when the camp was only two days old. She noticed first the sound: 'a continuous low-pitched keening, from a dense mass of human beings'.[12] Moira Conroy was struggling to bring order. On the third day of operation, as news got round of the camp's existence, there were over 9,000 hungry mouths to feed, and the ominous beginnings of outbreaks of measles and hepatitis. Every family was registered according to the weight of the children and given food and blankets—those without children had to wait, but were given supplementary rations.[13]

Large shelters, roofed with heavy duty plastic and half-walled, were built, each holding about 200 people. Inside, the sick and the starving lay on the mud floor, with only the blankets to cover them. Guards (local men on work for food programmes) tried to keep order, to prevent the weak and the sick from losing out, and the food trucks frombeing overwhelmed. The visitors were shocked to see how the guards needed sticks and guns to preserve order. Children, some of whom weighed literally half what they should, were carefully assessed for intensive or merely supplementary feeding. Once registered, the people took their blankets and joined queues for water and food (even here human spirit showed itself: one woman gave her blue blanket back—she wanted a red one.).

The food dispensed was high-protein biscuit and *fafa*—a kind of porridge made from grain, oil and water—and milk. For those used to the spicy *wet*, this was an insipid diet, and soon some of the biscuit found its way to the street market in Harbu, exchanged for hot chilli and spice. Twenty-five workers cooked the food in giant steel vats over open fires. After Harbu, Deirdre Purcell went north to Korem where Concern and other agencies looked after some 100,000 people. The army, conscious how easily such camps could become centres of guerrilla activity, kept a wary and intrusive eye on things. But she was assured that the situation was improving—only 42 people had died before 10 am that day. 'This is the innermost circle of degradation,' she wrote. 'Hell is not a poet's vision, or even other people, it is here in Korem under a baking corrugated roof . . . there are not enough beds for all so the aisles between them are covered in stretchers, pieces of sacking or cotton stretched between two branches. A teenage boy twitches on the floor in the last throes of life.'[14]

Returning a few days later to Harbu, she noted a dramatic improvement. 'In just two days there are more shelters, the people have been separated according to their local *kabeles* under the chairmanship of an appointed leader. Everyone at the camp had been fed twice on the fourth day. They would be fed twice again today. But they still come from the outlying regions, with the weaker on the backs of the stronger. Five orphans arrived last night. Their mother died on the roadside on the way to Harbu. Their father had died the previous day. The nine-year-old carried the baby and chivvied the other three into the camp. It took three hours. They left the mother where she fell.'[15]

Every death meant a loss—one cute little orphan boy, whom the nurses nicknamed Jack after Jack Finucane, died after a few days in the camp. Ray McClean remembered another child 'who was suffering from bloody diarrhoea, gross dehydration and bubbling pneumonia. I started the child on antibiotic. I saw the child on the following day, when it appeared to be dramatically improved. The next day I was told that the child had died in its sleep. I never did discover the reason why.'

Within a month Concern had recorded 10,000 people seeking aid in Harbu, and over 500 deaths. In December the death rate doubled as, ironically enough, heavy rains flooded the camp and caused many deaths from hypothermia and pneumonia. The nights continued cold in January, and nearly 700 died. In January the record of infections took another turn. Anne O'Mahony, who took over the medical administration of the camp in December, remembers the deadly sequence—measles, flooding, then cholera, an unidentified form of jaundice, typhus, chickenpox. After every outbreak precautions were put in place to prevent recurrence, and eventually things took a turn for the better.

Typhus could only be stopped by preventing the influx of lice, which meant that every newcomer to the camp had to be fumigated, head-shaven and given new clothes. The volunteers were acutely aware of how closely the shaven heads echoed the images of German concentration camps that are so seared into the European consciousness. It was, many felt, a humiliation too much. But, working as they always had to through interpreters, it was difficult for the volunteers to know exactly what the people felt: what desperate options they had exhausted; what simple relief there was in being sure of a meal. And, of course, these Ethiopians did not carry the film images of the concentration camps in their heads. Ethiopian nurse Tiruwork Asfaw, who worked in Harbu, was sure that the cleansing was not an issue for the people.[16] In corroboration, the oral verses collected by Professor Fekade, which comment on the humiliation of having one's children weighed like sacks of grain, do not mention such feelings. They do, however, record, as we have seen, the bitter gratitude felt towards the volunteer nurses from North America and Europe who came with food and medicine.

> As from a broken sieve,
> Does grain cascade from her hands,
> Mamma white woman, Mother to us all.[17]

The other witness was Dr Ray McClean, who had been active in Derry politics in the 1970s, serving as the first Catholic mayor of the city since the 1920s. He arrived in Harbu in December, just as the rains struck the camp such a blow. He described his first impressions. 'Late in the afternoon we pulled into a small town with a fairly wide, dusty street. The buildings were ramshackle, wooden framed and with a lot of sheeted corrugated tin in the construction. The street was alive with people, donkeys, goats and sheep, all of them with prominent ribcages bulging in threadbare bodies . . . ' As they pulled up to the camp they saw hundreds of people sitting patiently on the ground, waiting to get into the camp. 'Inside, the scene was grim. Rows of large shelters were built with black plastic sheeting, supported on wooden poles. Many of the shelters had collapsed under the weight of the heavy rains the previous night. Many adults and children were sitting quietly on the open ground. Most of the rain had evaporated under the heat of the midday sun, but many areas remained wet and muddy. In the distance I could see the nurses kneeling in the muck and dirt, tending to several small babies. The air was filled with the sound of dry, barking, incessant coughing.'[18] To ease problems caused by the collapse of the shelters, half the residents of Harbu had in fact been removed to another camp two miles away—this was of course a logistical nightmare, doubling problems of food, water supply, medicines etc.

After a brief tour McClean and Dr Michael Fanning from Dingle, the only other doctor on site, adjourned to the schoolhouse that the local authorities had given Concern as living quarters. In the large bare living room the volunteers had tea, mince stew and hard brown bread by candlelight. The talk was all of the incidents of the day. Bed was a cot in a large classroom in which all the men slept. The women (many more of them) slept in the other classroom. A visit to the lavatory during the night required an alarming journey to the outside latrine, a hole in the floor, with the accompaniment of howls from hyenas and bumbling attentions from oversized insects.

Up at 6.30 and on a breakfast of strong tea and brown bread, the volunteers faced a 12-hour day. McClean was plunged immediately into the camp's medical problems. 'In the shelters everyone lay on mud floors, under a variety of blankets. The very sick patients were often completely covered by a blanket, so that it was necessary to walk around the shelters and pull the blankets away to find the most seriously ill patients. All of the people were suffering from severe malnutrition, many of them had severe diarrhoea, with the resulting severe dehydration. A large proportion of the children also had pneumonia of varying severity. Three of the shelters had been re-served for the very ill patients. In those shelters the sound of con-stant coughing pervaded the air, with constant moaning from the mothers whose children had just died. The environment was in-vaded by flies. There were flies on the children, flies on the blankets, in the food, in the infected diarrhoea which was saturating the mud floors.'[19] (You quickly learned not to kneel to treat patients lying on the floor.)

Even for the most experienced volunteer Harbu camp, through November and December and into January, was a tough posting. Before a proper water tank was built (by the well-known Derry ac-tivist Paddy 'Bogside' Doherty) water had to be lifted from the con-taminated riverbed just below the camp. On the whole, it seems that nurses coped with the situation better than doctors, perhaps because the latter had responsibility but without the support struc-tures they were used to. One volunteer doctor was so appalled that she couldn't face it and left after half an hour in the camp.

Conditions began to get better with the arrival of a heavily funded team from Israel. They brought hundreds of good strong tents (all labelled 'From Jerusalem with love'—in English, of course, not Amharic), camp beds, pipes for water, huge blow torches for cook-ing food and heating water, even lighting for the alleyways between the sheds. All this equipment was tempting, but it came with a price. The Israelis were not interested in where Concern wanted to place the various hospital tents, food rooms, latrines etc.—they were going to lay the camp out exactly as it had been planned in Israel, and they wanted at least some of their team to remain on the strength. The Concern team felt 'taken-over', and the aggressive self-confidence of the Israelis did not help. It was about this time that the first airlift of Falashas, or Beta-Israelis, from Ethiopia to Israel, took place.

When Ray McClean returned to Harbu in April 1985 he was amazed at the transformation. 'Gone were all the old plastic shelters and their wooden supports. In their place were rows upon rows of neat, white tidy tents. The people moving about looked healthier, and were much better dressed. Above all the silent despair had lifted from many of the faces, and there was an atmosphere of hope in the air. I was delighted to see the excellent supply of clean water, which was being piped throughout the camp, and a complete series of water taps, set in new concrete to give ready access to clean water to everyone. A new latrine and sanitation system had been installed.'[20] Simply being able to rest the diarrhoea patients in cots meant that the flow could be controlled and did not form pools of re-infection on the ground.

Despite all these improvements very ill people, especially children, continued to pour into the camp. They had pneumonia, typhus and other diseases. Cholera, officially described as 'very severe diarrhoea', began to take its toll. Perhaps because things were less hectic, even approaching normality, Dr McClean found the first few days of his second visit extremely demanding. 'I felt as if I was living in some sort of hell on earth, where my companions were flies, diarrhoea, disaster and death.' The patients' fear and suffering penetrated the 'carefully prepared emotional cocoon', and the pain was personal and intense.[21] Late at night others revealed the stress they, too, had suffered: for instance, Bríd Kelly from Carrickfergus, who during the day worked coolly and effectively in the children's hospital unit, one night 'talked at length about her personal pain when she first arrived in the camp and her desperate need for more spiritual support, to assist her in facing the tragedy she found all around her.'[22] When Bono and his wife Ali visited Ethiopia at this time they came face to face with the horrors of famine. They visited Concern programmes in the northern province of Wollo and were deeply moved by the experience. In recent years Bono has become one of the great advocates of Third World debt relief.

But the situation did get better. By the summer of 1985 most of the camp inmates had taken their free bag of food and left, anxious to get back to their farms for the planting season. Except for orphans and the very old, the camp was rapidly being run down. Revealing of the trauma suffered, in a very un-African way the old and the orphans remained a problem until the local authorities put pressure on their families to take them in.

As the camp was finally being wound down, Jack Finucane was putting the finishing touches to his proposal that Concern work on behalf of the victims of the controversial resettlement programme. Resettlement was a drastic solution to the problems of those living on the exhausted soils of north Ethiopia, by which the government was to establish new internal colonies in the fertile south-western part of the country. The government would supply housing and seeds and equipment, as well as trained cadres to help. There was a long history of voluntary resettlement in Ethiopia. In the mid-19th century Emperor Menelik used land grants to his soldiers as a way of consolidating his control (a plan similar to the 'plantation' policy used in Ireland). Haile Selassie also encouraged a million people to move from the north to the south in the 25 years before the Revolution in 1974.[23]

After the Revolution the resettlement programme became the Derg's panacea—it was perceived as a remedy for all the country's major ills in one stroke. It was, wrote one scholar, 'a way of furthering a hotchpotch of economic, social and political objectives for dealing with famine, providing land to the homeless, increasing agricultural production, introducing new techniques, establishing cooperatives, removing urban unemployed and "undesirables", stopping charcoal burning, settling pastoralists and shifting agriculturalists, forming defences on the Somalia border and rehabilitating repatriated refugees.'[24] It is no surprise that the programme achieved none of these objectives.

But the resurgence of famine in what the people called 'the Cruel Days' (sometimes euphemistically just 'the Days'), focused the government's mind. A desperate plan was evolved to move over half a million people north-east to south-west across the country, three or four hundred miles, and re-establish them in new villages. Here they were to establish a new collective paradise where Christians and Muslims would live in productive socialist harmony in accordance with the tenets of Marxist-Leninism, under the guidance of cadres from the Workers Party of Ethiopia.

The humiliation of having to receive Western aid spurred the government into this radical solution to Ethiopia's problems. The new settlements would exploit the lush expanses of virgin land in the south-west of the country towards Sudan and the Rift Valley, it would relieve the pressure on the provinces of Wollo and Tigray, and it would at the same time initiate a socialist path of social and economic change. Peasants would be mechanised, their time would not be wasted in trading or tilling small private plots, and model villages would be evolved whose experience could ultimately transform the whole Ethiopian countryside.

The logic of resettlement attracted even those who felt that the middle of a major famine was not a good time to launch so ambitious a programme. Unfortunately, the execution of the programme was so brutal that most of the aid agencies refused to have anything to do with the settlements. Furthermore, the strongly Marxist tone of the whole experiment was deeply repellent to President Reagan and Mrs Thatcher, both of whose governments opposed the plan (stories of how supplies of whiskey for the Derg were given dockyard priority over famine supplies were commonplace). The first operational problem was the haste with which the plans were drawn up. The original action plan was produced in October 1984 and launched on 14 November—ten days later 15,000 settlers had already been moved. There was so little time that some of the resettlement sites were chosen after no more than a helicopter fly-over.

Many of the early settlers were more or less voluntary—dazzled perhaps by the golden pictures of new opportunities, and plentiful fertile land in the south-west. But soon enough the very strangeness of the new territory began to daunt people. An oral poet noted this with some humour:

> Going to a 'foreign' land
> Really makes one into a fool
> Having avoided the dog
> I was bitten by a hen.[25]

Quite soon local officials were having trouble getting enough recruits, and quotas were imposed, which of course put pressure on local authorities to fill their quota by what means they could. Tax offenders, urban unemployed, peasants living on slopes designated for afforestation, pastoralists and people living in very densely populated areas were all targeted. An incident at Ibenat camp in Wollo showed how ruthless the local authorities could be if they chose. For the camps were not popular with the authorities: they were centres of disease, they were expensive and they were disruptive.

One night in April 1985 the party secretary decided that Ibenat camp would be cleared, and at least 36,000 people were forcibly evacuated by the army. The camp was burned to the ground. The following day Jack Finucane visited the site with colleagues from World Vision and USAID. That night the *Washington Post*, no doubt tipped off by the Americans, phoned Jack and asked for an interview. The camp became front page news, and very political. Mengistu even admitted that his officials had made a mistake. In small numbers, people began to drift back to the area. Later that week Kurt Jansson, the UN coordinator, visited the camp with an RRC official and a BBC reporter. Concern and World Vision were asked by the RRC to supervise an orderly programme of return of the able-bodied. This incident merely alerted the naturally suspicious media to the possibilities implicit in the resettlement programme.

However chosen, the people due for resettlement would wait for transport in special camps (there was one near Harbu, but no Concern people were allowed access) before being bussed or flown to the settlement area. Bob Geldof, who witnessed one group boarding Russian Antonovs, compared the planes to the coffin ships that took the Irish away in the 1840s. 'The people,' he wrote, 'looked wretched. They had tiny bags on their backs and they held hands as they moved up the ramp of the plane. Few of them had seen aeroplanes before they moved to the camp and none of them had been in one.' Inside the plane the hold was so crowded that the people had to hold their children above their heads; because the planes were not pressurised they suffered from cramp and airsickness.[26] Most of the settlers went by road, and for the 50,000 or so ending up in Ketto (one of the areas in which Concern was to work) there was a particularly hard arrival. Nothing was ready: village sites had not been cleared, and medicine, cooking implements and clothing were all in short supply. Large temporary shelters were built, but these were crowded and insanitary. So many died in these shelters that people began to build their own wigwam-like hutlets away from the crowded main shelter. One of the Ethiopia Workers Party cadre wrote 'from morning till sunset you can see as many people as in Chanka's market, digging graves. From the bridge to the road you can hardly pass because of the stench.'[27] In a letter to Penny Jenden of Band Aid, Jack Finucane later estimated that 'over 70,000 people died during/after the move'. As he put it, this was not a nice tidy development project, carefully planned to the last gaiter button; it was a major human disaster.

The way the programme was carried out made it an easy target for criticism. Dr Claude Malhuret of Médicins sans Frontières explicitly compared Ethiopia with Nazi Germany in 1938 and Khmer Rouge Kampuchea in 1977. 'The situation is so bad', he was reported as saying, 'that no one should collaborate.' The expulsion of Médicins sans Frontières from Ethiopia merely confirmed that to support collectivisation was simply to sustain the bad policy of a vicious regime. Following Malhuret, many in the aid community argued that resettlement should be stopped, and the way to do this was for all agencies, including Concern, to refuse any further help, whatever the need on the ground.

This kind of moral dilemma is well known in humanitarian work. Do you offend against justice by collaborating with a corrupt regime or do you abandon people who have a right to expect your help? Concern tended to express its core values in mantras such as 'people to people' and 'respond to need'. These effectively ranked immediate direct aid higher than other long-term goals such as human justice. This was despite a consciousness that famines rarely occur in countries where democracy and human justice prevail, as Amartya Sen has pointed out. The alternative was not simply naivety—the newsletter of autumn 1980 agreed that 'refugees from this kind of situation [Kampuchea] doubtless contain both the helpless victims and the wilful exploiters of corrupt political systems; some people we would gladly help and some people who perhaps deserve it less'. On the other hand, however robust you are, situations do occur in which there is a real risk that the moral integrity of the helper may be compromised. However long a spoon you sup with, some situations are just too devilish. As always the question is—here, now, what should we do? Concern has tended to concentrate on using people to dispense services and aid to people, taking the view, as expressed in the newsletter that 'only action can lead us to solutions'.[29]

In 1986 Howard Dalzell, with long experience in India, joined the staff as agricultural adviser, and he brought with him a new vocabulary of sustainability of projects as an essential element in evaluation. At the same time, the enormous growth of the aid community since the 1960s, and their inevitable presence at every disaster spot, carefully presenting T-shirt logos to the television audience, have upped the stakes. Providing humanitarian aid has become a competitive business. Agency heads, with their own ambitions and careers to think about, have become national celebrities, being wheeled into television studios to tell us what to feel about this or that disaster. The resulting atmosphere is not conducive to calm debate.

It therefore took some clarity of purpose and courage for Jack Finucane to go against the received agency wisdom, and after discussion with the RRC, to propose a programme of medical and agricultural support to the seven-village settlement at Jarso, near Ghimbi in Welega province, to be financed by Band Aid and the Canadians. This programme began work in November 1985; Concern was the third agency to commit to helping the settlers, the others were the French Secours Populaire Français (which started work in March 1985) and the Austrian/West German Menschen fur Menschen (May 1985). The following year a larger project, in Ketto somewhat to the south-east, was agreed with the RRC.

The focus of Concern's $2 million programme was to help the 12,000 settlers to become self-sufficient as soon as possible. Working closely with the Ethiopian RRC, Concern was to build storage sheds in each village, provide clinics, grinding mills, roads, water supply and training. Specific agricultural inputs included grain, fertiliser, ploughs, the use of 26 tractors and, best of all, 625 oxen for the villagers. The oxen were a great success, providing an instant boost to the villagers' morale; men vied with each other to have a turn ploughing the land. The tractors were less so, since their use in deep ploughing threatened the fragile topsoil. There was, therefore, an element of relief work in the project, but a much larger component of development. An evaluation carried out a year later (November/December 1986) reported that 'Concern's contribution has provided great relief to the settlers and has contributed substantially to their achievement of food self-sufficiency.' Not that all was perfect: the metal sheets used in constructing the schools made them cold in the morning and too hot in the afternoon, and the 14.5 hp engines supplied to power the mills were too small.

Despite these encouraging words, the future of the resettlement programme as a whole remained problematic. The active programme of resettlement was discontinued in 1986, and then gradually the state began to withdraw its direct controls. The collective farms were dismantled, the state-run shops were closed, and the oxen were taken out of the collective and given to private owners. As Jack Finucane noted, instead of being the much-fêted 'children of the government', the settlers became the government's orphans. Some settlers went home to the north when they were able, and those remaining established more normal peasant styles of production. Despite political upheavals it seems that for those who stayed the experiment was eventually a success, cemented as life went on by children: 'more and more children born in Ketto know not the taste of *tef*; Wollo is to them merely a fairyland evoked in the adults' reminiscences'.[31]

At the beginning of 1988 volunteer Dr Ann Broderick was kidnapped by the Tigrayan People's Liberation Front—to everyone's relief she was released after four days, well but exhausted after being obliged to walk many miles across rough country.[32] A few months later Fiona Quinn (from Kildare) and Mary Coen (from Galway) and four local Concern workers were kidnapped from the resettlement area in Jarso and after twenty-nine anxious days were finally released.

As the Derg under Mengistu lost ground to the separatist forces, the country became increasingly disturbed, and so more and more difficult for Concern. Mengistu finally fled to Zimbabwe in 1991. A loose coalition of resistance movements was established, from which the Oromo Liberation Front (which controlled the settlement area) withdrew some months later. A sporadic civil war ensued, in the course of which thousands of settlers took themselves out of harm's way and returned to Wollo. Then a Concern driver was killed. Concern had already temporarily pulled its expatriate staff out of the area in July 1991 and again towards the end of the year. Finally, in March 1992, the team left that part of the country for good and since then has concentrated on Addis and areas to the north.

7: After twenty years

The local government is likely to be the most difficult partner with whom the operational NGO must deal. NGOs expend an enormous anount of energy in dealing with host governments and in trying to comply with their often highly unreasonable requirements. [However] let me say that the NGOs are often themselves at least partly to blame for difficulties that arise.[1]

The 20th anniversary of Concern fell in 1988, the year that Dublin noisily celebrated its millennium. Led by the enthusiastic lord mayor, Carmencita Hederman, all sorts of parades, parties and stunts were enjoyed by a slightly bemused public. How did one respond to a fully-helmeted Viking just off his longship—which was moored, to add to the mental confusion, just below the bridge dedicated to the memory of Matt Talbot?

To mark the anniversary, Concern decided to commission a ship, like the *Columcille*, to carry much-needed food to Africa—this time to Ethiopia. The *Svea Atlantic* was commissioned in Denmark and loaded, first in Dublin and then in Belfast with 2,000 tons of relief goods. Extraordinarily, the Catholic and Protestant unions, which normally maintained strict demarcation lines, agreed to work together, and when the ship was ready adjourned to celebrate at a nearby 'Catholic' dockers' club.

The ship left Belfast for Ethiopia in January 1990, and everyone was happy. Then suddenly an old-fashioned act of piracy started the international telexes rattling. The *Svea Atlantic* was only 27 miles from its destination—the port of Massawa on the Red Sea—when it was boarded and captured by members of the Eritrean People's Liberation Front. Two other vessels were seized at the same time. The ship's owners in Denmark sent alarmed messages to Concern, who in turn approached Lloyds of London and various embassies—Swedish, British, Russian—for news. The Ethiopian government were tight-lipped and unhelpful. Nothing was heard for five days and rumours of disasters began to fly—the pleasant commemoration of Concern's 20th birthday was turning into a nightmare. Meanwhile, protecting themselves from Ethiopian military searches, the EPLF quietly unloaded the cargo at night; during the day they sailed the vessel far out to sea to avoid capture. On 17 February the now empty ship and the unharmed crew were released. The EPLF subsequently claimed that the vessels had strayed into a battle zone, and they had towed the *Svea Atlantic* to safety—though their press release did not explain why 'safety' required that the ship be completely denuded of its cargo. Luckily Concern was fully insured, and after some quibbling from the brokers—was it, or was it not, a 'war zone'?—the money was repaid and reassigned for more supplies. From Concern's point of view, a few days of anxiety had been amply repaid by twice the initial value being delivered to Ethiopia!

As in the rest of Ireland, the social and political ethos in Concern was steadily changing. A curious demonstration of this was the mighty row which had broke out in Council quite soon after Aengus Finucane became chief executive. The Concern office had been purchased from the Little Sisters of the Assumption, who had left numerous statues and religious icons around the building and, most obviously, a large image of the Sacred Heart on a plinth between the two central first floor windows. The statue was nearly as tall as the windows, and made a conspicuous landmark in the street. Despite the self-proclaimed non-denominational status of Concern, previous chief executives had not felt inclined to do anything about these relics. Aengus decided quietly to remove them, including the altar in the former chapel. The very public statue on the front wall of the house was another matter. This could certainly not be removed without anyone noticing.

Sides were drawn up immediately for and against removal. In a split of opinion characteristic of the 1980s (the era of divorce and abortion referenda) Protestants and traditional Catholics lined up against liberals and modernising Catholics. The traditional Catholics argued that the Little Sisters had sold the house at a bargain price on the assumption that the statue would remain; it was this promise that persuaded the Protestants, such as Dick Bunworth, to support retention. The liberals and the modernising Catholics felt that for an ostensibly non-denominational agency the image was too overtly Catholic, and an old-fashioned form of Catholicism at that. Passions ran high. Eventually an EGM was called at which 106 members turned up (as many never attended any meeting before or since).

Pausing only to pass a motion to restyle the chairman the chairperson, the meeting moved swiftly on to the issue of the day. P. J. Howell proposed: 'In view of Concern's stated position as a non-denominational organisation and particularly mindful that Concern's overseas operations involve it with people of many and varied religious beliefs I propose that the statue on the front wall be removed'.

Sheila Convery and Kay O'Loughlin Kennedy declared that as acting chief executives in the absence of Raymond Kennedy they had given an undertaking to the Little Sisters of the Assumption that the statue would be preserved, and local residents had reinforced this request. Disappointingly, the minutes of the meeting do not give details of what was undoubtedly a lively debate: 'There followed many contributions from members on their views'. In the end the statue was saved and the motion resoundingly lost, 24 for and 82 against. The vote revealed a deep contradiction (as there had been since the beginning) between Concern's much stressed ecumenical aspirations and the actuality. In her contribution, Council member Elaine Lucey put the point bluntly when Concern was criticised for not providing family planning advice at its mother and child clinics in Bangladesh: 'Concern is basically Irish and Catholic,' she said, 'even though we are non-denominational, and the vast majority of Irish people, particularly outside Dublin, are against contraception.'

So the statue remained, though Aengus Finucane made sure its more gilded decorations were toned down. It was finally removed by the hotel company that took over the building in 1995, and now only the plinth remains.

Triggered by the vast and conspicuous needs of Sudan and Bangladesh, income from public donations and fund-raising events nearly doubled in 1988, reaching just £5 million. Total income rose from £5.3 million in 1987 to £11.5 million in 1988; if donations in kind are included, as they were in the 1988 accounts for the first time, the total came to £15.2 million. At this time, just over half of Concern's income came from donations and fundraising events. The core of this came from groups of neighbours encouraging each other and their friends to contribute; a now well-developed network of people throughout the country who had responded to Michael Doheny's films and who had loyally hung on. An analysis by the newly named 'development department' in 1986 showed the return on each different type of activity; 'special events', although they were, no doubt, the best fun for the participants, scored worst, returning £5.65 for every £1 spent; the Christmas Fast campaign, now in more than 40 centres across the country, returned £6.83 for every £1; the newsletter did better still, returning £12.88. Best of all, however, was the Giro scheme organised through the banks, which returned a whopping £35.80 for every £1.

The depressing problem of poor public donor response when there was no spectacular televised disaster had been sidestepped by the co-funding route, which in 1988 rose by 150 per cent and provided £6.3 million in cash and a further £3.7 million in kind (wheat, oil, blankets, seeds etc.). If the receipts in kind are included, income from co-funders now amounted to two-thirds of the whole. The single most significant new contribution came from the British Overseas Development Administration through Concern's Northern Ireland office, which had been started by Paddy Maguinness in 1980. Moving into a new office in Belfast, Paddy invited Chris Patten, the Overseas Development Minister in the British government, to open it. To everyone's surprise not only did he agree, but he spent several hours in the office learning about Concern's work. Patten, who had previously been in the Northern Ireland Office, evidently saw an opportunity for cross-border cooperation, and encouraged Concern to apply for British aid funds. When it did so, the funds were quickly and readily forthcoming.

By 1988 there were 105 expatriates in the field, but 43 of these were on what were then called 'semi-volunteer' terms, the first step to becoming a full-time aid worker. These were typically on their second or later assignment. The traditional volunteer still represented 60 per cent of expatriates, but this was a declining proportion. People in the field were increasingly becoming professional aid workers. For those who decided to go back to their previous lives, re-entry was sometimes difficult. So many volunteers had been out from Ireland (and not of course only from Concern) that an association, Comhlámh, had been founded to express the views of returned development workers. A recurrent theme was the difficulty many had coming to terms with Irish society again (in a TCD thesis, Jill Butler reported that this was a particular problem for those who had been out for two years and had not been sick during their stint). In 1979 a disillusioned piece in the Comlámh newsletter by Johnnie Johnstone expressed what many felt: 'I soon became tired of the patronising smiles of would-be employers when I said I had been a volunteer in the Third World and suggestions that I was too idealistic to be of use in a commercially-oriented business . . . my friends had grown away too. No job, no people who understood. I had done my little bit towards a new heaven and a new earth and I got a letter from the Department of Social Welfare saying I was out of benefit, and could not claim State Aid, and my dental applications had been rejected.' Returnees found their experience akin to a bereavement—loss of friends, work, purpose and the now-familiar environment. The whole experience, huge to the volunteer, was often treated quite lightly at home: one VSO returnee reported how his friends 'were only interested in the fun side and carnivals, treating my absence as an unpaid holiday'.

The work in Ethiopia, though controversial, had greatly enhanced the organisation's reputation, especially among the big donor agencies. Aengus Finucane, as chief executive, brought his great knowledge of the field and his international contacts to the job, and after six years was firmly in the driving seat. His ebullient personality, his continual presence (he lived in a flat above the office in Camden Street) and his assured charismatic leadership gave a sense of unity to the whole operation. The confidence of major donors was seen in their willingness to respond to Concern's requests, initiated, as he liked to describe it, on foot of no more than a telephone call.

Concern now worked in seven target countries—Ethiopia, Somalia, Tanzania, Thailand, Mozambique, Bangladesh and Sudan—where it was estimated the world's most acute problems of poverty lay. In Ethiopia there were 22 expatriate workers and 285 local staff. The emergency there had subsided, but there were serious worries about the viability of the Jarso resettlement camp, and the needs of the people in the war-torn areas of Eritrea and Tigray. The volunteers themselves, though no less idealistic, were generally older and more self-confident than their predecessors of ten or twenty years before. Their standards were higher, too, in matters of personal space and freedom. The children generally of much smaller families, they were no longer happy with the kind of communal living that had been acceptable before. They were also less willing to accept restrictions that the volunteers of the 1970s had taken for granted. Field director Jack Finucane, for instance, waged a determined campaign against volunteers driving themselves rather than using the drivers supplied.

Somalia was frankly a problem. Four local staff had been detained for some days without explanation, and the field director, Dominic MacSorley, was asked to leave in July. It was suspected the office's outgoing mail had been tampered with. There was obviously a question mark over whether Concern should continue in this field.

In the camps on the Thailand/Kampuchea border there was a worrying surge of refugees from Vietnam, and the three volunteers and over 1,000 local staff were bracing themselves for more. In Nampula in Mozambique two volunteers did their best to help displaced families suffering as a result of attacks by rebel forces financed by South Africa, as part of its regional destabilisation policy.

Tanzania was the exception to these strife-torn places. Its benevolent ruler Julius Nyerere, a widely respected figure throughout Africa, had stepped down in 1985, to be replaced by Ali Hassan Mwinyi. From the beginning of Concern's involvement, the activities had been closely controlled through the prime minister's office. The programme was tightly focused on agriculture/horticulture, community development and necessary engineering. Uniquely among the early fields, there was no medical component. In 1988 13 expatriates and 142 local staff were engaged in a variety of development tasks (in the early 1990s an emergency food distribution programme was initiated at official request). For instance, horticulturist John Little from Athy, County Kildare, explained in the summer 1988 newsletter how the most difficult task for his local colleague Augustine Shirina was to persuade farmers to plant tree seedlings supplied as well as the food crops. They had for generations used the rapidly depleting local woodlands as a free resource, and they could not see why valuable space should be taken up in this way. 'They forget that without trees in Malangali there will be no fuel wood or charcoal for cooking and heating, no building poles for roofing houses, no wood for furniture. If people keep cutting timber at their present rate in another twenty years the place will be bare even of a basic twig.'

In September 1988 the mighty rivers that are present in every part of Bangladesh, like veins in the human body, were over-swollen with Himalayan snows and burst their banks. The resulting appalling floods left three-quarters of the country (twice the size of Ireland) under water. Seeds were scattered, fields submerged, cattle drowned. The carefully guarded privacy of hundreds of thousands of family compounds, with separate huts for the women and young, was swept away. As the floods seeped into homes, families were pushed together to spend weeks perched on beds above the water. The floods covered tubewells, so the only water available was muddy and contaminated with sewage. On the spot, Concern volunteers were able to react immediately. Field director Theresa McDonnell and assistant field director Paul Crowe reported from the Kaliajure area: 'Damage is very extensive. Many villages have been destroyed and it is difficult to appreciate that villages did in fact exist in some places. Flood water has dropped by approximately 5 feet, but Kaliajure remains under water, the only means of communication is by boat and even that is difficult. You can imagine the desperation of villagers seeing their homes being slowly eaten away and crumbling into the endless expanse of rising water.' Among other responses, they filled a trawler with drums of clean water and ferried it around.

Estimates of the number affected varied, but at least 30 million people had to leave their homes. Sometimes themselves ankle-deep in the muddy, soiled water, Concern volunteers provided cooked rice for 35,000 families in Dhaka alone. As the floods subsided, volunteers designed and distributed 12,000 specially created packs with housing materials, blankets, cooking utensils etc.

Bad as Bangladesh was, perhaps the worst field in 1988 was Sudan. Concern had first entered the country in 1985, led by Theresa McDonnell, when staff members from Ethiopia went to see if anything could be done for the thousands of refugees from Tigray who had poured across the long border between Sudan and Ethiopia to escape the war.

Sudan is the largest country in Africa, with a population of some 25 million. The northern two-thirds containing the capital Khartoum is mostly desert, inhabited by Arabs. The southern third is inhabited by pastoral African tribes, predominantly the Dinka. More or less since independence in 1956, the politically dominant north had neglected the south, much as West Pakistan had neglected East before 1971. Economic and political power was concentrated in the Arab north, to the extent that the south, with perhaps a quarter of the population, had only 9 per cent of the secondary schools. After numerous coalition governments, a coup in 1969 brought Colonel Jaffar Nimeiri to power, and the pro-Arab policy was reinforced, to the point of the introduction of Sharia law in 1983. The southern-based Sudanese People's Liberation Army, led by John Garang, a Dinka, fought for autonomy. In 1985 a new leader, Sadiq al-Mahdi, came to power in Khartoum, exactly a hundred years after his great-grandfather had brought the British General Gordon to a sticky end in Khartoum. Al-Mahdi fought hard and viciously to prevent the SPLA gaining power. This was a desperate, cruel, proxy war, financed on one side by the Arab states and on the other by anti-Arab and anti-Moslem groups and governments.

'Both sides,' wrote the *New Yorker* in 1989, 'have deployed a silent weapon to kill women and children: starvation. It is as much a part of their warfare as automatic rifles and landmines. The government hasn't allowed food to go to towns and villages to which refugees from the south have fled, and the SPLA has blown up convoys and threatened to shoot down planes carrying relief food to towns— even towns populated by Dinka—that it has under siege. No one knows how many people have starved to death in recent months.'[2]

Concern's work began in Omdurman, and there were quickly 30 experienced expatriates and more than 700 local staff engaged in refugee and famine relief. In the first four months of operation over £800,000 was spent—by 1988 expenditure had reached £6.2 million, of which as much as 80 per cent came from co-funding sources. The programme included supplementary feeding, water, sanitation and elementary health services, as well as a mother and child clinic. Later development projects included education for small children, literacy and craft training for women, the building of schools and school latrines, as well as agriculture and forestry projects.

Sudan's infrastructure was extremely poor: there were only 3,000 miles of road, most of which were gravel or dirt-track; the telephone service was such that only three per cent of calls between the two largest cities in the country actually got through. The postal service was very unreliable—a letter from Dublin to Khartoum could take weeks or even months. In the country there were simply no means of communication at all, so runners and couriers had to be used. Telex worked possibly one day in six. The lack of communication meant that volunteers felt much more than usually isolated. Not to get their family's Christmas greetings until after St Patrick's Day made volunteers feel very far from the home country. Luckily there were people flying in and out from Dublin to bring post sacks with them, but the loss of one such opportunity through administrative mishap could cause bitter disappointment.

Within weeks of Concern's arrival in 1985, severe famine began to grip the country, and the programme was expanded rapidly throughout the southern White Nile province, laying the foundations for an extensive connection with local government, village sheikhs and other organisations that was to be extremely useful in subsequent years.

The real exodus from the south began in the middle of 1988, as migrants fled hundreds of miles to Khartoum, away from the increasingly savage civil war. Concern volunteers, taken from their normal development assignments, provided assistance en route, and looked after them when they arrived. The newsletter of summer 1988 reported that 'starving people on overcrowded trains are arriving in Khartoum, the capital of Sudan. They are fleeing the famine and war in their home areas in southern Sudan. The majority of them are members of the Dinka tribe.' Trains were so irregular and the needs of the people so immediate that Concern kept a 24-hour watch at the station, with a staff member sleeping on the platform. Some of the refugees came from as far as Aweil, over 600 miles, crammed 200 to a carriage, with others crowded on the roof. By the time they arrived they often had to be given instant food and rehydration therapy. One eyewitness told how some starved, exhausted and terrorised women took half-an-hour to climb down from the roof of the train.[3]

Then teams went down the line with special instant foods, cooking utensils and hydration packs. The towns on the railway were crowded with refugees waiting for a train to the capital. In Muglad, hundreds arrived every day, mostly destitute, without even blankets. Feeding centres were opened, and plastic sheeting for tents and clothes made available. By 1988 there were some 75,000 men, women and children being given aid. For some help came all too late. Volunteer Cathy Hennessy will long remember a particular incident: 'Slowly the man crawled towards me. He was a young man with an old man's eyes. He never took them off me as he slowly made his way over to where I was surrounded by sick children. The man was dying.'[4]

Getting to Abyei in the far south proved a major problem. Roads were impossibly bad, and there was (or so the government said, which turned out later not to be true) no air strip. So Mike McDonagh from Clare, late of the Mid-Western Health Board and one of Concern's legendary pioneers, eventually organised a donkey train. Mike was Concern administrator in Muglad at the time. The train consisted of 346 donkeys each loaded with 132 lbs of grain; they made the 120-mile journey in October 1988. It cost a fortune—not only did McDonagh have to buy the donkeys, but he also had to pay protection money to the local Arab militia chiefs. (This was a few years before Somalia introduced aid agencies generally to such necessities, and before it was widely realised that payments of this sort were very dangerous, not least because it gave men of violence a vested interest in the continuance of conditions which they had very often themselves helped to create.) The Arab tribesmen who hauled the food, however, certainly earned their money—at several points they had to carry the sacks of grain across swampy ground themselves before returning for the donkeys. Later, Mike organised a more conventional lorry convoy.

On 4 August, another horror—that night alone twice the *annual* rainfall for the region, eight inches, fell on Khartoum. The Blue Nile from the east, which meets the White Nile from the south at Khartoum, was already swollen by the heavy rains in the Ethiopian highlands. Immediately the overflowing waters poured into the crowded squatter settlements which surrounded the town. Concern emergency teams on the spot distributed plastic sheeting, blankets, clean water and feeding utensils from their stores as quickly as they could. Medical supplies struggled to combat the threat of epidemics. From Ireland came £850,000 worth of high-energy biscuits, water storage tanks, purification tablets and plastic sheeting.

In the shadow of the world-scale emergencies in Bangladesh and Sudan, Aengus Finucane (in his report to Council of September 1988) described his current difficulties with the perennial 'emergency relief *v* development' debate. How was he to balance an urgent response to the massive human suffering caused by emergencies with the important long-term development designed to reduce the vulnerability of the poorest of the poor—the so-called hard-core poor? This is a constant tension in Concern's history. For some people emergency response was Concern's natural home—where the organisation began (in Biafra) and where it demonstrably got greatest public support. For others, emergency response, while undoubtedly important—even unavoidable—was simply the urgent defeating the important. Serious emergencies occur, the argument went, when natural disasters hit inherently vulnerable or unstable environments;

reduce the vulnerability and instability by development projects and the people will suffer less from these natural incidents. A cyclone or a crop failure in Florida or Japan, say the development lobby, has quite a different impact on lives from one hitting Bangladesh. Vulnerability is the key.

Furthermore, since there was (is) no well-understood route to development, people began to realise that any action to that end could have as many bad as good effects. The complexity of human life being what it is, even the simplest, most unobjectionable action can have unforeseeable, negative consequences. A sad example comes from Bangladesh. What development work, one might have said, could be freer of negative implications than the sinking of a tubewell to provide plentiful clean water for a village? Yet the tens of thousands of tubewells Concern and other agencies have sunk in Bangladesh since independence have provided the country with a major health problem for the 21st century. So many wells were dug and so much water was used for irrigation that the water table sank. In doing so it exposed previously harmless saturated arsenic to the air, thus rendering it poisonous. When the water table rises again during the wet season, the poisonous arsenic is carried up the pump and into the drinking water, causing stomach cancers.

There was in Sudan another, complicating dilemma. The agencies knew of the aggressive, virtually genocidal, policies undertaken by the government, and yet said nothing. It was quite clear that the Sudanese government was uneasy with aid agencies, especially those with a predominantly Christian ethos. In 1986 it expelled Winston Prattley, the director of the UN relief operations in Sudan, and in late 1987 four relief organisations, including the specifically Christian World Vision and Lutheran World Federation, had been asked to leave. Most agencies, including Concern, held uneasily to the view that silent action on the ground (which could not occur without local and national bureaucratic support) would do more for the people than publicity and expulsion.

An employee faced with dubious behaviour on the part of his or her employer has three broad choices: exit, voice or loyalty. One can leave, one can try to change things by the risky strategy of complaint, or one can collude in (more or less) silence and get on with one's work. In some cases, there is a fourth option. Aid agencies caught in this dilemma have been suspected of leaking information to media or international bodies. This can easily backfire, but it was very successfully followed by Concern in 1988. Fr Gottardi Silvano, the parish priest of Abyei in southern Sudan, wrote to Concern administrator Mark Cunningham, thanking Concern for delivery of food. But he noted that the consignment had been designed to help 10–15,000 people, but the number of refugees had now escalated to 30–40,000. 'Due to the malnutrition,' wrote Fr Silvano, 'the death toll has increased to 45 a day.'[5] Most of the victims were children or old people. At this time the US agencies and government were holding back from helping Sudan's famine victims, inhibited by all sorts of diplomatic considerations. Somehow the letter got into the hands of the US Embassy in Khartoum, and was sent from there to the US Office of Foreign Disaster Assistance. OFDA's head brought the letter and a news film of the famine to George Schultz's attention, and suddenly the diplomatic niceties seemed irrelevant.[6]

The 'exit, voice or loyalty' issue can be a tough choice, entirely dependent on guesses as to how others, notably the local power élites, but also the media and the international community, will react. Aid agencies can even rationalise silence by presenting collusion as a positive decision not to interfere with the internal arrangements of the country. We have seen how Médicins sans Frontières and Concern made quite different judgements on the resettlement programme in Ethiopia. International media reaction is critical and this is dependent on happen-stance and the unpredictable response of individual gate-keepers. A typical example was when only a day before the first stunning Amin-Buerk film on the 1984 famine in Ethiopia was broadcast, the BBC offered a full set of pictures to a London newspaper. 'We're not actually interested in famine,' they were told. A few weeks later the tide had turned with a vengeance, and the newspaper was sending its own reporters to Ethiopia to get pictures.[7]

An international agency such as Concern, with a mandate to help the very poorest (who are almost by definition politically oppressed as well), must also keep an eye on how governments elsewhere will respond. For instance, as we have seen, activities on behalf of the Hutus in Rwanda in 1994 made getting access later to Tutsi-dominated Burundi doubly difficult. On the other hand, donors will not support agencies seen to be too compliant with intolerable regimes. At the same time the unpredictable consequences of speaking out tend to alarm the timid, the conservative and the prudent, just as Africa Concern's Libreville airlift challenged the cosy relationship between the Nigerian federal government and Joint Church Aid. In 1988, the agencies in Sudan, for as good and as bad reasons as Pius XII in respect of Nazi Germany, took the view that silence was the least-worst option.

Concern's approach in Sudan was eloquently criticised by Dr Abdullah El Tom, a Sudanese anthropologist, in its 1989 evaluation. 'The compromise,' he noted in a hard hitting passage, 'appears to be dear, stopping only short of complacency. By deciding not to embarrass the government and expose it to the world conscience, Concern partakes in the cover-up of the genocide. Why protect the very government which is to a great extent responsible for the death of 250,000 to 500,000 of its people in a single year?'[8] As it happens, this was unfair, as Aengus Finucane had given an interview to the BBC about the situation he had found in the refugee camp near the Dinka village of Muglad. Abdullah El Tom's next point was also strongly expressed, and pause-making. With government encouragement, he suggested, Concern located its camps neither in the starvation zone i.e. the south, nor in the centre of power i.e. Khartoum, but in-between, on the way from one to the other. But, 'in a capital-centred country like Sudan, citizens can starve in the bush without threatening the established order.' 'For this favour,' he wrote, 'the government must be grateful to Concern.'

Not long before the 1988 flood Concern's Bangladesh programme was also subjected to an evaluation; this one made an interesting but, for many, unwelcome contribution to the 'emergency *v* development' debate. Such reports were a regular feature of Concern's work, and in 1987 a formal policy was established that evaluations should take place in every field every five years. In October 1986 a development academic, Professor Charles Elliott of the development studies department at the university in Swansea, visited Bangladesh to carry out an evaluation of Concern's programmes, having previously undertaken a number of interviews in Dublin. His wife, a trained counsellor, accompanied him on the trip, and she sat in on the interviews, a presence somewhat resented at the time. The 63-page report, though signed by him alone, is written with the magisterial 'we', giving rise to such remarkable phrases as 'there is little doubt in our mind', and 'we are aware that we have set the Council a daunting task', and so on. A number of errors of fact, pounced on by field director Philip O'Brien, were dismissed, with a lordly wave, as 'piddling details'.[9]

Professor Elliott admitted that he was new to Concern in Ireland or elsewhere, and almost new to Bangladesh. But his grasp of development theory prompted him to suggest a root and branch redesign of Concern's involvement in Bangladesh. He recommended that Concern should stop trying to do development work in Bangladesh, and hand over virtually all its non-emergency activities to Bengali NGOs as soon as possible. Where there was no suitable local NGO, Concern should establish one, using existing local staff. His conclusions stemmed from his theory that conflict between community and government was an essential part of 'genuine development'. Development was ultimately political, and was 'fundamentally about equipping poor people with voice, influence and perhaps ultimately real power.' This can be done by NGOs, but only those which are community-based and local. This was far from the view expressed by Aengus Finucane in the autumn 1980 newsletter that 'our humanitarian aid is delivered in a political context. But we very quickly get out of our depth if we shift our emphasis from humanitarian to political.' As it happens, local NGOs, notably BRAC and the Grameen Bank, have been extremely successful in Bangladesh, but very much less so in Africa.

The volunteers, despite their 'remarkable personal qualities', did not meet with Professor Elliott's approval. Older, more experienced men and women, preferably with experience in other fields, should be recruited instead. His recommendations implied a very different kind of volunteer from what had hitherto been the norm. He thought that a volunteer should spend three months (out of a two-year term) immersed in learning the local language. He believed that they should then have read, wrestled with and understood a number of textbooks on Bangladesh development issues. Finally, Professor Elliott suggested that they should covenant, as part of the contract, that they would become involved educationally and/or politically in development issues on their return. To this end they must be 'properly briefed' about the educational/political tasks they were to face. Aengus Finucane's ideas were simpler. He thought that there were pressingly urgent tasks to be done, so each volunteer should grab the baton as quickly as possible, run with it as hard and as far as possible for the appropriate term, and then leave the field. If they then cared to get involved in fundraising at home, so much the better.

Professor Elliott had, however, correctly sensed Concern's distinctly non-academic approach to preparing and training volunteers. This had much in common with the way Holy Ghosts were sent to eastern Nigeria. The young priests were given little language tuition, and did most of their work through English; their specific training in Igbo culture and custom was sketchy, as was their knowledge of such practical parish matters as running a bank account.[10] Concern did introduce the volunteers to Bengali and a few became fluent speakers, but there was certainly no attempt to insist, or to impose anything like a three-month immersion course. Although they were certainly not professional development academics like himself, it was rather unkind of Elliott to describe the volunteers he met as 'under-educated and under-prepared', even if he assigned a rather special meaning to this, viz. that they failed ideologically 'to interpret the problems they encounter in their professional lives as symptoms of a political and social structure that is both cause and effect of the perpetuation of under-development.'[11]

Undoubtedly, Professor Elliott's most wounding finding was the way Concern related to its local staff. He apparently identified deep resentment among local employees about the policy of always using expatriate supervisors, and goes on: 'It is hard to exaggerate the anger and resentment among both the Bengali employees of Concern . . . and among Bengalis in the NGO sector and in government'. He pointed out that Concern was behind other international NGOs in this. He suggested that the very presence of volunteers in Bangladesh 'prevents the emergence of Bengali leadership and in that sense is actually anti-developmental.' It was very hard for field director Philip O'Brien (who had in 1983 appointed Mohammed Mobin as the first local manager) and his predecessor Jack Finucane to believe this, but they discussed the report in detail, and a number of steps, mainly addressing the questions raised about the status and opportunities of the local staff, were taken. A firm commitment to the country for at least another ten years was recorded in the 1988 accounts. On the other hand, Aengus Finucane was not one to be impressed by the swings and fashions of academic development theory. His final opinion of the report can be detected in his comment to Council: 'The present calamitous situation spells out again the harsh realities of this unfortunate country. It spells out again for us in Concern the need to stay on the ground with the poor (their numbers now vastly swollen) rather than indulge in flights of theoretical fancy when programming for Bangladesh.' For members of Council however, the Elliott report, backed by his careful briefings, was a first intimation that perhaps the Finucane way was not the only, or even necessarily the best, way to approach aid work.

The three-man evaluation team which arrived in Sudan in March 1989 was more widely constituted than that of Professor Elliott and his wife. It comprised Dr Abdullah El Tom (quoted above), who had recently started to work in NUI Maynooth, Brendan Parsons (the Earl of Rosse) ex-UN and later chairman of APSO and Hugh Byrne, deputy chief executive of Concern with considerable field experience. By this time Al-Mahdi had been overthrown in favour of Ahmad al Bashir, an Islamic fundamentalist. This was not a good omen, and civil war remained sporadic—it and its fellow-horseman of the apocalypse, famine, reappeared in 1998. And now, to add further complications, the Dinka were at daggers drawn with their traditional enemies in the south, the Nuer.

Although in the circumstances, priority was always given to emergency work, the evaluation team noted that both at head office and in the field there was a hankering after long-term development.

This was encouraged by Sudanese government officials who seemed genuinely to like Concern and the Irish. They had, for instance, given at least one of Concern's programmes a three-year as opposed to the more normal one-year licence. (The relationship was not always so sunny. In South Kordofan, which included large camps at Baba-nusa and Muglad, Concern was barely tolerated by the authorities; when they came into the camps its representatives were regarded as little more than spies.[12]) Nonetheless, the team believed that to try to combine emergency and development work was to attempt the impossible. 'Either the organisation should give priority to developing and maintaining long-term development projects *or* to emergency operations. There is no basis for assuming the latter can be undertaken at the same time, and by the same staff, as the former, as experience in the Sudan shows this is just not realistic.'

The evaluation team saw Sudan as a country whose difficulties were likely to continue for the foreseeable future, so it urged Concern to concentrate on emergency relief, even at the expense of the most worthwhile development projects. Few agencies, they report, have 'such an impressively successful experience of this than Concern, which clearly enjoys greater confidence of both the national and international authorities in this respect than just about any NGO. Indeed some of these authorities like USAID as well as WFP and UNICEF *count on* Concern to ensure safe delivery of food and materials.' Emergency work, they argued, was one sure way, as development was not, of reaching the organisation's target, the poorest of the poor.[13] 'It would', they conclude, 'be a double tragedy not to respond to this by giving this programme priority over all others.'

The team, however, agreed with Professor Elliott that 'localisation' of the staff should occur as soon as possible, and that more emphasis should be placed on training both volunteers and local staff. They found the volunteers 'well qualified, exceptionally highly motivated and doing an outstanding job under fairly difficult circumstances.' Like Professor Elliott they dreamed of longer-term, more experienced volunteers, ones who would not leave after two years 'just when he or she has built up enough experience to be really useful'. Local staff at all levels was the ideal, though there was the complicated issue of salary, which had to be attractive to compete with what gifted Sudanese could get in other Arab countries.

Neither this team nor Professor Elliott addressed the question of relations with co-funders which did, of course, affect what could be done on the ground. Perhaps too timidly, many in Concern believed that it was easier for an expatriate (bluntly, a white Westerner) backed by international accounting systems to gain the confidence and funding of the rich agencies in North America and Europe. With 80 per cent of the funds spent in Sudan coming from such sources, this was clearly a consideration. On the other hand, Council had authorised, as part of its general statement of policy in November 1987, a clear commitment to 'give a greater role in the management and implementation of its projects to nationals of the country in which it works'. Unfortunately, as the evaluation team discovered, this was so far just an aspiration: 'few if any of those we spoke to in Khartoum professed to be aware' of the policy, and 'certainly in the Sudan this is not yet a reality'.

The last word on this evaluation should perhaps be a team member's, in a personal comment at the end of the report: 'In Sudan I saw work that was on a par with anything that I had seen elsewhere. It is the same Concern—with the same opportunistic strengths, the same irritating flaws, the same potential for excellence.'

8: Killing fields

'Occasionally,' an American diplomat explained, 'you have to dance with the devil to do the Lord's work.'[1]

War in general, and civil war in particular, is now the single most obvious cause of under-development, poverty and human wretchedness. The indifference of nature (drought, disease or pest) pales into insignificance when compared to the effects of human wickedness. In countries such as Sudan, where you could recently buy an AK47 for the price of a chicken, untrained civilians, even children, can become deadly. Added together these sources of distress produce the testing ground of modern aid, where the aid itself can become an unwitting factor.

The international trade in weaponry, particularly light machine-guns and landmines, has made violence, suicide and war among the top ten causes of death worldwide in the 15–44 age group.[2] To finance arms purchases, rebel leaders loot their country's natural resources; it was thus the friendless Khmer Rouge sustained itself for years by selling rubies, sapphires and logging rights. In Angola, potentially one of the richest countries in Africa, the civil war was extended for years by the government pawning the oil resources of the west, and the rebels looting the diamond fields of the north. Enterprising warlords can even sell 'booty futures'—a share in the resources that the purchased guns will capture (as the Revolutionary United Front did in Sierra Leone).

For the first 20 years or so of Concern's existence the fundamental fact of international life was the Cold War. Unwilling to risk direct conflict the US and the USSR fought each other by proxy in Central America, in Asia and in Africa. To establish regional strategic footholds the great powers cynically provided kleptocrats, dictators and tribal warlords with their weapons of choice (including specialist torture equipment).³ Sometimes this would lead to almost farcical consequences. In 1977, the Soviets suddenly switched allegiance from their previous ally Somalia to the new Marxist government of Ethiopia. Hundreds of Soviet advisers were moved overnight from Mogadishu to Addis, and within months, 15,000 Cuban troops were employed to 'protect' Ethiopian borders. Now, heavily armed with new Soviet weapons and allies, the Derg was in a position to recapture large parts of the Ogaden desert that, with slightly older Soviet weapons, the Somalis had invaded a few years before.

By 1989, Gorbachev's *glasnost* programme was beginning to loosen the iron grip of the Party. Internationally Stalin's protective Iron Curtain cracked at the same time. In August the Hungarians repudiated their treaty with the East German government and allowed thousands of East Germans into the West. Now pressure came on the Berlin Wall—the 'Anti-Fascist Defence Barrier' as it was officially called—the great symbol of the Cold War. For nearly 30 years since its sudden erection in 1961 this brutally guarded line of concrete and barbed wire had haunted the Western media. Checkpoint Charlie, the main crossing-point between the Soviet and US occupied zones, was one of the most photographed and filmed places in the world.

In a profoundly satisfying expression of human freedom, in November 1989 thousands of unarmed East Germans mobbed the guards on the wall. The authorities, the ground under their feet shaken by the seismic shifts in Moscow, let them through. In emotional scenes that were televised across the world, 'Ossies' poured across the barrier, to be greeted by jubilant 'Wessies'. 'Here,' one was told as a 20-mark note was pushed into his hand 'have a beer on us'. Thousands of battered Trabants lumbered across the border, to be greeted with flowers and chocolates—even their notorious fumes were applauded as the perfume of freedom (at least for a while).

Meanwhile, across the world another revelation was in progress. In Houston, Texas, Boris Yeltsin made a tour of an ordinary supermarket. He and his entourage goggled at the profusion of vegetables, with radishes as big as Soviet potatoes, at piles of breads and cheeses, at thousands of tins and packages—30,000 items, as opposed to the hundred or so stocked by the average Russian store. They suddenly knew why their rulers would not allow Soviets to travel. They felt humiliated and profoundly deceived. Yeltsin's last vestiges of socialism slipped away from him. He now wanted revenge, and two years later he got it, by becoming President of Russia. The old Soviet Union disintegrated into 12 separate states.[4]

The new world order, released from the heavy hand of Cold War geo-strategy, was characterised by an acceleration of civil wars fought on ethnic or identity grounds, such as we have already seen in Ethiopia. Unlike the wars of liberation from colonial powers that preceded them, these wars are extremely destructive of civil society—the social, political and trading structures. Social leaders, such as professionals and intellectuals (or, as in Cambodia, anyone who wore glasses), are common targets. In addition, the extraordinary length of these wars turns fighting into a way of life for many young men. With severely depleted resources violence becomes a rational strategy, at least for yourself and your friends. What's more if poverty has given you little choice, fighting is liberating and full of possibilities for power and prestige. The post First World War cliché says 'war is hell', but hardly anyone in history has believed that—across the world (with the possible exception of China) the fighting man has been held in the highest esteem—in Celtic Ireland as in 20th-century Somalia.

These wars are so destructive that it is no surprise that eight out of the ten countries rated lowest in the UN's Human Development Index have suffered civil wars, in which more than 1,000 people a year were killed, in recent years; that half of the 'least developed' countries have experienced major armed conflict some time during the last 20 years; that countries afflicted by civil war have the highest infant mortality rates and the lowest per capita incomes.[5]

For hundreds of years, the countries of the Indochina peninsula had fought wars for territory among themselves. Sometimes the Cambodians would be ascendant, as when the Angkor Wat empire spread over half Vietnam; at others the Thai or the Vietnamese burst from their borders to claim sovereignty over more land and therefore more taxes from the unfortunate peasantry. After a hundred years of enjoying French 'protection', Vietnam eventually achieved independence, only to be then assaulted by the Americans in an attempt to stop Communist infiltration of the whole area. During the Vietnam war Cambodia, struggling to remain aloof, allowed the Vietcong to use camps inside its territory from which to assault South Vietnam. In 1965, with the tacit permission of Prince Sihanouk, then Cambodian head of state, the Americans began to bomb these areas. Thus began Cambodia's time on the cross. Some believe that more than a million ordinary Cambodians were killed, wounded or maimed as a result of the bombing of this ostensibly friendly country. Hundreds of thousands fled to the cities.

In 1973 the US renewed its bombing campaign, this time to prevent the shadowy Pol Pot and his Khmer Rouge from taking the capital. Although this second campaign had the immediate effect of forcing the Khmer Rouge to withdraw, in the end it accelerated the collapse of rural society that ensured its ultimate victory in 1975.

In the dry season of 1975, Saigon fell to North Vietnamese forces backed by the Soviets. In Cambodia Pol Pot, 'Brother Number One' of the Chinese backed Communist Party of Kampuchea, brought the Khmer Rouge into Phnom Penh on 17 April. The party instantly initiated an extraordinary attempt to re-invent itself, and cast out any vestiges of the hated West. The first step was to eradicate all urban living. 'A day after their entry into Phnom Penh the Khmer Rouge emptied the cities, breaking up families, clearing hospitals and marching the entire population into the countryside. Eyewitnesses saw the sick and injured being forced to get up and stagger from the city.'[6]

Men and women from the cities were called 'new people'. They were class enemies and so dispensable—the Party cadre sneered: 'keeping you is no gain: losing you is no loss'.[7] New people were made to hack rice fields, canals, dams and villages out of the malarial forests, all under the supervision of the 'old people' from the villages. This was only the start. In the next four years, the regime became an international by-word for brutality. Cadres destroyed schools, hospitals, factories, machines, vehicles, and even typewriters. Intellectuals and professionals were exterminated (just 54 doctors managed to survive, by disguising themselves as peasants). By the time the regime was toppled in 1979 it is estimated that over a million, out of an initial population of some nine million, had been executed or had died of starvation, disease or overwork in collective camps.[8]

During the 1970s the whole south-east Asia region became a turmoil of refugees.[9] A communist government also came to power in Laos in December 1975, and hill tribes and resistance fighters were forced out. From Vietnam first came the people closely associated with the defeated government of South Vietnam, and then from 1979 the 'boat people', who were Vietnamese of Chinese origin fleeing the anti-Chinese repression of the government. From Cambodia the increasing paranoia of the Pol Pot regime killed millions and forced thousands more across the border. In 1979 the Vietnamese, goaded by a constant stream of Khmer Rouge attacks invaded Cambodia. More refugees fled the fighting and the resultant starvation and disease.

Thailand, relatively peaceful and prosperous, was the first destination. This was not a responsibility the country accepted enthusiastically. Indeed at one point, in June 1979, Thai soldiers rounded up some 42,000 Cambodia refugees and brutally pushed them down a steep hillside back into Cambodia; since the border was mined several hundreds, perhaps thousands, were killed.

Eventually, however, the Thai government announced that it would open its borders to all refugees. Within hours of that decision, it seemed that as many as 350,000 refugees would have to be accommodated. UNHCR asked Concern to help create an instant camp at Sa Kaeo (Ban Kang). Justin Kilcullen, an architect from Mount Merrion in Dublin (later chief executive of Trócaire), was the first technical person on site, and described his experience for a special Concern newsletter. 'We found 30 acres of empty bush, one bulldozer and a few workmen. This had to be transformed into a settlement for 90,000 refugees who were expected within the next five days. We began ploughing out roads and digging trenches for toilets. Almost immediately refugees started to arrive. As there is little water on the site, lorries delivered water from a nearby river.

Convoys of supplies began to arrive. In the middle of the chaos, two rainstorms converted the camp into a swamp. Endless convoys of buses emptied the refugees hungry, sick and bereft of possessions into this sea of mud. For nine days we worked an exhausting four-teen hours a day, 6.30 am to 8.30 pm. Dr Joe Barnes, a Dubliner, took charge of a "ward" in the emergency field hospital catering for nearly 1,500 patients. Buses full of sick arrived in the dark. We had to carry them through ankle-deep mud and lay them on soggy mats. When I left on Wednesday, with a dose of malaria, the patch of cleared land I had first seen nine days before was now a crowded settlement of 30,000.'[10] Although the camp was now 'awash with engineers', it took time before conditions became anyway satisfac-tory. Aengus Finucane, who had been asked by UNHCR to report on the camps described the conditions in Sa Kaeo a month after establishment as execrable. 'I have not seen, in many years of camp experience, a situation as humanly degrading as exists in Sa Kaeo. There is not the remotest vestige of privacy as men, women and children defecate in full view of and within feet of the camp living areas . . . UNHCR cannot continue to be associated with situations like this and command respect.'[11]

Fifteen such holding camps were established on the Thai-Cam-bodian border and Concern worked in four of these. The largest was Khao I Dhang, where 112,000 people were held. The camp was divided into zones, with Concern taking responsibility (under UNHCR) for zones 3 and 7 comprising some 25,000 people. When Anne O'Mahony started in 1982 there were 23 separate agencies involved in health in that camp alone. Although conditions were relatively good, the camp was tightly controlled by the Thai mili-tary; every piece of medical equipment and supplies had to be indi-vidually checked-in every day. This was so time-wasting that eventually one staff member was delegated to do nothing but check equipment in and out. Field director Aengus Finucane led a team of 23 volunteers. Sanitation and feeding programmes were established, together with mother and child clinics, education, and social welfare activities.

Khao I Dhang camp was, as Concern's Munster organiser John

Miller reported to the summer 1980 newsletter, 'a sprawling net-work of bamboo grass huts and shelters. Each family has very little space in which to live. Interiors of these huts are dark, overcrowded with often up to ten people living in a small area.' Yet for him the overwhelming impression was of the friendliness of the people: 'walking through the narrow alleys or entering the huts and shelters, I was greeted by warm smiles and friendly glances. Wherever I went children would follow: "OK, Hallo, Goodbye". The only English they knew.'

Not everyone was able to cope with camp life. Concern monitored its feeding programmes and found that it was able to identify first children and then mothers (often widows or deserted wives) who were struggling to survive. A rehabilitation and development programme was set up, based on experience from Bangladesh, and using an advisor from the Bengali NGO BRAC. There was also a youth programme and other educational and craft programmes, to try to give the thousands in the camps some focus to their lives.

Come the cool of the evening, as Michael Doheny, a veteran observer of camp life, noted, 'the whole camp population seems to be out on the "streets". Little markets have sprung up everywhere and they are crowded; organised games like football, volleyball and others are in full swing. Water tanks are surrounded and motley groups—men, women and children—await their turn to draw their ration. It is a cheerful scene and the greetings and the exuberant cries, the smiles that greet us everywhere give no indication of the pain of loss that lies deep in the hearts of many. In these last moments of light, as the sun sets on another day of exile, there is a calmness which induces reflection. Many eyes must look eastward to their homeland and think of what they have left behind . . . and of the loved ones that are missing or dead.'

The exile was to last for another 14 weary years. During that time the camps were not insulated from the political struggles at home. Each camp had its own political allegiance, as well as the more or less sinister presence of guerrilla fighters. Not everyone stayed in the camps all the time, but it was not to be until 1993 that political and military conditions finally allowed all the refugees to return.

After so many years of hope deferred, some of those going home had sadly unrealistic expectations: 'I have a lot of money,' one woman told Dominic MacSorley, brandishing a $50 note as she left. 'I will be able to support myself until I find my son.' She had not heard of her son for 15 years, and monetary values had changed enormously since she had left Cambodia. Here was another field of activity for Concern—to help the reconstruction of the shattered infrastructure of the country. With perhaps one in eight of its citizens killed or missing since Pol Pot's regime came to power, there was much to do.

Just before the Cambodian refugees finally went home, another vicious civil war erupted, bringing another series of grim camps and more images of starvation in the shadow of warfare into people's living rooms. The place this time was Somalia, on the Horn of Africa, whose chronic problems erupted in 1992. There was, naturally, a long and complicated history, but the immediate problem stemmed from long-time President Siad Barre's frantic attempts to stay in power. During the re-invasion of the Ogaden desert by Ethiopia he had in panic flooded the country with weapons donated by the US, by Italy and other countries. Foreign aid to Somalia (now that it was no longer pro-Soviet) soared to $80 a head, the highest in Africa. Much of this was spent on weaponry. To shore up his position Barre increasingly leaned on his own clan, which in turn stimulated armed opposition groups based on clan affiliation. He was finally chased from his luxurious Villa Somali in 1990. Then the trouble really started. One of the opposition parties, the United Somali Congress, split, with the ex-head of the secret police General Aideed as one of the key warlords. As journalist Scott Peterson, who later regularly stayed in Concern houses on his visits to Somalia, put it: 'The power vacuum was readily filled by the ferocious ghosts of Somali warriors past. Fortified with the endless firepower of Barre's Cold War arsenal, a new and altogether modern version of the invincible Somali gunman began to transform his country, sucking the once noble, often brutal attributes of Somali nomadic life into a vortex of irresistible violence.'[12]

In the old days a Somali warrior had his spear and his camel—

the range of possible violence was limited by the simple fact that to kill someone with a spear requires energy and concentration. An AK47 in the hands of a teenager muzzy with *qat* requires only indifference. And when he and his friends career around the city in a 'technical'—a heavy machine-gun bolted on to a land cruiser with its canopy ripped off—nobody cares to get in their way.

A temporary ceasefire had been negotiated, but the food situation was still critical when Jack Finucane visited Somalia in late April 1992. He urged that Concern get involved as soon as possible, and by 8 May supplies and personnel were on the way. First to arrive were Mary Considine from Longford and Kevin Byrne from Dublin. By August there were 10 expatriates and 300 local staff running 10 feeding stations for severely malnourished children. The worst by far was Baidoa, in the sorghum basket of the country. Normally a town of 60,000 people (a bit larger than Galway) its population had now swelled to 100,000. The newcomers were usually exhausted and hungry, having walked many miles. Every day a truck passed through the town collecting the dead for burial outside the town. In August 3,194 were collected in this way (a total that does not include those buried by their relatives). On 22 September, after heavy rains overnight, 470 bodies were collected. Seventy per cent of the dead were children.

Garda Kevin Spain, a volunteer, described his day in the camp at Baidoa. It had rained heavily during the night. 'We arrived at the first centre and met one of the workers, he said there had been some deaths. Just inside the door he pointed to a bundle under a table, it was covered with a blanket. Anita [Ennis] pulled back the blanket and there lay a child dead. The now familiar knot in my stomach was back. It was a disgusting sight and no child alive or dead should look disgusting. This was not a child who had found peace in death, this was a child who had died, crouched wet, cold, alone and in agony . . . the women and children were lined up in large rectangular shelters sitting on plastic sheeting which was saturated, everywhere was mucky and the people were drenched and cold even though the sun was getting hot at this stage.' Work began immediately to establish proper shelters, and soon the children were set to work collecting stones in 1kg Kerrygold tins. In the middle of all this Audrey Hepburn, UNICEF's goodwill ambassador, arrived with a film crew. 'She sat in among the sickest children who Eileen [Gilsenan] had now moved under the shelter of the tree out of the blazing sun. She sat beside a young child and stroked her head and face, she was kind and gentle, but the woman who had made millions laugh and cry in her films could not change the blank expression on this little girl's face.' Half an hour after Audrey Hepburn and her crew left, the child was dead.

The civil war completely disrupted the local economy. To their dismay aid workers simply *had* to hire their own bodyguards, even their own technicals, to travel through the country. Shockingly, neither they nor their humanitarian supplies were safe from plunder and destruction. Working thus in a war zone was a turning-point for many in the NGO community. In one feeding centre the militia regularly stole all the blankets handed out to children, who were left to shiver in the rain, so the agency had to cut the blankets up before handing them out, so that they were only of use to the smallest children.

This lack of respect for aid agencies and their work was a phenomenon of the 1990s. In that decade 40 International Red Cross personnel were killed in Chechnya and Rwanda alone, compared to the 15 who lost their lives in all conflicts between 1945 and 1990. In Somalia looting, casual murder and intimidation meant that food aid intended for the interior often rotted on the quayside because the greed and violence of the militias made it too dangerous to distribute. This was a brutal world, in which cargoes of *qat* always took precedence over food in the docks, and when food aid did arrive the militia always took their fill first. Shiploads were even turned away from the port by gunfire as rival militia fought for the food aid even before it arrived.

Clan warfare broke down to sub-clan fighting, which in turn fragmented into family against family. UN Secretary-General Perez de Cuellar deplored the Somali 'nightmare of violence and brutality,' and despairingly despatched an envoy to make peace. Scott Peterson recorded how in the Concern feeding centre on Mogadishu

University campus little Adad died from a stray bullet while he was being breast-fed: he was his mother's second child to die. Now, despite all that nurse Margaret O'Mahony could do, the third, little Shukri, was dying too. Gently the mother, whose name is not recorded, took off her daughter's special feeding wristband, thus accepting defeat. She then lay down beside her scarcely breathing child and softly began the song of death. 'Can you imagine', Margaret asked the journalist, 'back home, losing even one of your children?'[13]

Deeply shocked by what he had seen himself in Somalia, and by the reports from Concern staff, Aengus Finucane issued an emotional press release. 'I saw sights,' he wrote, 'that equalled and surpassed the worst I have seen in Biafra, Bangladesh, Karamoja, Ethiopia and other disaster areas over 25 years. I saw a father, a mother and their child huddled together in death. They had made it to a spot across the road from a Concern feeding centre and there died. An ordinary wheelbarrow carried off the mother with her child piled in beside her for burial in a shallow grave up the road. Then the wheelbarrow came back for the father's body.' He was convinced that only a substantial UN peace force could solve the problem by enforcing mass disarming of the militia. Mike McDonagh, Concern field director in Somalia, agreed: 'It's ridiculous that any 12-year-old boy with a gun can disrupt a multi-million dollar relief operation.'[14]

Then Aengus Finucane suggested to President Robinson, elected two years before, that she follow the example of Foreign Minister David Andrews and visit Somalia and Kenya to draw international attention to the disastrous situation. In early October Mary Robinson flew into Baidoa from Kenya in a small plane. As her entourage whisked through the town her vehicle was nearly rammed by a stray technical which swerved aside at the last minute, killing a donkey. (A few days before a Red Cross feeding station nearby had been attacked by local technicals, though the looters were driven off.)

Arriving at one of the camps she was initially overwhelmed by the hundreds of emaciated children and women and babies. In her book on the visit she wrote: 'I knelt down beside one woman and asked her to show me her baby. She was almost too weak to lift the small bundle, but I saw the sores on the scalp and flies crawling over the baby's eyes and mouth . . . I moved on to another woman picked at random because I had caught her eye. She was embarrassed that her clothing was so poor. She said "We have no clothes. It's cold at night and my child is cold." I moved to the next woman. Her baby was very light and frail and began to cry as I lifted it, and then stopped. I became aware that none of the babies was crying. As I held the tiny baby I heard Irish photographers saying "Look this way, President", and just that time I did.'[15]

The presidential party stopped for a lunch break at Concern headquarters, where staff obviously enjoyed the benison of celebrity, one whom all greatly respected. There was much laughter and teasing, house jokes, and a general cheerfulness that was a welcome relief from the emotional experiences of the morning.

That afternoon they flew out of Baidoa to Mogadishu. On the flight the President remembered 'so many hot, dry hands, brittle bones, tiny bundles of young Somalihood. I remembered the gesture of humiliation by a woman trying to cover her knees, a person who had probably been comfortable in Somali society two years before.' Some of the people in the endless queues were educated, spoke English, had perhaps been local professionals.

Her next stop was at the settlement at Mandera, an enormous sprawling gathering of straw and plastic huts just across the border in Kenya. It could hardly be called a camp—it was just where 55,000 people had fled from the famine in Somalia. There was not a single proper latrine; food supplies were not getting through (according to UNHCR rules they were too close to the Somali border to be classified as refugees); disease, especially measles and typhoid, was just starting to appear. At this time Concern was not working there, though as a result of what they saw on this visit they decided to move in at once. The President and David Andrews visited the graveyard, where by the shallow graves a flock of vultures shuffled and flapped.

Back in Nairobi the President gave an emotional press conference, in which she stressed over and over the shame she felt that such conditions should be allowed to last—'I felt,' she said, with tears glistening in her eyes, 'shamed by what I saw, shamed, shamed

. . . What are we doing that we have not got greater conscience for it?' It was, she repeated, 'not acceptable that human beings are in the degrading, humiliating situation in which they find themselves— we really have to stand back and say: it diminishes all of us as human beings.' Her long statement was broadcast almost complete on RTÉ, and made a deep impression on her viewers. For Concern and other Irish aid workers her words were an enormous morale booster. Not only did she specifically praise the work of the Irish agencies, but her general approach deeply reinforced their own feeling that what they were doing was worthwhile. More impressively still, this was not a once-off; when she got back home the President asked for regular updates on the situation, and Concern executives felt they had access to a sympathetic and effective ear in the Park.

Two months after the enormous publicity generated by President Robinson's visit, the UN agreed that the US military would lead a multi-national force to intervene in support of the New World Order with 25,000 US troops, backed by 13,000 from other countries including Ireland. Initially Concern enthusiastically welcomed the US intervention, for the troops gave practical support to NGO efforts. They helped in the construction of feeding centres and the refurbishment of schools. However, the local conditions were too much, and the eventual failure of this mission was to be used for years as a precedent against similar armed interventions, notably in Rwanda where perhaps thousands of lives might have been saved.

Concern's work at the feeding stations, at mother and child clinics went on, and as the number requiring intensive feeding fell, plans were being laid for an ambitious schools programme. In the suburbs of Mogadishu, for instance, the Pan Africa feeding centre catered for over 2,000 people a day, most of them from nearby displaced persons camps. But the environment was increasingly dangerous. In December the BBC reported stories of shooting in Baidoa, but although Mike McDonagh described this merely as 'inter-clan fighting', he noted that Goal and MSF had pulled out. However, in the dying months of his presidency Bush wanted a quick clean victory with as few body bags as possible. So disarmament of the militia, which would in truth have been difficult and dangerous, was taken off the agenda. As one diplomat put it: 'If we can't disarm New York or Washington, how can we disarm Mogadishu?'

In February, Concern was given a vivid reminder of just how dangerous things were. Twenty-three year old Valerie Place, a staff nurse from St James's Hospital Dublin, who was mostly involved in running the Pan Africa feeding centre, was travelling to Baidoa. A lone gunman shot at her car and the bullet hit her chest. She died soon afterwards. Her body was flown home, accompanied by Aengus Finucane in what he later described as 'the saddest journey of my life'. She had, as he put it 'paid the ultimate price of loving and caring in a situation of conflict fraught with risk.' Although a few Concern expatriates have died during their tours of duty, mostly from sickness, she is the only one to have been killed.

Remorselessly, the need for Concern's work went on, but the security situation deteriorated badly, and by August of 1994 Jack Finucane, Horn of Africa division head, visited Somalia and after a series of discussions with the then field director John Kilkenny, decided it was simply too dangerous to continue.

Just as Concern pulled out of one troubled land, it was plunged into another. Rwanda is roughly one-third the size of Ireland and in 1992 had a population of 7.5 million. Since the Belgian colonial period the country had experienced often bitter ethnic rivalry between the Hutus and the Tutsis. The root of the conflict, in this the most densely populated country in Africa, lay in the struggle between these groups for land, and hence wealth and power.

The minority Tutsis had special memories of the years when the Hutus' frustration at their subordinate economic position had burst out in a killing rage—1959, 1963, 1973, 1992. In 1990 the predominantly Tutsi Rwanda Patriotic Front invaded from the north, and made considerable gains. These successes greatly worsened the Tutsi-Hutu relations in the country. In early 1994 the extreme Hutu party assassinated the presidents of Rwanda and Burundi, and within hours a pre-planned campaign of brutal killings began. Roadblocks and marauding gangs of *interhamwe* (those who attack together) picked off moderate Hutus and leading Tutsis. Hutu hitmen provocatively murdered ten Belgian UN soldiers; the Security Council, terrified by memories of Somalia, withdrew UN troops just when they might have been of use.

Country director Dominic MacSorley's report described how militia bands fortified with banana beer 'were bussed from massacre to massacre. Many killings occurred in churches and stadiums where people had sought refuge. In mid-April 5,000 people were packed into a sports stadium in Kibuye in the west of the country. Gunmen shot at the crowd, throwing grenades, forcing people to run back and forth while the militia went in to finish them off with machetes. This type of killing was repeated throughout the country. No one knows how many people participated in the massacres. For many there was no choice, kill your neighbour or be killed. The entire Hutu population had been called to participate, creating a conspiracy of implication.' For the Irish staff it was especially shocking to learn that Rwandan Catholic priests and nuns had taken active part in the killings.

This was the most concentrated mass killing since Hiroshima, yet it was astonishingly low-tech. Most of the 800,000 or so killings were done, neighbour to neighbour, with a machete. As so often before, the experts had been proved wrong. It turned out that the science of the atom bomb or the Holocaust, or even the international arms trade, were not, after all, essential. All that was needed was enough hatred.

From long experience the Tutsis knew that there was only one thing to do—flee. Within days of the first killings thousands of refugees began streaming across the extreme southern border into Tanzania. The French army set up a protective area in the south-west of Rwanda, which quickly became host to a million internally displaced refugees. Then the rope was given another twist—the predominantly Tutsi RPF renewed the civil war, and in the chaos captured the capital, Kigali, in July. Public radio broadcasts, which not long before had urged the destruction of cockroaches (the Hutu term for the Tutsi), now gloatingly urged the Hutus to flee or be massacred. Three days later one million more refugees, among whom were many of those who had carried out the killings, started crossing into Zaire. Hundreds of thousands camped in and around Goma. By July there were nearly two million refugees in the Great Lakes area: 1.3 million in Zaire, 200,000 in Burundi and 600,000 in Tanzania, generally housed in enormous camps.

In the Lake Kivu area the good water supply was quickly overwhelmed (Oxfam had laid in equipment suitable for an expected 50,000 refugees). Since there were very few latrines, the water was quickly contaminated. Cholera, endemic to the region, broke out with alarming speed and ferocity, eventually killing as many as 50,000 people. In response to the epidemic Concern began relief operations on 29 July in Goma, setting up emergency feeding stations and a sanitation programme. In fact this was to be Concern's largest operation yet—over 70 volunteers in the Great Lakes area.

Indeed, the scale of Concern's involvement in the Great Lakes crisis was astonishing. As in many new fields the first task was to 'sell' the organisation to local officials—to highlight its special skills and what made Concern distinct from the hundreds of other humanitarian actors. This done, Concern's response was whole-hearted. In the four years 1994–7 more money was spent there than had been spent in either Ethiopia or Bangladesh since 1971. The £18 million spent in 1994 was equivalent to the organisation's total budget in 1992. The number of volunteers employed across the world (one-third of whom were in the Great Lakes area) was over 200, more than ever before, and given the present reduced usage of volunteers a number not likely ever to be exceeded. There were also over 2,600 local staff, bringing the global total to 7,300—once again more than ever before. Concern was not, of course, alone; over 200 agencies came to the camps in the region, with varying effectiveness. The influential Joint Evaluation of the international response to the Rwandan crisis noted a 'wide variation in the effectiveness of the agencies working on the ground'.[16] Some agencies sent volunteers on tours as short as two weeks, speaking neither French nor Kinyawanda, with little or no experience of cholera, and with drugs limited to those their donors happened to supply.

Even for experienced Concern personnel these huge violent camps were extremely stressful. No expatriate stayed after dark. Despite the bright sun, no one could forget that these unsmiling young men had been actively involved in extreme acts. It took some courage to drive every day to the clinic or the feeding centre, while, as you walked among the huts, everywhere silent men stood, and watched. The suspicion and tension were palpable.

At the same time, because of the intense media interest the so-called 'battle of the T-shirts' took place, with agencies jostling for public attention and for the high-profile, media friendly activities such as establishing cholera treatment centres or working with un-accompanied children. As the Evaluation reported, only a few agencies (including Concern) were prepared to work in the sanitation sector. In 1995 the government actually expelled 38 NGOs, and as the news cameras went elsewhere, others left, so that by 1996 there were fewer than 70 agencies active in the country. This crisis marks the end of an era when journalists from Jonathan Dimbleby in Ethiopia in 1974 to Scott Peterson in Somalia had relied on the NGOs to be on the ground and the most knowledgeable. From now onwards the media would be first. Thus, in a recent air trip to a remote part of Afghanistan, Dominic MacSorley and Phil Miller found themselves the only NGO workers among 45 on the plane. All the rest were journalists.

Tragically, this was only the start of Rwanda's anguish. There were revenge killings in the camps and in Rwanda itself; there was continual pressure from the Democratic Republic of Congo (ex-Zaire) for repatriation, but this was stiffly resisted by the *interhamwe* elements in the camps who feared the Tutsi-dominated government's justice programme. Eventually, in 1996, the Rwandan-backed army attacked the camps and one and a half million refugees streamed back into Rwanda, as suddenly as they had come. Concern established a series of transit centres to provide temporary food and shelter for some of the thousands as they tramped back to their villages, struggling with their few possessions. In the misery of the long, crowded treks, children often became separated from their parents. An important part of Concern's work was to help these children, and a tracing system was established to reunite them with relatives. This tracing system was one of the most effective programmes established in Rwanda. As a measure of its success, the guidelines established by Willa Addis (assistant country director) were later adapted by the Rwandan government and also by Save the Children.

The government faced appalling problems. Over half of the population had been killed, wounded, uprooted or returned from long-term exile (as a result of fleeing from previous slaughter campaigns) in four years. Now they all, Tutsi survivors, Hutu Power *interhamwe* and returned exiles, had to learn to live together in a small cramped country. Western literature is full of deeply felt descriptions of the fear and loathing felt by Holocaust survivors decades after 1945; the Rwandan government had little choice but to try to reconstruct a society with, as it were, Gestapo and Jewish survivors cheek by jowl.

The infrastructure was not promising either. A quarter of the country's housing stock had been looted or damaged. The killings had naturally concentrated on younger men, so one-third of households were now headed by more or less traumatised women, and in the 25–29 age group as few as 67 men survived for every 100 women.[17] There were perhaps a quarter of a million orphaned children, and 80,000 households headed by children. Land was still short; genocide survivors had often taken over the property of returning refugees, and tension was high. Weapons carefully buried before leaving were unearthed, and by 1997 the hate broadcasts that had stimulated the 1994 massacres were again being heard. Some 100,000 persons—so-called *genocidaires*—were in prison awaiting trial for their activities during the killing time. These included many women, and at least 2,000 children accused of active participation. International aid agencies urged the release of these children, though the climate made it likely they would be ready victims of revenge attacks.

As the Rwandan government sought, with agonising slowness, to recreate its legal system, it continued to cram the prisons with suspects. Conditions in these prisons got worse and worse—in one prison visited by Jack Finucane and Dominic MacSorley it was so crowded that the men took it in turns to stand or lie down. (As in the H-Blocks, the internal arrangements in the prisons were run by local leaders. The guards stayed out.) In another they were shown an underground room in which they had to jostle through the silent, crowded bodies; it was hot and rank, lit by one feeble, low-wattage bulb. As they got to the middle of the room, the light suddenly went out and they were plunged into absolutely darkness, surrounded by suspected killers. It was a bad moment.

Both men were hugely affected by these visits and immediately set out to improve conditions. Since the government did not feed the prisoners, their wives had to bring food every day (sometimes from afar). Concern set up a series of food programmes which allowed the women time to build up their lives in other ways. As the government's justice programme grew, the numbers in the six prisons that Concern was feeding doubled in a year.

It was during this programme that another of those controversial actions that has identified Concern's character as an agency was undertaken. The women's *cachot* (communal prison) in Gitarama contained 219 women (one of whom was a nun) with 33 infants; the women were all suspected, with reason, of active participation in the killings. The conditions were very crowded, with poor sanitation and food preparation. The women were confined to their cell block for most of the day. So Concern acquired a field next to the *cachot* and persuaded the authorities to allow them to build a walled courtyard, with a simple shelter. This enabled the women to leave their cell block and hugely improved their general welfare. It is unlikely that the well-meaning from Dublin 4 or Ballydehob who subscribe their £20 a month have in mind prison-building for genocide suspects.[18]

Nobody looked back on this time in Rwanda with much pleasure, though there were moments to savour. In four years, Concern cared for 32,500 children who had become separated from their parents as a result of killings or mass treks to and from the camps. For Anne O'Mahony, who worked with these children, the tracing programme was 'the most heartwarming programme I have ever been involved with in my 17 years with Concern'.

Among the children Concern looked after was '*Inconnu*' (Unknown), a little boy, perhaps six years old. He was disabled, paralysed down one side and apparently mute. He turned up at one of the feeding centres in 1988, listless and unresponsive, hiding goodness knows what trauma. Florence, a 17-year-old Rwandan in the centre, took an interest in the boy; she fed him, took him to the hospital, helped him with his exercises. At last, coaxed by her, he began to take his first steps and to utter short basic sentences. Concern staff were anxious to find a home for him, but any questions about his past made him visibly distressed. Staff were reluctant to leave him in an orphanage, but there seemed little alternative, until Florence asked if she and her family could adopt the boy. Inconnu himself thought this was a wonderful idea and her family saw the boy as a gift from God. The legal formalities were quickly arranged, and the boy happily left the hospital with his new family. Visiting later, Concern workers found little Inconnu (he had decided that was his new name, and did not want another), extremely happy and integrated into his new family.

9: Making a difference

*Compassion is a rising star, even if it is from time to time
obscured in the skies. But it will only rise if people push it, and
the way they can do that is by deciding whether they are
content with the old style of compassion, which meant helping
others to clear one's conscience (and there was no need to speak
to them, writing a cheque would do), or the new style, which
means discovering others as individuals, exchanging understanding with them.[1]*

When the modern NGO movement started, in effect with the Biafran
war, aid seemed a simple business. The public responded to the television pictures of starving babies and donations poured into the
agencies whose job was to channel the money and goods involved as
expeditiously as possible to the intended beneficiaries. Ordinary
people gave hardly more thought to exactly how the aid was to be
channelled, or the conditions in which it was to be received, than
they might to the fate of a few coins given to a street beggar. In the
field, however, needs were so pressing and conditions so difficult
that inevitably there were logistical mistakes and, following them,
accusations of incompetence or even callous indifference. THOUSANDS
OF TONS OF FOOD ROT ON THE QUAYSIDE AS WOMEN AND CHILDREN
STARVE ran a typical headline. Although this was rarely true, the public
held on to a dark suspicion that barely 20 pence in every pound got
through—and yet strangely they *still* wanted to subscribe their bit.

After a few experiences where aid was misapplied or wasted donors and agencies increasingly realised that goodwill and energy were
not enough—practical skill in very difficult conditions was also required. Médicins sans Frontières, for instance, reached this point in
1977–9 when the charismatic founder Bernard Kouchner was even-

tually replaced by Claude Malhuret and others. MSF's experience in various refugee camps had convinced them that a much more professional approach to management and logistics was essential. A salaried administrative system, and formal departments responsible for fundraising, logistics and medicine, were established. Direct mail fundraising boosted MSF's income from \$4.3 million in 1982 (not very different from the £2.8 million spent that year by Concern) to \$33.7 million at the height of the 1984 Ethiopian famine.[2]

An increasingly professional management, with staff moving from one agency to another (it was a great source of pride when 'alumni' of Concern began to appear in key roles in UN agencies) had its own social science terminology. The 'Third World' was no longer talked of, as one field director admonished head office in 1993, nowadays the term was 'least-developed countries'.

Professional management in Concern and other agencies ultimately would require men and women to devote their whole careers to the work. This was quite a different order of commitment to the two years or so asked of the volunteers. Among other things it meant shouldering a lifetime's compassion for distant strangers, a stance that flies in the face of the natural priority given to family and friends. There is something at least unusual about this posture.[3] We are adjured to look after those at home first—why attend to the street children in Addis Ababa, when there are street children in Dublin? Then, a volunteer might be asked: 'What's so special about *you* that you have to go to Sudan or Angola or Sierra Leone, places about which you know little (not even the languages they speak)—why you?' And then, the common model of lifetime compassion was the driven saint, such as Vincent de Paul or, in our own day, Mother Teresa. Few professional development workers aspired to such heights of self-sacrifice. Some of the new caste might choose to work on the ascetic lines of the old missionaries; most, however, expected to provide their families with similar lifestyles and ambitions to those of their school and university contemporaries.

Although Aengus Finucane still had, in his favourite phrase, 'fire in the belly', and a clear vision of what he wanted Concern to do, there were others (mainly on the staff, but in Council as well) who were sympathetic to different attitudes. Conscious that many of the volunteers lacked the public self-confidence displayed by American or British aid workers—a common theme in Ireland in the 1970s and 1980s—Aengus had persuaded Council to fund ex-volunteers to attend development studies courses in Swansea University and elsewhere in return for a commitment to further overseas service. There they were taught to step back from the immediacies of the field to explore wider issues. When they came back to Dublin they looked with a colder eye on Concern's activities, their minds full of such questions as:

— how far is our activity a neo-colonial intrusion on the local society?

— how far does our development work justify or even require manipulation of existing social arrangements to achieve justice?

— how far is what we are doing shaped by our ideas, or the donors', rather than what the recipients want?

— how far are we committing ourselves only to activities which are susceptible to neat proposals and neat accountancy returns?

— how do we decide who to help and when? [4]

Sometimes this study led to disillusionment; after all, by 1995 Concern had spent some £227 million directly in the field, and from the seclusion of a library in Swansea, or even in the bustle of Camden Street, it was difficult to see how this drop in the bucket had made much difference at all. Doomwatchers of all sorts, notably the prestigious Worldwatch Institute with its annual *State of the World* publication, hammered home the message that the world was in a bad way and only likely to get worse. Massive population increase, caused by declining infant mortality rates, simply put more pressure on food supply and on the environment (desertification, deforestation, overuse of water). It was not just people who were suffering—World Wildlife Fund experts claimed that 40,000 species of animals and plants were being hurried into extinction every year as a result of human activity, notably by the destruction of the Amazon rain forest. It was, as bestselling authors such as Isaac Asimov and Paul Ehrlich told us, probably too late to save the world from spinning into an irreversible decline. And if the occasional FAO report suggested that there really was more food out there than before, ordinary human wickedness was sure to thwart good intentions. Everywhere, it seemed, there were kleptocrats stuffing Swiss bank accounts while their people starved, governments and rebels both using food supply as a weapon of war, leaders living in comfort while their followers were trapped in the squalor of segregated camps, whiskey or *qat* imports given dockside priority over food during famine. Over meals in Concern houses across the world volunteers swapped horror stories, such as that of the mutilations in Sierra Leone. In an attempt to rally his supporters, the country's president had urged them to 'rebuild Sierra Leone with their strong right hands'. By way of response, rebel forces began to hack off their prisoners' hands, often employing drug-crazed boy soldiers with machetes for the purpose. Thousands of men were mutilated in this way.

In the field also, although it was obvious that famine relief camps, the feeding stations and the mother and child clinics had made a difference, there was increasing emphasis on the broader causes of emergencies and on combating the root causes of poverty. On the level of 'people to people' countless thousands of lives had certainly been improved. Concern had built bridges and rebuilt houses, planted trees against desertification, and advised thousands of farmers on how to get the most out of their land. In camps and slums, Concern had occupied the precious years of youth with basic primary education programmes. It had established tracing schemes for war orphans, and devised Young Shoulders programmes for older children whose parents had died from war or AIDS and had been left to look after siblings. In camps and urban slums Concern workers organised clean water and sanitation schemes, as a contribution to human dignity and health safety alike. A particular focus from the early days in Bangladesh has been on women's skill training programmes, whereby women, who are so often in traditional societies the poorest of the poor, are enabled to provide better lives for themselves and their children. A class in sewing followed by a small loan to buy a sewing machine, can help a woman feed her family. There are also adult literacy programmes, and work with street children and sex workers.

None of these schemes amounted to saving the world. Some, particularly the emergency relief feeding schemes, were hardly more than rescue operations, on the simple but profound belief that 'a not-dead baby is better than a dead baby'. Could we not, it was asked, avoid camps altogether, by getting food to where the people lived, even in leaky distributive systems? As it happens, Bangladesh, the country in which Concern has worked longest and has devoted large human and material resources, *is* materially better off today than it was in 1971. But the most devoted fan of the organisation would not claim that this was because of Concern's presence.

Parallel to the academic explorations of aid came a collective disillusion with communalism. In the 1980s and 1990s young women and men were more individualistic and more demanding than the previous generation—they had been told, even if they did not quite believe it, that it was good to be greedy. The deep sense of religion that had focused the goodwill of previous generations was also waning. When Aengus Finucane was field director in the mid-1970s he could expect 17 out of 20 volunteers to attend his Mass; ten or 15 years later only three or four would be there. The 1990s in Ireland saw the first of a series of scandals involving clerics which cumulatively damaged the Church. Perhaps surprisingly, this diminution of the Church's moral and ethical authority did not affect the generosity of the Irish people as contributors to appeals.

As aid agencies became professionalised so too did donors: they demanded to be formally reassured that their funds were responsibly spent. This was not new. Large donors had always insisted on rigorous procedures and Concern's files show evidence of bureaucratic admonishment. In 1985, for instance, the EEC complained that reports and financial statements were not in accordance with rules, as the official pointed out: 'I refer you to letter 17739 of 11 July 1985 . . . ' In the same month in 1985 Band Aid explained that no second tranche payments would be made until the first tranche had been properly reported on and accounted for. In November 1988 Jack Finucane sent a characteristically vigorous note to his field managers about their preference for operating over report writing.

"'I'm too busy,'" he wrote, 'really means I am too lazy or too poorly organised and I am not interested in management.' Reporting, he stressed, is part of good management and good management is the basis of the success of any project.

To prevent any appearance of signing blank cheques, donors began to demand that projects should be sustainable by the recipient country, so that the donor was, as it were, merely providing seed money. Furthermore, the agency's 'exit strategy' was critical. If there was a proposal to establish a programme for mentally handicapped street people, the donor wanted to know how this was going to be handed over to local administration and when. Under this scrutiny, and in special fear of doing more harm than good, projects designed to help the desperately needy in the developing world were subject to stringent tests of viability. In the pursuit of the best, donors demanded years of experience and multiple qualifications for quite mundane jobs. Paradoxically, these requirements cumulatively imposed a much higher standard of security than is happily accepted by the Western business world where the great majority of new product launches fail and one in four new company start-ups come to nothing.

The aid community was taught also to deplore anything that smelled of welfare—food for work programmes were the furthest one could go in that direction. This was another double standard. Visitors from Bangladesh, such as Mohammed Mobin (later assistant country director in Cambodia), quickly discovered that Irish people, like all Westerners, are protected from cradle to grave by a fine web of welfare, from child benefit to old age pension, *none* of which is available in Bangladesh. Nobody expected Irish unemployed men to work in exchange for dole payments. Why then, asked Mobin and his colleagues, did the aid community so deplore welfare elements in their overseas programmes?

Well-presented proposals were usually expected to follow the Logical Framework approach; originally developed by USAID in the 1960s it had gradually become the norm. The key to this approach was the emphasis on quantified performance measurement. The question for each level of the hierarchy of objectives was: what measure or measures will indicate that we have (or have not) achieved what we set out to achieve? As Dr Basil Cracknell explained to a Concern workshop in 1990: 'the number of kilometres of road built, or outboard motors supplied to fishermen, or of research papers produced' might be appropriate measures. The simple emphasis on quantification was very much of its time. Not even the American experience in Vietnam—where it is said, just a few days before the Tet offensive, that the number of Vietcong reported as killed finally exceeded the entire population of the country—had driven home the critical difference between a numerical target and an achievement. The Logical Framework matrix did, however, force the proposer to identify such elements as required inputs, expected outputs and objectives, indicators of achievement and finally and, importantly, external conditions and risks that might imperil the project's completion.

This matrix was only one of the ways in which management jargon and business thinking crept into Concern's everyday vocabulary, a development that not everyone felt happy with. As Hugh Byrne put it in a 1993 note to Theresa McDonnell, then heading the policy review committee: 'Since the Craig Gardner report [on organisational structure, delivered in 1991] we are increasingly using management terminology. I have no difficulty with that, unless it is used wrongly to imply that Concern is now *only* a business, and that the lowest rather than the highest commercial ethics apply to it.'

We have noticed the shift towards professional management within NGOs and the changing policies of donor agencies which were occurring in the arly 1990s. The decade of the 1990s was also to bring a series of high profile emergencies, two of which were discussed in previous chapters, which were to impact substantially on the work and finances of the organisation.

The public had traditionally responded generously to emergencies. At donor level, new arrangements were put in place in the early 1990s to deal more urgently and effectively with emergencies. In 1992, the EU established the European Community Humanitarian Office (ECHO) while in the US the Office for Disaster Assistance (OFDA) was set up. These new arrangements meant that the donor community were better equipped to deal with emergencies and were devoting more resources to them. However, with overall aid budgets static or falling, this meant it was becoming more difficult to access resources for long term development work. These trends were to have important consequences both for Concern's fundraising work and for its finances over the course of the 1990s.

At the beginning of the decade, although donations from the public were less important than they had been in the past, they were still the single largest source of income. An estimate from 1990 suggested that Concern, receiving £14.03 million, was second in public esteem to Rehab which received £30 million; the other aid agencies, Trócaire (£7.4 million) and Goal (£1.8 million) received considerably less.[5] It was natural to imagine that the impact Concern had made in the Republic could be replicated elsewhere. However, when Paddy Maguinness started up the Northern Ireland office in 1980, he quickly discovered a key difference between Concern on its native ground and elsewhere. After years of fundraising effort since 1968 Concern was 'rooted', as he described it, in the Republic. The organisation's leaders such as Raymond Kennedy, Michael Doheny and Aengus Finucane were familiar presences on television TV screens. Everyone knew someone who had been a volunteer; the annual Christmas Fasts were regular social occasions as were the numerous golf tournaments, debates and other events.

A particular advantage of the South was the homogeneity of the population. This made it relatively easy to approach—by the newspapers and radio and television programmes nearly everyone received, or the well-established system of church gate collections. In Northern Ireland, Paddy Maguinness had to learn that things were very different. This was, after all, a place in which what Freud called the 'narcissism of minor differences' had been brought to a fine art. Everything in the North was focused on the religious divide, even in apparently indifferent matters. There were, for instance, separate Catholic and Protestant cancer charities each appealing to, and drawing from, only its own community. People were 'placed' by the tiniest turn of phrase. For instance, Paddy could not understand why the office was not attracting Protestant recruits; he consulted the

Fair Employment Agency who told him to use the phrase 'mid-Ulster' in the advertisements. 'Where,' asked Paddy, 'is mid-Ulster?' 'Ah,' said the agency man, '*That's* your problem, you're a Catholic.' So the next advertisement asked for a development officer for mid-Ulster, and, as the agency had promised, attracted several Protestant applicants. As it happens, this acute sensitivity to religious difference had been equally true in the South until the 1960s, where the religious affiliation of everything from grocers' shops to scout troops was known. In this context the deliberate ecumenism of the Africa Concern board seems braver and more forward-thinking than might today be realised.

In the North, Concern's PR people struggled for long to explain how it was that an agency headed up, from Dublin, by a Catholic priest and represented in Belfast by a 'Paddy Maguinness' could possibly be non-denominational. It took until the Somalia crisis in 1992 for Northern Ireland's largely Protestant-controlled media to begin to pay attention to Concern, and another couple of years before the Northern Ireland office was able to plug into British aid funds.

In the South, there was a ready acceptance of Concern and a ready audience for its campaigns. Not that money just flowed into the coffers—every penny had to be worked for, especially if there was no eye-catching disaster to rivet attention. Numerous and vocal local charities made the generation of donations from the public a much more competitive business. The development department had to produce a constant stream of new ideas and refresh the good old favourites such as the Christmas Fast (tip: start your 24 hour fast immediately after your evening meal). There was the Junior Fast, an environmentally friendly 'water-watcher' scheme, an Advent calendar, a CD from Mary Black and numerous sporting events. Typical of these was the golf tournament held in St Helen's Bay golf club in memory of volunteer Patrick O'Connor from Wexford who had died of malaria in Mozambique. This is now an annual event, organised by the O'Connor family, and raises as much as £20,000 each year for Concern.

In 1994 Concern cashed in on World Cup fever by setting up a supporters' book (£1 a signature). The resultant book of signatures was to be presented to the team, with all proceeds to Concern except for a prize of a free trip to the US for three lucky winners. (Goal and UNICEF also had World Cup related fundraising events that year.) The department made sure that statistics went to the newspapers, stimulating feel-good coverage, for example in the *Dundalk Democrat*: 'Dundalk people have once again shown they have hearts of gold when it comes to supporting a worthy cause, for they have dug deep into their pockets with a massive response to the Rwanda Crisis Appeal'. To be fair, they did raise more than £60,000.

Whatever about the innovative efforts to raise money from the public, the overall finances of the organisation were determined both by the range of its programme and by donor funding both for emergencies and for long term development work.

We have seen the enormous effort that went into the two big operations in Somalia and Rwanda in the first half of the 1990s. But to appreciate the range of Concern's activities we must be aware of many other places and programmes. Concern began the 1990s with staff in twelve countries: Bangladesh, Cambodia, Ethiopia, Mozambique, the Somalia/Kenya border, Sudan, Tanzania, Thailand, Uganda, Laos and Iraq (with programmes providing food and shelter for Kurdish refugees in the northern no-fly zone).

The 1993 annual report noted that Concern now had 13 fields, of which two, Angola and south Sudan, were new. It had spent £29 million overseas, of which half was spent on emergencies in Somalia, South Sudan, Bangladesh, Ethiopia and Angola and on looking after the refugees from Burundi in Tanzania. The other half of the money was spent on a wide range of programmes running from HIV/AIDS support to urban and rural development. The organisation employed just over 4,600 people, of whom 141 were expatriates. The emergency fields tended to be heavy users of staff, so Bangladesh, which was struggling with another severe flood, employed 1,300 local staff and 25 expatriates. Sudan employed 500 local staff and 13 expatriates.

Total income in 1993 was £31.5 million, down slightly on the 1992 peak of £36 million which had been stimulated by the huge response to the Somalia appeal. A full 91 per cent of this went overseas, with 2 per cent being spent on development education and administration, and 5 per cent on promotion. Donations from the public were just under 39 per cent of income, and virtually half of income now came from various official sources, mostly the European Community, Britain and Ireland, but also the US, Switzerland and France.

In response to this considerable increase in overseas funding, the organisation's name was changed slightly, to Concern Worldwide. Although it was a pity to spoil the old simplicity of the logo, this name could be registered in the UK and elsewhere, as 'Concern' alone could not. In all, funds came from over 60 official and NGO sources, a total which gives some idea of the constant pressure for information and reporting imposed on head office and the field directors. Only 7 per cent of funds came from NGO co-funders such as Comic Relief, Care USA, Terre des Hommes, Intermon (Spain) and many others.

Table 9.1 *Sources of income 1993*

	£m	per cent
Public donations and fundraising	9.0	29
Donations in kind	6.3	20
European Community	5.3	17
British government	3.3	10
Irish government (inc. APSO)	2.1	7
United Nations (4 agencies)	1.2	4
USAid	0.6	2
Deposit interest	1.2	4
Other co-funding sources	2.5	8
Total	*31.5*	*100*

As these changes to the operating environment gathered force, Aengus Finucane was approaching the normal retirement age, and had not been well—a series of infections picked up on field trips were taking their toll. People began to wonder how long he would stay as chief executive—not that he showed any interest in retirement himself. He had for years been the motivating teacher, translating his own ideals (derived from his formation as a Holy Ghost and his experiences in Nigeria), into Concern action. Volunteers in the field received a constant stream of memos from Dublin about this or that detail of how they were to live their lives: they could take the bus, but not the train; they were not to live alone; they could have this kind of R&R but not that kind. In this role, he acted as a kind of charismatic parish priest for the whole parish of volunteers. On his travels from field to field he met the volunteers, listened to them and talked to them, often at great length, far into the night. His focus on the task of helping the poorest of the poor was inspiring and absolute. If a volunteer complained about some inconvenience, he would say: 'I wish I had your application form with me. I don't remember anything in that about wanting use of a car, or a private room, or weekend R&R. I thought you wanted to help the people.' Annoyed, and a bit humbled, the volunteer would simply have to accept his values.

In his 16 years as chief executive Aengus Finucane built a close bond between Concern's culture and what its staff did on the ground. The relationship was constantly reinforced by his regular presence in the field, his unmistakable feeling for the local people, and his stories reinforcing his own (and now Concern's) values. It also grew out of a set of shared Christian attitudes. Now, as the new ideas from development theory and business management were increasingly adopted, this carefully fostered unity between theory and action changed. Activity went on much as before, but the authorisation and justification that used to come so solidly from the culture drained away.

In May 1993, Aengus Finucane circulated a discussion paper outlining the 'severe strains' the system was under. Concern's income had doubled in 1990 and again in 1991; it was slightly down in 1993, but still twice what it had been only three years before. There were more expatriate and more local staff in the field than ever before; a new development was the deployment of 'local' staff outside their own field; for instance, staff from Bangladesh went to Africa and Cambodia. [6] As before, Bangladesh was the proving ground of this development, where volunteers were increasingly employed as technical advisors only. In belated support of Professor Elliott's theory, the very strong local agencies in Bangladesh such as BRAC and the Grameen Bank clearly showed that when (if) they were available, local workers could provide all the inputs that volunteers had done in the past. This was obviously desirable from numerous points of view. However, there was a trust barrier to be surmounted—Bengalis were discovered to be fine managers of local projects, but were, at that time, felt not to have a wider global view; and then it was thought that in financial matters they were more vulnerable than foreigners to local pressure.[7]

One of the most successful of such locally run projects was the disaster and environment management unit established by Mohammad Mobin in 1991 which consolidated the lessons learned in the various floods in 1978, 1987/8 and 1991. The unit's expertise has been called on even in India. Since 1997, it has more and more drawn on the knowledge and motivation of local NGOs to do the work on the ground.

As demands from donors for sustainability, empowerment of local people and so forth hardened, good projects became harder to formulate. As Aengus Finucane told Council: 'Our ability to generate funds has outstripped our capacity to apply them (while maintaining standards)'. Strain began to be felt by the home staff as the activity became more complex and sophisticated. As we have seen, over 60 separate foreign organisations were providing funds. At the same time, Concern was making substantial project grants to third parties in Iraq, Pakistan and Sudan, all of which had to be established and monitored.

Finally, and most seriously, the financial control system was struggling to cope with the doubling of the flow of cash. The auditors, Stokes Kennedy Crowley, had initiated a meeting earlier in May 1993 to express their concern that 'striving to keep up with the day-to-day handling of income left inadequate time for financial management'. Among other things there was a serious question about the investment management of the pension fund, a question that was typically not high on anyone's agenda, until it became a crisis.

The increased flows of pure cash needed tight control, but so did the frequent changes of exchange rates for sums received in dollars, sterling, pesetas, Swiss francs and so on. The lack of a financial director to manage the whole area was, they felt, a mistake.

To handle this 'embarrassment of riches', as he put it, Aengus Finucane proposed to put into action a Craig Gardner organisational review of a year or two before, one of whose objectives had been to clarify relations between senior staff and Council. At the beginning of the 1990s there were six departments: finance, home (fundraising and education), international (overseas fundraising), personnel and administration, and two overseas divisions. It was now proposed to put a new layer of three directors between the division heads and the chief executive. The three posts were established as follows: Eamon Keating, finance director, newly recruited from Ryanair; Howard Dalzell, overseas director and Paddy Maguinness, development director and deputy chief executive. A number of new units and posts were also established. Of course, there were cost implications to this restructuring: expenditure on head office administration went up from £420,000 in 1991 to £670,000 in 1993.

Hardly had the three directors settled into their new jobs when the organisation was hit by the consequences of the Rwanda massacres. As the news of the killings broke in April and May 1994, it was obvious to experienced watchers that this was a situation in which Concern would have to become involved. But the public did not really react until news of the cholera outbreak in the refugee camps flashed on to television screens in July. Then, belatedly, the response was immense. By the end of the year, Concern had taken in £45 million, 50 per cent more than the previous year, and three times the 1990 income—embarrassment of riches, indeed. This included £14 million in food and non-food items such as seeds, tools, educational materials, household utensils and medical supplies, all of which had to be warehoused, controlled, transported and delivered. Concern took on an extra 2,600 staff in the field, including 75 more volunteers. We have seen in the previous chapter the scale and intensity of Concern's activity. Incredibly, Concern managed to put £40 million to use in recipient countries, nearly half of which was allocated to the Great Lakes area.

The following year things came down with a bump. Income dropped suddenly from £45 million to £30 million—but, of course, it was less easy to reduce expenditure in the field. As a result, expenditure exceeded income by £1.3 million that year and by £2.97 million in 1996. At the AGM in May 1996 Aengus Finucane tried to put this in context, but it was clear from his analysis how dependent Concern was on the surges of income associated with high-profile emergencies. As he ruefully put it, 'chronic poverty, no matter how extreme, does not generate anything like the same funding response as do emergencies and disasters. The same is even more true with regard to "development" projects.'

The problem for Concern in 1996, as Aengus Finucane saw it, was that a large, effective, but costly, organisation had been built up, with many rehabilitation programmes in hand for which it was difficult to obtain official funding. Furthermore, given that half of the income had been coming from official sources, there was the beginnings of a worrying new trend. Official donors were increasingly decentralising decision-making to their local representatives working with local NGOs. Finally, since 'we are experiencing the longest disaster-free period we have known since the mid-1980s', Concern's overhead costs were under severe pressure. (This may seem odd to those conscious only of the highly publicised crises such as Ethiopia and Rwanda. In reality crises and disasters are so common that a period of two and a half years without one was indeed unexpected.) What he did not mention at the AGM, but what was causing his colleagues some concern, was the cost of establishing a US office.

Concern had been in the US in one way or another since Michael Doheny had begun establishing contacts in California in the 1970s. The agency had long had good relations with US embassies and aid bodies in many of the fields. US officials had often encouraged Concern to establish itself in North America, which would enable it to channel considerable additional funds through the organisation. But the regular coverage of Concern's work on CNN during the Somalia crisis had convinced Aengus Finucane that a scaled-up presence would enable it to tap into the residue of goodwill supposed to reside in the Irish-American community; corporate America and the various sources of official US aid were also to be targeted. However, establishing such an office was an expensive business. There were initial staff problems, and there were unexpected difficulties in raising money from the public and from corporate America. This was to change significantly for the better when Siobhán Walsh took responsibility for the US office and Aengus built relations with the corporate sector.

As expenditure bit deeper into a reducing income, the atmosphere between the chief executive and the three directors became uncomfortable. Each had his own ideas as to how the problem should be solved, and they were all articulate and forceful in expressing them. Naturally, the debate did not escape the watchful eyes of the staff, for whom this was an unsettling time. An added complication was Aengus Finucane's personal position. He was to be 65 in 1997, the normal retirement age in Concern, although in fact his contract did not specify this. He wanted to stay in the organisation to which he had given so much.

In June 1996, a gloomy mid-term report estimated that the deficit was likely to exceed £3.4 million—this proved to be overly pessimistic. All income sources were performing variously badly, and expenditure in the fields was only slightly down, if at all. The organisation was indeed, as the chief executive told the officers in August, going through 'a lean time'; the concurrent strategic review process would have to take these new elements into serious consideration. In September, after considerable debate Council set a new home overhead budget of £3.75 million, a slashing reduction from the original £5.6 million. A further £1 million was to be cut from the overseas budgets. This statement, famously called the 'stake in the ground' ('mistake' more likely, muttered the disenchanted) was not achieved without numerous tense meetings, within Council, between Council officers and senior employees, and between employees themselves.

The atmosphere in Camden Street grew fraught. Despite denials, everyone knew there would have to be redundancies—and given the kind of organisation Concern was, this was extremely uncomfortable. In the end, 14 people took voluntary redundancy or early retirement; their re-entry into other jobs was greatly aided by freely-given counselling and help from ESB personnel staff.

Aengus Finucane, whose sickness had kept him out of the office first for weeks and then for months over this period, was fighting both for his vision of Concern and his own position. He told Council officers in September that 'Concern is under-managed because it is over-managed'. He proposed a return to the former management structure, and asked Council to confirm his own position for another three years in order to facilitate a reorganisation. At a major meeting in October, Council finally considered this suggestion. Since many members of Council had worked with him in the field, and all saw him as the embodiment of the present spirit of Concern, this was an agonising moment of decision. In November, he offered his resignation, and his retirement as chief executive was accepted effective from April 1997 when he reached 65. In the event he remained until the end of June when his successor, David Begg, came on board.

This was a major turning point. Aengus Finucane had been central in the life of Concern since he first went to Bangladesh in 1972. He had devoted his life to the poorest of the poor in far-off places, and was now retiring from the front line. His new task was to be an ambassador for the office in the US. When the new chief executive was appointed there was also a significant generational change, taking Concern away from its roots in the Biafra conflict.

10: A new era

Sunday 8 February 1942 The words of a Russian Zionist addressed to God during the times of the pogroms constantly go through my head: 'You can wait; for you a thousand years are as one year—but we cannot wait.'[1]

The new chief executive, David Begg, who took up his post in July 1997, had made his name in the trade union movement. His arrival signalled a significant generation change, since he was nearly 20 years younger than his predecessor, a 20 years in which Ireland changed more than it had perhaps since the Great Famine. While his predecessor followed his missionary vocation in the warm tropical nights of Uli airport, bundling Africa Concern's aid into lorries, he had been studying electrical engineering at Kevin Street College of Technology.

As he took office, Ireland was just beginning to realise a period of unprecedented prosperity; the Celtic Tiger was purring comfortably. To the astonishment of the old imperial power, a British parliamentary report declared that average income per head in Ireland was now $10 more than in the UK. Reinforcing this message were posters all round Britain with a finger pointing, like Kitchener's in the famous First World War appeal, saying 'We need you back in Ireland!' addressed to Irish workers who had emigrated to Britain. On the building sites, wages in Ireland were notably higher than in Britain. Mindsets change more slowly than economies, however; when a few asylum seekers sought to share this prosperity there was consternation in some sections of the Irish public and press.

Bertie Ahern took office in 1997 with a slender majority bolstered by Independents. Tony Blair, on the other hand, came in on a landslide. The IRA grudgingly declared another ceasefire, and this time it was just enough to allow substantive talks between Sinn Féin and the Unionist party to start. The Irish peace process was born. A less positive process was starting with the revelation that Charles Haughey had received £1.3 million from chain-store boss Ben Dunne, and the forced resignation of the new foreign affairs minister Ray Burke over allegations that he had received large donations from property developers in north Dublin. The tribunals in Dublin Castle, which, like Dickens' celebrated case Jarndyce *v* Jarndyce, seem to benefit mainly lawyers, began their weary journey of discovery. Later in the year, memories of Baidoa and the emotional press conference in Nairobi were stirred as Mary Robinson left the presidency to join the United Nations, and was replaced by Mary McAleese.

After graduating from Kevin Street, David Begg joined the ESB; and then in 1979 he became a full-time trade unionist, becoming general secretary of the Postal and Telecommunications Union in 1985 and of the newly-merged Communications Workers Union in 1991. He became a member of the executive council of the Irish Congress of Trade Unions in 1986. For ten years he had been an active member of Trócaire's management board and this time had given him an active insight into development matters but, apart from some time spent in South Africa advising trade union members of the ANC, he had no field experience. He had seen the Concern job advertised and applied.

His immediate concern on appointment was to meet the staff and get a feeling for the problems to be faced. This process involved something of a culture shock. Concern prided itself on being a value-driven organisation. Though autocratic in decision-making, Aengus Finucane had encouraged debate and discussion about aims and objectives. Furthermore, most of the staff had once been volunteers in the field, and this gave a special possessive intensity to their loyalty to the organisation as *they* understood it. Change was not, therefore, to be advanced lightly or without challenge, at any level. This was far from what his previous experience had led David Begg to expect. As he said, 'My idea was that it was the chief executive's role to challenge people about how their work is done—in Concern everyone had an opinion, so I had never been in a place where I felt so challenged.'

David Begg was not, as we have seen, a field man, and this was a significant caste mark inside Concern. He brought to the job quite a new approach. For, if Aengus Finucane was management as educator, David Begg was management as strategist. He brought disciplines and a view of control very much based on the business model— interestingly, but also a bit disconcertingly, his attention was coolly on where the organisation would be in five years. Those who loved Aengus Finucane missed the intensity and the sociability (a drink in the Bleeding Horse across the road, talking late into the night, the stories).

In a normal business, policy divisions follow lines of personality—each side sees itself as determined, thoughtful and courageous and the other as simply stubborn, opinionated and reckless. In Concern there were certainly such divisions (with allegiances hardening in recent years by expectation of change at the top) but there were also strong ideological opinions such as do not arise with the supply of electricity.

There were two broad camps, described by David Begg as the 'trads' and the 'mods'. The trads tended to be especially comfortable in relief and emergency situations; they took the view that you did not need to define poverty—what you saw was obvious, and it was the agency's role to do something about it. They were unenthusiastic about talk of 'mission statements' and 'core values', not to mention the wider use of business language generally. The mods, on the other hand, tended to see poverty not as a problem but as a symptom. They were concerned to identify the root causes of poverty in a particular situation, feeling that without that understanding anything that was done was at best palliative and at worst positively harmful. They were conscious of the need to help people to help themselves, casting doubt on traditional development projects such as well-sinking and bridge-building, and even expressing scepticism as to the usefulness of emergency work. This dichotomy was not unique to Concern, as Nicholas Stockton of Oxfam avowed: 'I have frequently heard the development lobby dismiss the relief people as a bunch of cowboys and boneheads. Likewise, I have heard the relief lobby dismissing the development people as a bunch of dithering pinkos who couldn't fight their way out of a paper bag.'²

The immediate *casus belli* was the ongoing strategic review, which had been rumbling along for some time, partly because of Aengus Finucane's lack of enthusiasm for the project. The trads generally took the view that, if you had to have a strategic plan at all, it should be as short and as unconstraining as possible. For the mods, on the other hand, the strategic plan partook of the nature of a manifesto.

Adding to David Begg's discomfort was the fact that his reading tray was filled with new books whose advice generally seemed to be that Concern should become solely an advocacy organisation with no presence in the field at all, except in so far as it supplied support for local NGOs. How was he to reconcile this high thought with all the detailed activity on the ground—in Dimla in Bangladesh, for instance, under the management of Imran Ansari, where the rural development programme included group formation, community development programmes, leadership training and awareness raising, all designed to develop capacity, as well as more traditional programmes such as savings and loans schemes, pond digging, sanitation, tree plantation, non-formal primary education, tubewells, and training for traditional birth attendants? Not to mention the understanding that Concern's authority, and hence its ability to raise money at all, stemmed precisely from its presence and activity in the field.

After much discussion—some of which, as the review itself noted, generated rather more heat than light—the agency's first full-scale strategic plan was finally published in February 1998. It is an imposing document, over 40 pages long, and starts with a critical analysis of how some of the strengths Concern had built up over the years were now less relevant. Among these was the ability to respond quickly to large-scale, famine-type emergencies. These had been primarily due to countries' 'inept economic policies and low preparedness' combined with adverse military and political situations and were, it was felt, likely to be a thing of the past. (The 2002 crisis in southern Africa is, let us hope, an exception to this conclusion.) Absolute poverty, however, which required a different type of response, was widespread and rising. Other core strengths that the planners thought were losing value were:

— the strength in expatriate personnel, who were less useful than local staff in complex emergencies involving high security risks;

— the strength in operating projects, which was likely to be discounted by donors, who preferred local NGOs, and host governments increasingly seeking to control the work of international NGOs;

— the strength in using media to highlight emergencies, which was likely to be less effective given a more analytical media and a more sceptical donor public, who, it was thought 'tend to attribute more blame and responsibility to victims of emergencies and of poverty in general than has been common'.

The strategic review reiterated as the prime core objective the alleviation and ultimately the elimination of 'absolute poverty', in which people are 'at worst on the verge of death because of their inability to meet essential physical needs' and at best struggling to supply themselves with food, clean water, shelter and health. The review distinguished between development and emergency work. Emergencies were subdivided into complex and 'free-access' emergencies. Complex emergencies, where the plight of the poorest was made worse (if not originally caused) by adverse military and political situations, poor security and often outrageous violations of human rights, were becoming common. As we have seen, Concern had struggled in such environments in Somalia, Sudan and Rwanda, not to mention Angola and Sierra Leone. There was frankly not much that could be done in such cases, apart from developing as much local technical and operational expertise as possible. For so-called 'free access' emergencies, on the other hand, where the local government was willing to allow Concern to participate in the rescue and rehabilitation function, there was a much clearer way forward. Here new, more sophisticated, systems were to be established for rapid emergency response, including pre-stocked foodstuffs and other supplies, and development of better skills in camp management, emergency nutrition, public health and social services (notably basic primary education, which had been a priority of Concern's from the earliest days). One of the specific outcomes of the evaluation of the Rwanda experience had been the establishment of an emergency supply store in Rotterdam.

In development fields the strategic review proposed that, rather than increasing the numbers of expatriate volunteers, more emphasis be given to strengthening the capacity of local actors such as local NGOs, community and even state organisations. The review recognised that willingness to work with such organisations implied accepting their ideas as how best to reduce poverty, and even the local people's definitions of who is poorest, subject to Concern's core values and considerations of good stewardship.

All of this activity required money, and David Begg's immediate focus was on consolidating the financial base. To this end, his appointment in 1998 of Sally-Anne Kinahan (from Oxfam Ireland) to the key marketing post was one of his most successful initiatives. Under her leadership a strategy was developed to deal with the problem of 'crisis-dependency' that had dogged Concern since the end of the Biafran war, remained. Over and over again Concern has seen its income collapse once the heart-rending immediate emergency is over. For the agency it was frustrating to see that just then, when so much valuable work could be done to lessen the people's long-term vulnerability, funds would shrink. The question, therefore, was: how could the organisation establish a regular flow of income to sustain its ongoing fieldwork in the absence of an emergency? In the past, solutions have ranged from holding back a higher proportion of the emergency donations in reserve to increasing reliance on institutional donors, such as the EU, to whom detailed argument about development could be made. The strategy chosen was to develop regular monthly giving, by standing order, in order to provide a financial base for planning and for funding long-term development work. This strategy proved successful and by 2002, over 100,000 supporters had committed to regular giving.

The number of fields rose rapidly: there were 19 in 1998, and by the end of David Begg's term in 2001, there were 27, typically with a mix of emergency and development programmes in each. The activities recorded in the 1998 Annual Report showed showed the wide range of Concern's work.

Afghanistan: Following devastating earthquakes in February and

May, Concern provided basic shelter programmes in 20 villages, with housing, water and health schemes in the far north east areas of Rustaq and Chah Ab.

Angola: Programmes included work with the Ministry of Health in Malanje Province, primary health care posts and rural rehabilitation programmes in Ekunha, Huambo Province and also in Kunhinga, Bié Province. Unfortunately, at the end of the year full-scale war erupted again, and access to rural areas became limited.

Bangladesh: This country suffered some of the worst flooding ever recorded in 1998. Concern responded with emergency relief programmes distributing 4,411 tonnes of rice and oral rehydration supplements, and vegetables to 40,000 families. Meanwhile the ongoing programmes in community development included providing health and nutrition services to 469,000 mothers and children, establishing several hundred community groups of both urban slum dwellers and landless farmers, and continuing the women's training centres and the primary education programme.

Burundi: As the security situation improved, Concern was able to establish feeding and health centres in Cibitoke Province and a seed and tool distribution programme was initiated in Buruni. In December an emergency programme housed 2,800 families.

Cambodia: Over 1,000 primary teachers were trained; access to clean water was established in 20 schools, numerous fish ponds were dug through food-for-work programmes, livestock management was improved through the facilitating of village livestock associations.

Congo: 1998 was a difficult year because of the local security situation. Work stopped for several months because of fighting. A refugee resettlement programme was established in south-eastern Congo, and in north Kivu the school rehabilitation project struggled in very difficult circumtances to complete six new schools.

Ethiopia: In Kalu Woreda Concern established a four-year rural project which included rehabilitating water resources, training in soil and water conservation, infrastructure support, and food distribution in a food for work programmes. There was also a widely-praised community-based development programme in the capital Addis Ababa which included the building of houses, community kitchens and latrines, access roads and skill training programmes.

Haiti: Emergency response to Hurricane George was provided. Working with a local partner, AAPLAG, the first womens' community savings scheme was set up in the offshore island Gonave; on the same island a community agricultural store was begun, and extensive training in improved farming practice provided.

Honduras: Hurricane Mitch hit the country in late October with devastating force. Over 50 main roads and 84 bridges were destroyed; schools and water supply systems were smashed. More than a million people (out of a 6 million population) were displaced. Concern set up a base in nothern Honduras and began distributing food, clothes, medicine, shelter and construction materials, as well as water and sanitation equipment to ten municipalities with a population of over 100,000.

Korea: After a series of natural disasters in the mid 1990s, north Korea applied for UN assistance in 1995. Concern's work began in 1997, with a 'winterisation' programme by which 16,000 warm jackets were distributed among farming communities, kindergartens and nurseries; a coal distribution programme supplied 4,215 tonnes to a similar range of outlets.

Laos: The main programmes were for returning refugees, rural development andextensive school-building. The work with the refugees proved particularly successful, and at its end, Concern established four new programmes focusing on capacity building, sustainable development among the Laotheung people, a micro-finance service and a disaster preparedness project.

Liberia: Concern focused on support for over 80,000 returning refugees, and collaborated with local, national and international agencies in the repair of infrastructure and the provision of water and sanitation services to 73 villages.

Mozambique: A full, diverse programme was in progress, covering education, health, agriculture and community development. In Niassa Province, for instance, the community development programme sunk wells, built schools, set up nutrition and health posts, organised agricultural groups concentrating on goats, rabbits, vegetables and cereals. Two local organisations received funding.

Rwanda: Since the returning refugees had been reduced to a trickle, Concern's transit centres were closed in September. This was the end of a highly acclaimed programme which had looked after 32,490 children. Work with prisoners continued, as did a housing scheme through which 1,075 houses were built in Butare, Giterama and Ruhengeri.

Sierra Leone: Continuing political instability made this a dangerous station, and some staff had their lives threatened. Work with internal refugees continued, with emergency shelters and latrines built in camps. Families returning to their villages after spending years in the bush were helped with seeds and tools.

Somalia: Concern shifted the focus of its education project to working with local communities to provide education services. Other activities included a water programme for southern areas devastated by the 1997 floods, and seed and tool distribution to farmers in that area. To help these farmers, 31 damaged irrigation canals were rebuilt using local labour paid in cash. 4,000 farmers in 14 villages benefited from this programme.

Sudan: A major humanitarian crisis erupted, putting almost 2 million people at risk. Concern concentrated on enhancing food security and building community capacity. Shelter materials, seed and equipment were distributed to communities that had been looted by government-backed militias. A nutrition crisis in the south inspired a massive food aid operation; as well as distributing food, and providing supplementary feeding centres, two Concern staff were seconded to the World Food Programme to help coordinate the work.

Tanzania: A strategic plan to run to 2002 was completed, focusing on long-term development and enhancing the emergency response capacity. On the ground, programmes included food security, work with local bodies and committees, completion of three bridges to improve transport infrastructure, water suverys and well building, youth work and school refurbishment. In Kigoma region a therapeutic feeding centre was established to help severely malnourished refugees from Burundi.

Uganda: A cholera epidemic in Kampala called for an emergency response in which 27,000 people benefited from various measures to reduce mortality, including garbage collection and disposal, rehabilitation or construction of latrines and unblocking drainage, construction of water stand pipes, and general public health awareness. On a longer term perspective, Concern supported local institutions in HIV/AIDS work, especially focusing on the link between poverty and HIV/AIDS. Other community development work in the south of the country facilitated local partners in establishing local groups and community projects.

In the 1990s project after project showed how carefully delivered developmental work on the ground can improve lives. From so many possible case-studies, a small sample must suffice to give a flavour. In Tanzania, Concern built roads that opened up whole areas such as the Malenganakali ward; this enabled farmers to receive better prices for their produce and to buy inputs more cheaply. A regular bus service meant that the sick could be quickly moved to nearby Iringa. In that area Concern has been associated with the planting of trees for ten years, radically changing the area's appearance. One man told an evaluation team that after some years away, he had recently walked right past his village without recognising it.

In Chimoio city, Mozambique, Concern became involved in an education project with the aim of improving access of the poorest children to education—nearly half of primary age children did not attend. A recent description of the project commented: 'various approaches and methodologies were used to achieve this aim. The project uses participatory methodologies in order to encourage poor people to help themselves, promoting a capacity building approach with communities, local and national governments and other stakeholders and developing partners. Parents and communities are involved in school management as well as being involved in physical construction; local government personnel are involved in planning, training and management of activities and a local NGO, Magariro (meaning 'doing things the local way') is carrying out activities with community groups.' Among other involvements, a teachers' credit fund was established, as well as a teachers' resource centre and a mobile library (which have now been taken over by the City Department of Education). In three years attendance jumped by 28 per cent, and the techniques described have been used by other service delivery agents.

Thousands of miles to the east, in Khaliajuri, Bangladesh, long-time Concern worker Lovely Amin evaluated the effects of the micro-finance programme facilitated by Concern. Micro-finance programmes, of which the most widely known is the Grameen Bank, have enormous potential for improving the lives of the poor, especially rural women. By lending and repaying tiny sums of money, these programmes enable the women to improve their own lives and that of their families. Lovely Amin found there were other benefits. For the first time women members of the programme were elected as local Ward Members; the participants improved their ability in independent decision-making, notably in family planning issues. In a rural area where traditional and cultural beliefs were very strong, the programme had stimulated a change in the respondents' perception of themselves and their traditional roles. But it was not just the women themselves who reported benefits from the scheme: 'husbands, mothers-in-law, key informants also reported positive changes as a result of the micro-finance programme'.

Further east still, in Cambodia, Concern initiated a programme to replace the dramatic loss of forest which had been accelerated under the Khmer Rouge regime. Refugees returning to their villages were having to walk miles to collect enough wood to cook their rice. In village after village the need to regenerate the forests came up as a top priority. Technically, all forest land was the property of the government, so the initial direct approach was simply to plant over 400,000 trees—unfortunately many of the trees were damaged by grazing animals and the larger saplings were often cut down for fuel. 'Rather than set up a security system to keep the local people out' as one report put it, 'we asked them to help us find a better solution to the problem.' The ownership difficulty was a significant problem; villagers believed that even if they were allowed to manage the local forests in the short-term, once the trees reached maturity the forestry department would simply come in and cut them down for sale. However, Concern managed to persuade both the villagers and the local department of forestry to allow locally formed committees to be established, setting rules for the management of the forests. Grazing, cutting trees for fuel, harvesting forest plants and vines were all controlled. The scheme worked. The forests developed rapidly, with a huge leap in the numbers and varieties of plants growing in the newly-regenerated forest lands. A study in 1998 proved that an acre of managed forest could produce as much net income as an acre of rice paddy. The legal position was still, however, potentially unfavourable—other agencies had run up against severe difficulties. So a new programme was established which, as well as training other agencies in Concern's process, aimed to form a national network of interested parties with the ultimate aim of changing the law. Members of the network included NGOs, environmental groups, village committees, the Buddhist movement and even local forestry staff, in support of local management schemes. Through public meetings, dissemination of Concern's economic research and targeted lobbying of key government ministers, the Community Forest Network eventually succeeded in inspiring a forestry law which recognised local forestry rights.

Epilogue

In September 2000 a stirring and happy reunion of volunteers took place in Dublin. Ostensibly held to celebrate the organisation's 30th anniversary, it was, in practice, a statement of closure of an era. Over 500 volunteers attended, as did the key founders Kay, John O'Loughlin and Raymond Kennedy. Aengus Finucane and David Begg were there, as were ex-chairpersons Eanna Johnson, Phena O'Boyle, Peter Kierans, P. J. Howell and Tom Arnold and current chairperson, Tom O'Higgins. President Mary McAleese gave a warmly congratulatory speech, and then tactfully withdrew. It was undoubtedly the happiest, noisiest and, perhaps, the most emotional party in Dublin that year. Volunteers (including several from abroad), proud of their mutual achievements, were delighted to meet old friends, to catch up with old colleagues (even if they didn't always recognise who they were talking to: 'By the way,' Áine Fay, country director in Bangladesh, was asked, 'have you seen Áine?') And they retold the old stories, of local staff they had known, of Aengus' visits, of evenings in the African night.

The favoured route to change in the 20th century was that of born-again conversion, revolution or re-invention, whereby lives were to be changed forever by one impatient, heroic act. This mechanistic approach has been responsible for a great deal of grief, in Russia, Germany, China, Cambodia and a hundred other countries. Perhaps the 21st century will, by contrast, favour a more organic route, that of persistently adding one small improvement to another and then to another.

In fact, this has been happening. Official statistics provide us with some hope: things do get better. Driven by a halving of infant mortality since 1968, especially in the developing world, both population and life expectancy across the world have risen markedly. As more children survive, families feel secure enough to control further births, and so since 1990, when 87 million people were added to the world's population, numbers born each year have gone steadily down. And despite tremendous growth in population over those years, the number judged by the FAO to be actually starving (i.e. insufficiently nourished to perform light work) has gone down from 917 million in 1970, to 792 million in 1997. (Still far, far too many, of course.) This is largely because the Green Revolution has ensured greater yields, allowing developing world available calories per head to climb from 2,100 in 1968 to nearly 2,700 today. Not only are people living longer, in better health and with less hunger, they are richer—there are for instance six times as many televisions per 1,000 in the developed world than there were thirty years ago. The apparently unstoppable advance of the Sahel has halted, and countries such as Burkino Faso are becoming green again. These are only a few of the positive signs.

By a multitude of tiny improvements initiated by the people themselves, their leaders, and the international community, conditions have changed for the better. Concern was and is a specifically Irish contributor to the process, focusing its attention on the poorest. Every baby saved from hunger, every farmer helped to grow two ears of corn where one grew before, every tiny loan from a microfinance scheme, every sanitation scheme providing a little dignity to an urban slum, is one of those minute improvements.

There are still immense problems, of course, but the reason for hope is that immense problems have been solved. For instance, although famine has not been, like smallpox, more or less eradicated, we can certainly say that the world community knows what to do and has the apparatus to resolve any incipient large-scale famine threat. This was not true even twenty years ago.

Concerted effort focused on specific circumstances can improve lives. Above all there is the constant demand for help from the poorest of the poor, who simply need, in justice, as much help as they can get.

So the work will go on.

Appendix 1: Concern's core values

The following core values were explicitly enunciated for the first time in February 1998. This is the current formulation.

Extreme poverty must be targeted. The quality of our overall endeavour must ultimately be measured by its contribution to the rapid elimination of the extreme form of poverty defined by the United Nations as 'absolute poverty'.

Our other values, stated below, are subsidiary to this central value:

Respect for people comes first. Poverty, no matter how extreme, reduces people's choices—not their competence and abilities. Respect is shown to all people with whom we engage; and in particular in our overseas work, we respect the integrity and dignity of the poor with whom we work.

Gender equality is a prerequisite for development. The establishment of equality of opportunities between men and women is fundamental to both the achievement of fairness and to poverty elimination.

Development is a process, not a gift. Development is a process that occurs in people and is achieved by them at their pace, either on their own or with outside facilitation. We hold as a fundamental tenet that people living in absolute poverty have, in varying degrees, personal capacities, local resources and external opportunities for their own self-development. It is imperative that our work builds on these resources

Greater participation leads to greater commitment. At home and overseas participation in decision-making leads to a greater and more sustained commitment to achieving developmental objectives. We believe in a high level and quality of participation by the poor in decision-making about development initiatives taken in partnership with them.

All governments have responsibility for poverty elimination. Most of the poverty endured by countless numbers of people living in the developing world cannot be solved without changed national and international social, economic and political structures. Concern engages in advocacy to this end.

Emergencies call for rapid response. We value the importance of being able to respond quickly, effectively and creatively to people unable to meet their basic needs, especially in sudden onset emergencies.

Democracy accelerates development. Lack of equity in the distribution of power within and between societies retards the struggle against absolute poverty. Participatory democratic environments are the most favourable settings in which states, markets and people can together solve the problem of global poverty.

The environment must be respected. The destruction of the environment poses a major threat to our target groups. We acknowledge the importance of protecting the earth's environment and the need to ensure that our development and advocacy work promotes the concept of environmental responsibility and the conservation of natural resources and their sustainable management.

Good stewardship ensures trust. We hold money in trust for all of our donors and for their intended beneficiaries. This creates a responsibility to ensure we are accountable and to give value for money both to our donors and to our project participants.

Experience is the best teacher. Our current policies, strategies and practices have been developed through our learning over the years. We value the ongoing process of learning and of participating in networks with other organisations to share experiences and learn from them.

Appendix 2: Income and expenditure

	Chair	Chief Exec.	Revenue (£000s)			Expenditure (£000s)				Notes
			Cash	Kind	Total	Field	Non-Field[1]	Total	Non-field %	
Africa Concern										
1968/69	V. Grogan	JK	458		458	394	20	414	5%	2
1969/70	V. Grogan	JK	618		618	547	39	586	7%	3
1970/71	V. Grogan	JK	117		117	120	30	150	20%	4
1971/72	V. Grogan	JK	143		143	146	31	177	18%	5
1972	V. Grogan	JK	46		46	37	20	57	35%	6
Concern										
1973	Sir A. Esmond	RK	34		34	28	15	44	34%	7
1973/74	Sir A. Esmond	RK	460		460	186	63	249	25%	8
1974/75	Eanna Johnson	RK	519		519	475	90	565	16%	
1975/76	Eanna Johnson	RK	482		482	442	97	539	18%	
1976/77	Eanna Johnson	MD	683		683	618	133	751	18%	
1977/78	M. Fingleton	AT	732		732	504	254	658	39%	
1978/79	M. Fingleton	AT	1,071		1,071	851	188	1,039	18%	9
1979/80	M. Fingleton	AT	2,285		2,285	1,294	294	1,588	19%	
1980/81	M. Fingleton	AF	2,289		2,289	1,899	300	2,200	14%	
1981/82	M. Fingleton	AF	3,415		3,415	2,828	617	3,445	18%	10
1983	M. Fingleton	AF	2,932		2,932	2,846	486	3,332	15%	11
1984	P. O'Boyle	AF	6,866		6,866	3,165	575	3,740	15%	
1985	P. O'Boyle	AF	7,349		7,349	6,868	698	7,566	9%	
1986	P. O'Boyle	AF	5,920		5,920	4,951	789	5,741	14%	
1987	P. Kierans	AF	5,315		5,315	6,099	790	6,889	11%	
1988	P. Kierans	AF	11,529	3,709	15,238	12,682	945	13,627	7%	
1989	P. Kierans	AF	11,387	3,730	15,117	12,827	1,136	13,963	8%	12
1990	P. Kierans	AF	10,350	3,686	14,036	13,884	1,335	15,219	9%	13
1991	P. J. Howell	AF	19,494	13,799	33,293	30,335	1,839	32,174	6%	
1992	P. J. Howell	AF	27,124	9,049	36,172	25,438	2,503	27,941	9%	
1993	P. J. Howell	AF	25,209	6,262	31,471	30,086	3,037	33,123	9%	
1994	P. J. Howell	AF	31,317	14,060	45,378	40,740	4,614	45,354	10%	
1995	T. Arnold	AF	18,567	11,633	30,200	28,066	3,876	31,943	12%	
1996	T. Arnold	AF	17,019	7,596	24,615	24,634	2,947	27,581	11%	
1997	T. Arnold	DB	19,087	2,634	21,721	18,204	2,604	20,808	13%	
1998	T. Arnold	DB	23,777	1,162	24,939	20,771	3,147	23,918	13%	
TOTALS			256,594	77,320	333,914	291,965	33,512	325,381	10%	

1. Non-Field includes all expenditure on administration, fund-raising, promotion and development education
2. 29 July 1968 to 30 June 1969
3. 1 July to 30 June
4. 'Field' includes £40,000 net shipping costs
5. 'Field' includes £41,000 net shipping costs
6. 1 July to 31 December 1972
7. 1 Jan 1973 to 30 June 1973
8. 1 July to 30 June
9. incorporation of Cork Branch
10. 18 months to 31 Dec 1982
11. Calendar years from now on
12. 1st published valuation of donations in kind
13. £2m in and out for the Svea Atlantica not included

Appendix 3: Field directors 1968–98

Field directors are listed in order of their taking charge of the field; the dates record the opening of the field.

India 1971
Raymond Kennedy

Bangladesh 1972
Raymond Kennedy
Aengus Finucane
Jack Finucane
Philip O'Brien
Theresa McDonnell
Paul Crowe
Aine Fay
Paul O'Brien
John Kilkenny
Noel Malony

Yemen 1973
Michael Brosnahan
Jimmy O'Toole
Mary Humphries
Fintan Farrelly
Seamus Connolly

Ethiopia 1973
Brian Pearce
Jack Finucane
Fintan Farrelly
Tom Lavin
Brian Nugent
Moira Brehony

Tanzania 1978
Philip O'Brien
Theresa McDonnell
Pat Shanahan
Bernie Bloomberg
Brian Nugent Jan Rotte
Jo Thomas
Paul Murphy
Paul O'Brien

Thailand 1978
Aengus Finucane
Ciaran Kitching
Ciunas Bunworth
Brian Nugent
Dominic MacSorley
Garvan O'Keeffe

Uganda 1978
Aengus Finucane
John Phillips
Moira Brehony
Aine Fay
Louise Supple

Mozambique 1984
Ciunas Bunworth
Mariana Quinlivan
Peter O'Mahony
William Carlos
Kate Corcoran
Jo Thomas

Sudan 1985
Theresa McDonnell
Moira Conroy
Nick Pyatt
Tom Lavin
Anne O'Mahony
Paul Murphy
Moira Brehony

Somalia 1986
Mark Hogan
Dominic MacSorley
Anne O'Mahony
Mike McDonagh
John Kilkenny

Cambodia 1989
Garvan O'Keeffe
Dominic MacSorley
Anne O'Mahony
Rod MacLeod
Noel Malony
Louise Supple

Liberia 1991
Mike McDonagh
Beatrice Killen

Laos 1992
Mike McDonagh
Maire Mathews
Jan Rotte
John Kilkenny
Mark Capaldi

Angola 1993
Mike McDonagh
Marcus Oxley
Beth Matthews

South Sudan 1993
Toireas Ni Bhriain
Paul Murphy

Burundi 1994
Orla Quinlan
Rob Williams
Dominic MacSorley
Willa Addis

Rwanda 1994
Mike McDonagh
Dominic MacSorley
Anne O'Mahony
Zaire 1994
Mike McDonagh

Michael O'Reilly
Dominic MacSorley
Pierce Gerety

Haiti 1994
Patrick McManus
Rod McLeod

Sierra Leone 1995
Mike McDonagh
Noel Malony
Anne O'Mahony
Toireas Ni Bhriain

Afghanistan 1998
Aine Fay
Will Power

Honduras 1998
Mike McDonagh

Appendix 4: Volunteers 1968–2001

These are the volunteers recorded in the curent Concern files; it is possible that some may have slipped through the net. If so, Concern would be glad to know.

Samantha Aarvold
Hilary Abbey
Stephen Abbey
Barbara Adams
Danielle Aebisher
Gerard Agterberg
Jean Francois Aguilera
Maria Ahern
Shakeel Ahmad
Alauddin Ahmed
Siobhan Airey
Pervez Akhter
Magdalena Alemany
Costa
Mary Allen
Ita Ambrose
Sandi Anderson
Sinead Andrews
Paul Anticoni
Rachel Anticoni
Jane Armitage
Fitsum Asseffa
Mary Austin

Colm Joseph Baker
Oliver Bakewell
Angela Balfe
Olwyn Ballantine
Derick Barrett
Joan Barrett
Mary Barrett
Susan Barrett
Teresa Barrett
Jacinta Barrins
Aidan Barry
Deirdre Barry

Hilary Barry
Rosemary Barry
Val Batchelor
David Beary
Hans Bederski
Peter Behan
Catherine Bell
Patrick Belton
Mark Belton
Ted Berth
Robin Biddulph
Andy Bidnell
Maureen Billiet
Lyndsay Bird
Turlough Bird
Robert Blackmore
Tony Blackmore
Rona Blackwood
Breda Blanche
Dorothy Blane
Eduardo Blasco Delgado
Kathleen Blennerhassett
Catherine Blishen
Bernardus Bloemberg
Mashilda Bloemberg
Peter Bofin
Elizabeth Bogue
Mary Bolger
Thomas Bolger
Anna Bolger
Tango Bolton
Brian Bonar
Maureen Bonfield
Annalies Borrel
Aileen Bourke
Sandra Bourke

Frances Bowen
Rita Bowen
Robert Bowen
Niamh Bowes
Rachel Bowler
Mary Boyle
Nicola Boyle
Ros Boyle
Siobhan Boyle
Andrew Brachi
Jo Bradford
Clare Brady
Francis Brady
Malcolm Brady
Miriam Brady
Noelle Brady
Aicha Brahmi
Jonathan Brass
Eamonn Brehony
Anne Brennan
Michael Brennan
Vivienne Brennan
John Breslin
Ann Broderick
Marie Broderick
Liz Broe
Nuala Brogan
Jane Brogan
Breda Brophy
Fr. Michael Brosnan
Andy Brown
Heather Brown
Judith Brown
Mary Browne
Bernard Browne
Ellen Buckley

Elizabeth Bunde
Ciunas Bunworth
Brendan Burgess
Christine Burke
Eileen Burke
Mairead Burke
Robert Burke
Ronagh Burke
Linda Burns
Maria Burton
David Burton
Catherine Butler
Catherine Butler
Gillian Butler
Jacqueline Butt
Warren Buttery
Anna Byrne
Bernadette Byrne
Colm Byrne
Edward Byrne
Hugh Byrne
Pauline Byrne
Kevin Byrne
Marianne Byrne
Martin Byrne
Mary Byrne
Michael Byrne
Monica Byrne
Ned Byrne
Noreen Byrne
Monica Byrne

Marian Cadogan
Ethna Caffrey
Sheila Cahalane
James Cahill
Siobhan Cahill
Maura Cahill
Rose Caldwell
Geraldine Callaghan
Anne Callanan
Anne Cameron
Julie Cameron
Anne Campbell
John Campbell

John Campbell
Noel Campbell
Brian Canavan
Anna Cannon
John Canny
Phillipa Cantillon
Mark Capaldi
Isabelle Cardinal
Freda Carew
Ann Carey
John Carey
Kathleen Carey
Irene Carlos
William Carlos
John Carlow
Arthur Carlson
Ailish Carr
Bronagh Carr
James Carroll
Kevin Carroll
Maria Carroll
Anne Carroll
Matthew Carter
Rachel Carton
Desmond Carville
Ann Casey
David Casey
Deirdre Casey
Francis Casey
John Casey
Marie Casey
Patricia Casey
Catherine Casey
Irene Casey
Diarmuid Cashman
Adrienne Cassidy
Catherine Cassidy
Rodrigo Castro
Clare Chamberlain
Monica Chambers
Dan Chambers
Martin Charlton
Sarah Chave
Anne Choiseul
Sr. Theodora Chompala

Philip Choudhury
Marie Christie
Ratri Chukiatwong
Catherine Claffey
Angela Clancy
Sara Clancy
Suzanne Clancy
Margaret Clapson
Peter Clarke
Colleen Clarke
Dorothy Clarke
Eamonn Clarke
Kathy Clarke
Michael Clarke
Niall Clarke
Jimmy Clavesillas
Maire Clear
Raymond Cleary
Michael Cleary
Conor Cleere
Nigel Clerkin
Harry Clifton
Mary Clifton
John Coakley
Susan Coakley
Joseph Cockerill
Mary Cocoman
Finbarr Cody
Mary Coen
Tim Coffey
Dom Colbert
Cathy Cole
Anthony Coleman
Martina Coleman
Niamh Coleman
Alison Collie
Barbara Collins
Noreen Collins
John Collins
Martina Collins
Stephen Collins
Vivien Collins
Martina Collins
Marie Collison
Leonard Comerford

Volunteers 1968–2001

Paul Comiskey
John Connell
Bernadette Connolly
Eidin Connolly
Seamus Connolly
Sheila Connolly
Anne Conroy
Moira Conroy
Carmel Considine
Deirdre Considine
Mary Considine
Ann Conway
Clare Conway
Tim Conway
Linda Cook
Robert Cooke
Patricia Cooney
John Cooney
Justin Corbett
Sophie Corbett
Kate Corcoran
Deirdre Corcoran
John Corcoran
Marie Corcoran
Mary Corish
Eva Corral
Mary Corridan
Lorraine Corrigan
John Corristine
Margaret Corristine
John Patrick Cosgrave
Olivia Cosgrove
Dave Costello
Grainne Costello
John Costello
John Costigan
William Cotter
Paul Cotterill
Nigel Cowman
David Thomas Cox
Eamon Coyle
Ciaran Coyne
Elizabeth Coyne
Christine Creedon
Susan Cremin

Torcuil Crichton
Maria Cronin
Mary Cronin
Una Cronin
Marie Cronnelly
Paul Crook
Raymond Crotty
Anne Crowe
Paul Crowe
Phyllis Crowe
Therese Crowe
Dominic Crowley
David Crowley
Margaret Crowley
Therese Crowley
Jillian Crowther
Dolores Crudge
Brian Cullen
Elizabeth Cullen
Maurice Cullen
Moira Cullinan
Alice Culliton
Eric Cummings
Anne Cummins
Mary Cummins
Mark Cunningham
Melissa Cunningham
Terry Cunningham
Ann Cunningham
Fiona Cunningham
Jennifer Cunningham
John Cunningham
John Cunningham
Pamela Curley
Paul Curley
Anne Curran
Susan Curry
Pauline Curry
Martina Cusack

Jo Da Silva
Torunn Dahl
Caroline Dalton
Martin Dalton
Angela Daly

Helen Daly
Mary Daly
Mary Daly
Eleanor Daly
Ellen D'Arcy
Mary D'Arcy
Margaret Darragh
Veronica Davey
Karen Davies
Alice Davis
Stephanie Davis
Graham Davison
Sheila Dawson
Susan Dawson
Mark De Guilio
Pedro De La Cruz
Josephine De Wergifosse
Ita Deacy
Margaret Deasy
Joan Deegan
Nicki Deeson
Paul Delahunty
Margaret Delaney
Maria Delaney
Mary Delaney
Maximilien Delville
Alice Dempsey
James Dempsey
Margaret Dempsey
Marybelle Denis
Michaela Dennis
Pauline Derby
Margaret Desmond
John Devane
Sheila Devane
Rose Dew
Janet Dewhurst
Pauline Dewhurst
Vivek Dharmaraj
Juliet Dickey
Frances Dignam
Sharon Dilger
Margaret Dillane
Patrick Dillon
Elizabeth Dineen

Stephan Dix
John Richard Dixon
Richard Dixon
Tom Dobbin
Anne Dodan
Nora Doheny
Fr Michael Doheny
Breege Doherty
Des Doherty
Frances Doherty
Neil Doherty
Thomas Doherty
Helen Dolan
Ann Donald
Peter Donkin
Margaret Donnellon
Ciaran Donnelly
Dermot Donnelly
Michael Donnelly
Patricia Donnelly
Mary Donohoe
Peter Donovan
Aine Doody
Maureen Doohan
Anne Doolan
Imelda Dooley
Dolores Dowd
Enda Dowd
James Dowdall
Margaret Dowling
Michael Dowling
Deborah Downes
Maeve Downing
Agnes Doyle
Andrew Doyle
Bernard Doyle
Brendan Doyle
Gary Doyle
Jim Doyle
Kaye Doyle
Mary Doyle
Maura Doyle
Michael Doyle
Eithna Drake
Louise Drew

Patrick Dromey
Sr Catherine Droszcz
Marlyn D'Sa
Veronique Ducos
Arabella Duffield
Mark Duffield
Ann Duffin
Brendan Duffy
Helen Duffy
Patrick Duffy
Sinead Duffy
Brendan Duggan
Malachy Duggan
Rita Duggan
Mary Duignan
Naoise Duignan
Mary Dunbar
Rachel Duncan Brown
Colette Dunne
Elizabeth Dunne
Mary Dunne
Yvonne Dunne
Jackie Durcan
Maria Durnin
Catherine Dwyer
Celine Dwyer

Amanda Edwards
Fiona Edwards
Joseph Edwards
Patti Edwards
Fr. Peter Egan
Mary Egan
John Elliott
Mary English
Reginald English
Anita Ennis
Paul Enright
Brigid Enright
Elizabeth Erraught
Vivienne Evans
Irene Julia Evison
Steve Evison

Brian Fagan

Anne Fahy
Teresa Fahy
Patricia Fakhouri
Michael Fanning
Helen Fanning
Mary Farragher
Jimmy Farrell
Kevin Farrell
Catherine Farrelly
Fintan Farrelly
Clare Fay
Gabriel Fay
Geraldine Feehan
Bernadette Feeney
Brigid Feeney
James Feeney
Joseph Feeney
Mary Feeney
Peter Feeney
Deirdre Feghahat
Margaret Felton
Ana Maria Fernandes
Joao Fernao
Victor Ferreira
Eileen Ferrins
Joanne Ferris
John Finn
Mary Finn
Mary Finnan
Jean Finnemore
Frank Finucane
Fr. Aengus Finucane
Fr. Jack Finucane
Adrian Fitzgerald
Geraldine Fitzgerald
Gerard Fitzgerald
Maria Fitzgerald
Mary Fitzgerald
Aidan Fitzpatrick
Deirdre Fitzpatrick
James Fitzpatrick
Margaret Fitzpatrick
Margaret Fitzpatrick
Marion Fitzpatrick
Barbara Fitzpatrick

Volunteers 1968–2001

James Fitzwilliams
Mary Flanagan
Anne Flannery
Mary Flannery
Colette Fleming
Yvonne Fleming
Monica Flinn
Mary Flood
Maree˜ Flynn
Emer Fogarty
Josephine Fogarty
Pauline Fogarty
Ann Foley
Connell Foley
Judith Foley
Leonora Foley
Carmel Foran
Alison Forder
Maria Forrest
Kate Forrester
Lara Fossi
Rachel Fowler
Conor Fox
Noelin Fox
Sophie Francis
David Fraser
Susan Fraser
Katherine Fullam
Martha Fulton
Bridget Furlong

Breda Gahan
Mairin Gallagher
Anne Gallagher
Brid Gallagher
Karen Gallagher
Michele Gallagher
Maura Galvin
Rita Galvin
Pauline Garry
Neill Garvie
Catherine Gately
Kathleen Gately
Rita Gault
Brian Gavin

Bernadette Geoghegan
Emma Geoghegan
Lawrence Geoghegan
Pierce Gerety
Anne Ghadims
Anne Marie Gibson
Aidan Gillan
Maureen Gillan
Barbara Gilroy
Mary Gilroy
Eileen Gilsenan
Fionnuala Gilsenan
Paul Ginnell
Ann Glynn
Colleen Glynn
Grania Glynn
Michael Glynn
John Glynn
Esther Gonzalez
Joe Goodwin
Concepta Gordon
Roberta Gordon
Carmel Gormally
Monica Gorman
Peter Gorman
Niall Gormley
Michael Gott
David Gough
Deirdre Gough
Geraldine Graal
Katherine Grantham
Annemarie Gray
Karin Gray
Nola Constance Greene
Nancy Greene
Brian Grennan
Roger Grennan
Gerry Grey
Joseph Gribben
Veronica Griffin
Anne Griffin
Margaret Grogan
Nuala Guilly
Wayne Gum
Nick Guttman

Mary Ann Guzman

Anne Hadcroft
Carmel Hadnett
Patricia Hallanan
Etta Halliday
Eileen Halligan
Kenny Hamilton
Donal Hand
Maura Hanly
Kathleen Hanrahan
Eveyln Haran
Neil Haran
Donncha Harkin
Kathleen Harnett
Arabella Harris
Kathy Harris
Helen Harris
Jane Harris
Audrey Harte
Thomas Harte
Amanda Harvey
Colin Haskins
Barbara Haslam
Hans Hassemer
Noreen Hastings
Adrian Steven Hatch
Kay Haughton
Francis Hayden
Michael Hayden
Daithi Hayes (O'Aodha)
Rachel Hayhow
Geraldine Heagney
Anne Healy
Eithne Healy
Paul Healy
Angela Healy
Annette Hearns
Bridget Heenan
Phyllis Heeney
Attracta Heffernan
Mary Heffernan
Kathy Hegarty
Marion Hegarty
Mary Hegarty

Brigid Hehir
Eric Heitzman
Andre-Bob Helbios
Ed Henderson
Mary Elizabeth
Henderson
Catherine Hennessey
Sean Hennessey
Margaret Hennessy
Shaun Henry
Fiacre Hensey
Jean Hermes
Nannerl Herriott
Frank Heslin
Joanne Hession
Ian Hester
Geoff Heyes
Mary Hickey
Mary Hickey
Anne Hickey
Patricia Hickey
Elena Higgins
Elisabeth Higgins
Gerard Higgins
Mary Higgins
Ray Hilliard
Karen Hillyer
Michael Hilton
Nicholas Hilton
Karen Hingley
Tom Hockley
Elsa Hodgins
Diane Hodgson
Eileen Hodnett
Rose Hogan
Sean Hogan
Dale Hogland
Elaine Holland
Mary Holland
Denise Holland
Maria Holmes
Bernard Holt
Joy Holverson
Rosemary Hood
Jennifer Hopps

Annette Horne
David Horrocks
P. J. Howell
Sean Hoy
Sheila Hudner
Catrin Hughes
Caitrin Hughes
David Humphrey
James Hunt
Maria Hunt
Seamus Hunt
Valerie Hunt
Thomas Huntington
Rosemary Huntington
John Hurd
Annabel Hurlstone
Nigel Hussey
Ian Hutcheson
Geralyn Hynes
Jim Hynes

Charlie Jackson
Beth Jackson
Jeffrey Jacobs
Ingrid Renee Jager
Lorna Jamieson
Pat Jamison
Walter Jeanty
John Jefferies
Neville Jefferies
Elinor Jenkins
Ann Johnson
Ethna Johnson
Victoria Johnson
Dara Johnston
Joe Johnston
Barnaby Jones
Kevin Jones
Rose Jordan
David Joyce
Eileen Joyce
Tobias Joyce
Tony Joyce
Mal Juchaniewicz

Aminata Kallon
Mark Kane
Darina Karanth
Jody Kasprow
Anne Kavanagh
John Kavanagh
Mary Kavanagh
Michael Kavanagh
Mary Kavanagh
Anne Keane
Finny Keane
Kate Keane
Neil Keane
Sinead Keaney
Richard Kearney
Rita Kearney
Theresa Kearney
Joseph Kearns
Paul Keating
Clare Keegan
Olivia Keena
Eugene Keenan
Gerard Keeney
Philomena Kelf
Cora Kelleher
Donal Kelleher
Lu Kellett
Anne Louise Kelly
Anthony Kelly
Brigid Kelly
Catherine Kelly
David Kelly
Joan Kelly
John Kelly
Joyce Kelly
Lorcan Kelly
Mary Kelly
Mary Kelly
Mary Kelly
Philomena Kelly
Terina Kelly
Mary Kelly
Brid Kennedy
Bridget Kennedy
Brigid Kennedy

James Kennedy
Karen Kennedy
Mary Kenny
Michael Kenny
David Keogh
Mary Keogh
Roisin Keogh
Maeve Kerney
John Kerr
Maureen Kerr
John Kerr
Sarah Keylock
Isabelle Kidney
Mary Kidney
Ann Kiely
Peter Kierans
Angela Kiernan
Azelda Kiernan
Mary Kiernan
Cathy Kilcoyne
William Kilduff
John Kilkenny
Margaret Kilkenny
Frances Killeen
Beatrice Killen
Geraldine Killian
Deirdre King
Sheelagh King
Brenda Kingston
Julia Kingston
Robert Kinnear
David Kinross
Jim Kinsella
Susan Kinsella
Catherine Kirkwood
Oliver Kirkwood
Kate Kirsopp
Fr. Ciaran Kitching
Elizabeth Knaggs
Alex Krick
Christina Kyne
Mary Kyne

Jayne Ladbrook
Clare Lafferty

Peadar Lafferty
Siobhan Lagan
Robert Lambert
Jean Lane
Vince Langdon
Charlotte Langeveld
Bernie Lardner
Eileen Larkin
Peter Lavelle
Thomas Lavin
Ellen Lawless
Sr Monica Lawless
John Lawlor
Louise Lawlor
Mary Lawlor
Ruth Lawlor
Maria Lawlor
Sarah Le Breton
Siobhan Lee
Kathleen Lee
Sean Lee
Mairin Lehmann
Jimmy Lenehan
Eamonn Lenihan
Gerry Lenihan
Pat Lenihan
Mary Lennon
Susan Lennon
Grainne Leonard
Aidan Leonard
Tinne Lernout
Simon Levine
Alyson Lewis
Elizabeth Lewis
Sibylla Lewyska
Ronat Lillis
Fr. Sebastian Lioncar
Christine Lipohar
Mary Liston
John Little
Barbara Lloyd
Finbarr Loftus
Kieran Logan
Teresa Lonergan
Jean Long

Sian Long
Carol Lorenz
Dieter Lorenz
Barry Lorton
Deborah Lott
Agnes Lucey
Margaret Lucey
George Lumsden
Vivienne Lusted
Barry Lynam
Bernadette Lynch
Breda Lynch
Catherine Lynch
Catherine Lynch
Dympna Lynch
Elizabeth Lynch
Finola Lynch
Liam Lynch
Madeleine Lynch
Maeve Lynch
Maria Lynch
Michael Lynch
Timothy Lynch
Joan Lynch
Catherine Lyng
Hugh Lynn
Anne Lyons

Robert MacCabe
Diarmuid MacDonncha
Gus MacEntire
Andrew MacGregor
Colin Mackay
Mary Macken
Michelle Mackin
Pamela Mackle
Anne MacMahon
Ann MacNamara
Charlie MacNamara
Mary MacNamara
Peader MacRory
Daithi MacRuairi
Dominic MacSorley
Stewart Maginnis
Dara Maguire

Tina Maguire
Gervaise Maher
Helen Maher
Mary Maher
Paul Maher
Bernadette Mahon
Luke Mahon
Ann Malone
Leah Malone
Nora Malone
Sophia Malone
Imelda Mannion
Karine Mantey
Alex Marcelino
Jennifer Marfleet
Bernard Markey
Karen Markey
Patrick Markey
Andrew Martin
Bridget Martin
Bryony Martin
David Martin
Dr. Therese Martin
Eamonn Martin
Mary Martin
Mary Martin
Mary Martin
Emily Mates
Beth Mathews
Donal Matthews
Maire Matthews
Patrick Matthews
Carole Maunder
Stephanie Maxwell
Peter McAleer
Frances McAllister
Darine McArdle
Frances McArdle
Raymond McArdle
Ann McAteer
Eunan McAteer
Geraldine McBrien
Rory McBurney
Keith McCabe
Rosemary McCaffrey

Therese McCaffrey
Caroline McCaffrey
Desmond McCall
Kevin McCambridge
Peter McCanny
Peter McCarron
Assumpta McCarthy
Charles McCarthy
Elizabeth McCarthy
Geraldine McCarthy
Gerry McCarthy
Jim McCarthy
Marie McCarthy
Moira McCarthy
Sheila McCarthy
Eilis McCarthy
Maire McCarthy
Patrick McCaughey
Ray McClean
Linda McClelland
Cliff McConkey
Susan McConnor
Martin McCormack
Selina McCormack
Michael McCoy
Teresa McCreery
Patricia McCrink
Mary McCrossan
Kevin McCrudden
Lorna McCullagh
Geraldine McCullough
Grainne McCullough
John McDermott
Terence McDermott
Mairead McDonagh
Mike McDonagh
Damian McDonald
Elaine McDonald
Jim McDonnell
Sean McDonnell
Nuala McDonnell
Catherine McDonough
Monica McElvaney
Mary McEnery
Michael McEnery

Orna McEntee
Nuala McGarvey
Siobhan McGee
Anne McGeough
Connie McGilloway
Patrick McGivern
Patrick McGloin
Patrick McGloin
Maureen McGlynn
Carmel McGoldrick
Jacqueline McGovern
Margaret McGovern
Mary McGovern
Fergal McGrane
Shane McGrath
James McGuire
Rita McGuire
Tony McGuire
Mary McGuirk
Brigid McHugh
Teresa McHugh
Breda McHugh
Rosie McIlroy
Matthew McIlvenna
Ann McKay
Mary McKeon
Marion McKeown
Joan McKiernan
Jules McKim
Susan McKnight
Patricia McLaughlin
Patrick McLeish
Anne McLoughlin
Cliona McLoughlin
Fiona McLysaght
David McMahon
Elaine McMahon
Meabh McMahon
Veronica McMahon
Patrick McManus
Michael McMullen
Christopher McNally
Brian McNamara
Susan McNaughton
Carmel McNeill

Mary McNiece
Cathal McNiff
Bridget McNulty
Aidan McQuade
Denis McSwiney
Malachy McVeigh
Tom Meadley
Stephanie Meagher
Brigid Meagher
Bernadette Meagher
Catherine Meehan
Charlotte Meehan
Martin Meehan
Sean Meehan
Maria Meilak
Mary Mellerick
Wendy Melville
Gerldine Merkx
Teresa Merry
Jean Messadoui
Sarah Methven
Louise Michael
James Miley
Edith Milham
Jacinta Miller
Phil Miller
Cameron Milne
Sjouke Minkema
James Minogue
Pauline Mitchell
Bisetegn Mitiku
Takeshi Miyazaki
Thomas Mockler
Enda Moclair
Gaye Moffat
Vivien Moffitt
Anne Molloy
Desmond John Molloy
Nora Molone
Imelda Moloney
James Moloney
Noel Molony
Eddie Moloughney
John Monaghan
Marian Monaghan

Dominic Moncilovic
Donna Mooney
Irene Mooney
Sheelagh Mooney
Una Mooney
Alice Moore
Anne Moore
Dermot Moore
Kaye Moore
Martina Moore
Mary Moore
Niall Moore
Mary Moran
Olive Moran
Paul Moran
Catherine Morgan
Michelle Morgan
Margaret Moriarty
Margaret Morris
Alistair Morrison
Janet Morrison
Richard Mowll
Kieran Moylan
Carmel Moylan
Paula Mularkey
Mary Mulhern
Aidan Mulkeen
Eamonn Mullan
Mark Mullan
Margaret Mullen
Sr. Mairead Mullen
Olivia Mulligan
Carmel Mulrine
Jacinta Mulrooney
Lynn Mulrooney
Patricia Mulvin
Maire Murnion
Phelim Murnion
Paul Murphy
Martin Murphy
Caitriona Murphy
Colin Murphy
Gillian Murphy
Evelyn Murphy
Gerard Murphy

Jane Murphy
John Murphy
Kieran Murphy
Lucy Murphy
Maria Murphy
Maria Murphy
Mary Murphy
Noreen Murphy
Pat Murphy
Tony Murphy
Vera Murphy
Wendy Murphy
Winifred Murphy
Christina Murphy
Catherine Murray
Catherine Murray
Jacinta Murray
James Murray
Joseph Murray
Kate Murray
Catherine Murray
Padraic Murtagh
Mary Myers

Cronan Nagle
Sabina Nagle
Imelda Nagle
Rosalie Nally
Johnathan Napier
Jez Newall
Denis Neylon
Toireas Ni Bhriain
Sile Ni Fhlatharta
Brid Ni Laochdha
Aine Ni Loingsigh
Orla Ni Ruadhain
Danielle Nicholson
Frode Nilsen
Eileen Nolan
Jim Nolan
Padraig Nolan
Patrick Nolan
Dr. Nolan
Catherine Noonan
Mary Noonan

Mary Noone
Sarah Ann Norman
Nicolas North
Sheila Norton
Brian Nugent
Elizabeth Nugent
Judith Nyhan

Sheila O'Beirne
Phena O'Boyle
Rossa O'Briain
Anne O'Brien
Anne O'Brien
Bernadette O'Brien
Brendan O'Brien
Brendan O'Brien
Bridget O'Brien
Cindy O'Brien
Deirdre O'Brien
Desmond O'Brien
Eithne O'Brien
Ellen O'Brien
Irene O'Brien
Sean O'Brien
Paul O'Brien
Philip Daniel O'Brien
Thomas O'Brien
Ann O'Byrne
Ross O'Callaghan
Ide O'Carroll
Deirdre O'Connell
Denis O'Connell
Frances O'Connell
Helen O'Connell
Mary O'Connell
Mary O'Connell
Mary O'Connell
Maureen O'Connor
Nora O'Connor
Pamela O'Connor
Pat O'Connor
Siobhan O'Connor
Patrick O'Connor
Alva O'Dalaigh
Catherine O'Donaghue

Diarmuid
O'Donnabhain
Anne O'Donnell
Jim O'Donnell
Paul O'Donoghue
Maria O'Donoghue
Thomas O'Donoghue
Anne O'Donovan
Michael O'Donovan
Vera O'Donovan
Vera O'Donovan
Ann O'Dwyer
Anne O'Dwyer
Catherine O'Dwyer
Eileen O'Dwyer
Cecily O'Flynn
Mairead O'Flynn
Thomas O'Flynn
June O'Gorman
Patricia O'Gorman
Aine O'Grady
Marie O'Haire
Patrick O'Halloran
Eileen O'Hanlon
Eileen O'Hanlon
Joan O'Hanlon
Maureen O'Hara
Thomas James
O'Higgins
Denise O'Kane
Gerry O'Keefe
Catherine O'Keeffe
Garvan O'Keeffe
Gerard O'Keeffe
Josephine O'Keeffe
Margaret O'Keeffe
Frances O'Keeffe
Ann O'Kelly
Catherine O'Leary
Mary O'Leary
Sheelagh O'Leary
Fiontan O'Loinsigh
Rosalyn O'Loughlin
Maura O'Loughlin
Anne O'Mahony

Denis O'Mahony
Nollaig O'Mahony
Margaret O'Mahony
Peter O'Mahony
Kieran O'Malley
Monica O'Malley
Patrick O'Malley
Patrick O'Meara
Eamon O'Mordha
Angela O'Neill
Barbara O'Neill
Bernie O'Neill
Elizabeth O'Neill
Mary O'Neill
Mary O'Neill
Maurice O'Neill
Philomena O'Neill
Susan O'Neill
Fionnuala O'Reardon
Ben O'Regan
Cyril O'Regan
Patrick O'Regan
Barbara O'Reilly
Carole O'Reilly
Cleo O'Reilly
Fiona O'Reilly
Harry O'Reilly
Jenny O'Reilly
Justine O'Reilly
Margaret O'Reilly
Margaret O'Reilly
Mary O'Reilly
Mary O'Reilly
Michael O'Reilly
Monica O'Reilly
Patrick O'Reilly
Peter O'Reilly
Sheila O'Reilly
Vincent O'Reilly
Aine O'Riordan
David O'Rourke
Ellen O'Rourke
Niamh O'Rourke
Patrick O'Rourke
Eidin O'Shea

Kathleen O'Shea
Noel O'Shea
Susan O'Shea
Noelle O'Shea
Monica O'Shea
Christopher O'Sullivan
Angela O'Sullivan
Ann O'Sullivan
Ann O'Sullivan
Catherine Mary
O'Sullivan
Deirdre O'Sullivan
Deirdre O'Sullivan
Eithna O'Sullivan
Ann O'Sullivan
Helen O'Sullivan
Paul O'Sullivan
Margaret O'Sullivan
Mary O'Sullivan
Mary O'Sullivan
Maura O'Sullivan
Michael O'Sullivan
Michael O'Sullivan
Michael O'Sullivan
Pauline O'Sullivan
Peggy O'Sullivan
Gerard O'Sullivan
Helen O'Sullivan
Maggie O'Toole
Stephen O'Toole
Michael O'Toole
Jeannette Oldham
William Oliver
Angela O'Neill
Michaela Ongwae
Yoshio Oshima
Nora Owen
Marcus Oxley

Gerry Pais
Marian Pallister
David Parker
Evelyn Patton
Brian Pearce
Eilish Pearce

Linda Pearson
Stephane Petitprez
Bernadette Phelan
Michael Phelan
John Phillips
Victoria Phillips
Keith Pickard
Maura Pidgeon
Geraldine Pierce
Mariza Pinto
Valerie Rip Place
Valerie Place
Rosemary Pointon
John Poole
David Potter
Frankie Potter
Antonia Potter
Antoinette Powell
William Power
Angela Power
Kathleen Power
Steve Power
David Pratt
Jack Preger
Mary Prendergast
Alice Price
John Prince
Julie Pringle
Nicholas Prins
Janet Probyn
Juliette Prodhan
Mohammad Prodhan
Nick Pyatt

Finbarr Quigley
Anne Quilty
Mary Quinlan
Orla Quinlan
Maranna Quinlivan
Deirdre Quinn
Dolores Quinn
Eileen Quinn
Fiona Quinn
Grainne Quinn
Mary Quinn

Muireann Quinn
Patricia Quinn
Mary Quinn
Brigid Quirke
Christina Quirke
Daniel Quirke
Mariah Quish
Philip John Quist

Mary Raleigh
Charlie Rapoport
Susan Rea
Katherine Redmond
David Regan
Mary Regan
Paul Reidy
Donal Reilly
Margaret Reilly
Susan Reilly
Alex Reynolds
James Reynolds
Maura Reynolds
Ronan Reynolds
Amy Rial
Maria Ribeiro
Catherine Rice
Dorothy Richmond
David Ritchie
Sr Patricia Robb
Caroline Roberts
Elizabeth Roberts
Timothy Roberts
Niall Roche
Sheila Roche
Ann Marie Rogan
Breda Rogers
Terry Rogers
Annette Rolfe
Ann Rooney
Sheila Rotheram
Jan Rotte
Paulette Rowe
Terry Russell
Bernadette Ryan
Brigid Ryan

Imelda Ryan
John Ryan
Margaret Ryan
Mary Ryan
Mary Ryan
Mary Ryan
Rowena Ryan
Sheila Ryan
Theresa Ryan
Colm Ryder
Joan Ryder
Pauline Ryder
John Rynne

Katy Sadler
Peter Salama
Gwen Sali
Paul Sallon
Peter Sargent
Darius Sarshar
Martha Sawyer
John Scahill
Suzanne Scally
James Scanlan
Bridgid Scanlon
Julienne Scanlon
Patricia Scanlon
Linda Schexnaydre
Kathy Schiel
Evanna Schorderet
Liz Schweiger
Rachel Scott
Hannah Scrase
Sadie Scullion
Cormac Scully
Paul Scully
Adam Sendall
Les Serff
Rosa Serra Pujol
Patrick Shanahan
Mary Shanahan
Margaret Shanahan
Anthony Shanley
Geraldine Shannon

Lorna Shannon
Ursula Sharpe
Kate Shaw
Chris Sheehan
Clodagh Sheehan
Fiona Sheehan
Jim Sheehan
Ita Sheehy
Joseph Sheehy
Richard Sheehy
Patrick Sheehy
Nora Sheerman
Martin Shields
Eamon Shields
Michael Shiels
Aisling Shine
Ted Shine
Mark Shinnick
Erica Shipman
Rachel Shirley
Irwin Shorr
Anthony Sills
Paul Simkin
Isabel Simpson
Roland Sims
Garth Singleton
Nicola Singleton
Robin Singleton
Andrew Skally
Catherine Skelly
Paul Skinnader
Kathleen Skinner
Julie Slinger
Bernadette Smith
Margaret Smith
Mary Smith
David Smyth
Margaret Smyth
Stanislava Sofrenic
Joan Somers
Kevin Spain
Noreen Spain
Sandra Spain
Mary Speight

Peter Spink
Lynne Staite
Dawn Stallard
Tommy Standun
Teresa Stankard
Dolores Stankard
Michael Stapleton
Jimmy Steele
Dolores Steinglass
Ian Charles Stephan
Kieran Stewart
Tim Straker-Cook
Felicity Stringer
Sally Stucke
Louise Supple
Margaret Swan
Mary Sweeney
Mary Sweeny
Margaret Sweetman
Hugh Swift
Mary Syron

K. S. M. Tarique
Peter Tarleton
Michael Tarmey
Derrick Tate
Garrett Taylor
Jean Taylor
Ray Taylor
Simon Taylor
Monica Teahan
Melvin Tebbutt
Janice Terhaar
Gordon Terris
Bob Thelen
Jo Thomas
Valerie Thompson
Patrick Thornton
Manfred Tiedeken
Margaret Tiernan
Elizabeth Tighe
Vanessa Tilstone
Eamonn Timmins
Fergus Timmons
Roger Timony

David Tipping
Candace Tkachuck
Clare Tobin
Phil Tomalin
Kenneth Tormey
Jackie Trainor
Mary Tran
Derek Treacy
Mary Treanor
Phil Tubb
Brian Tubbert
Jane Tubbert
Phil Tuite
Aideen Tully
Mary Tully
Catherine Tunney
Jarlath Tunney
Anne Tynan
Sinead Tynan
Jacqueline Tyrell

Kim Dewi Umemoto
Pauline Underwood

Patrick Vahey
Robert Van Den Berg
Ellen Van Der Munnik
Erna Van Goor
Bill Vandenberg
Olivia Varley
Danielle Verjus
Nathalie Vezier
Jettie Vije

Teresa Wadge
John Wallace
Patricia Wallace
Stephen Wallace
Simon Waller
Catriona Walsh
Avril Walsh
Catherine Walsh
Deborah Walsh
Catherine Walsh
Elizabeth Walsh
Geraldine Walsh
Jessie Walsh
Kathleen Walsh
Liam Walsh
Marie Walsh
Mary Walsh
Marie Walsh
Siobhan Walsh
William Walsh
Claire Walshe
Tamsin Walters
Ita Ward
Noel Wardick
Peter Warren
Rachel Watson
Steven Watt
Alan Waugh
Olivia Webley
Elizabeth Weight
Keith West
Elizabeth Westaway
Sheila Wharton
Margaret Whelan

Mary Whelan
Rowena Whelan
Sheila Whelan
Damian White
Dara White
Maeve White
Gordon White
Marion White
Noreen White
Patrick Whitmarsh
Jennifer Whyte
Jon Wilkinson
Bill Williams
Michael Williams
Rob Williams
Alison Williams
Ann Wilson
Nicola Wilson
Tamsin Wilson
Mary Wolfe
John Wood
Richard Woodward
Francis Woulfe
Andrew John Wren
Louise Wright
Rebecca Wrigley
Denise Wyer
Joan Wynne
Margaret Young

Jean Yuan

Deborah Zalman

Notes and references

Chapter 1

[1] M. Black *A Cause for Our Times: Oxfam, the First Fifty Years* Oxford: Oxford University Press 1992 p 159

[2] J. Gunther *Inside Africa* London: Hamish Hamilton 1955 p 4

[3] C. Hibbert *The Dragon Awakes* London: Penguin 1984 p 231

[4] J. S. Mill *On Liberty* [1859] London: Everyman 1964 p 73

[5] The new West African federation was named Nigeria at the suggestion (in a letter to *The Times*) of Flora Shaw, a cousin of George Bernard. She had spent her childhood in Kimmage Manor, which was sold to the Holy Ghosts in 1911.

[6] Gunther *op. cit.* p 732

[7] *Missionary Annals* Dublin: Holy Ghost Fathers July/August 1968.

[8] K. Doheny *No Hands But Yours: Memoirs of a Missionary* Dublin: Veritas 1997 p 53. Kevin Doheny and his brother Michael, both Holy Ghosts, appear and reappear in the early history of Concern.

[9] J. Horgan in *The Irish Times* 19 March 1968

[10] O. Mooney 'The Irish Holy Ghost Order's involvement in the Nigerian Civil War 1967–70' unpublished M.Litt thesis p 102

[11] J. A. Daly CSSp and A. G. Saville 'The History of Joint Church Aid' unpublished typescript 3 vols 1971 p 84. This extraordinarily painstaking book was written by a Holy Ghost Father and a representative of the World Council of Churches immediately after the ending of the civil war, at the request of the Joint Church Aid committee. To give a sense of the detail, the chapter describing Africa Concern's activities is No. 54 and runs from page 843 to page 888. It includes quotes from letters no longer in Concern's archives. I am grateful to the late Fr Jimmy Dunne, archivist of the Holy Ghost Provincialiate in Dublin, for allowing me access to one of the very few copies extant of this valuable work.

[12] F. Forsyth *The Making of an African Legend: The Biafra Story* revised ed. London: Penguin 1977 p 210

[13] Daly and Saville *op. cit.* p 166

[14] 'Kwashiorkor' means 'first-second'. It typically strikes when the first child is weaned as the second is expected, and the newly weaned child is unable to cope with the starchy adult diet.

[15] M. Draper *Shadows: Airlift in Biafra and Nigeria 1967–70* Aldershot: Hikoki Publications 1999 p 135

[16] Forsyth *op. cit.* p 203

[17] E. Staunton 'The case of Biafra: Ireland and the Nigerian civil war' *Irish Historical Studies* vol xxxi no 124 Nov 1999 pp 520–21

[18] See A. Finucane 'The changing role of voluntary organisations' in K. Cahill (ed) *A Framework for Survival* New York: Basic Books 1993 p 180

[19] Daly and Saville *op. cit.* p 740

[20] Just at the time Seán Hopkins went to Amsterdam to buy the ship for Africa Concern some £800,000 had been raised in Holland for Biafran relief, following a dramatic documentary on Dutch television. When Seán's arrival was reported on the evening TV news, this seemed an obvious place for the organisers to start spending the money. Extraordinary events like this reinforced Africa Concern's sense of the rightness of their mission. Mensen en Nood was part of Caritas Internationalis.

[21] Daly and Saville op. cit. p 78

[22] C. S. Andrews *Man of No Property* Cork: Mercier Press 1982 p 275

[23] Mooney, p 103. In line with this dismissive attitude, the Irish government significantly underestimated the amount of money Africa Concern had at its disposal. In a memo of February 1969 a confidential estimate put the Joint Biafra Famine Appeal's fund at £278,000 (itself twice the government's contribution). However, the annual accounts for the year ending 30 June 1969 showed that Africa Concern had received £400,000 from the Joint Biafra Famine Appeal and a further £60,000 from outside sources. These figures were comfortably exceeded the following year.

[24] Daly and Saville *op. cit.* p 861

[25] *Ibid.* p 851

[26] *Ibid.* p 898

[27] J. de St Jorre *The Nigerian Civil War* London: Hodder and Stoughton 1972 p 404

Chapter 2

[1] T. Vaux *The Selfish Altruist* London: Earthscan 2002 p 70

[2] R. Challis *Sowing the Seeds: The History of Gorta* Dublin: Gorta 1986 p 28

[3] M. Black *op. cit.* pp 155–60

[4] The St Lô story is described in P. Gaffney *Healing Amid the Ruins* Dublin: A. & A. Farmar 1999.

[5] During and after the civil war Michael Fingleton had been in Nigeria, first in Lagos and then in the east, administering the Catholic bishops' funds there.

[6] The memorandum and articles of the new company were certified on 8 December 1972. The subscribers were: Seán MacCormac, R. A. Morgan, Rev. Ivan Briggs, J. O'Toole CSSp, Deirdre Morley, Nóirín Kennedy, Donnacha Ó Cinnéide, Eanna Johnson and Michael Doheny CSSp. John O'Loughlin Kennedy witnessed the signatures. The Minister issued a special licence that the word 'Limited' could be omitted.

Chapter 3

[1] C. Moorhead *Dunant's Dream: War, Switzerland and the History of the Red Cross*

London: HarperCollins 1998 p 120

[2] Figures from UNHCR *The State of the World's Refugees: Fifty Years of Humanitarian Action* Oxford: Oxford University Press 2000 Annex 3 pp 310–11

[3] The Spanish have not been given sufficient credit for re-inventing guerrilla (partisan) warfare during the Napoleonic wars, and, at the end of the century, designing the only effective military response.

[4] T. Pakenham *The Boer War* pb London: Futura 1982 p xvii

[5] A. Solzhenitsyn *The Gulag Archipelago* vol. 2 pb London: Fontana 1976 p 17. A great advantage, as the Germans later found, of imprisoning one's own people as opposed to foreigners was that the International Red Cross was paralysed, since it had no mandate to intervene in internal matters.

[6] J. Steinbeck *The Grapes of Wrath* London: Heinemann 1939. Chap. 22 onwards classically describes the life in Weedpatch Camp (officially Arvin Federal Government Camp).

[7] H. Marcuse *Legacies of Dachau: The Uses and Abuses of a Concentration Camp 1933–2001* Cambridge: Cambridge University Press 2001 p 26. 'Arbeit Macht Frei' means 'Work brings freedom'.

[8] W. Shawcross *The Quality of Mercy: Cambodia, Holocaust and Modern Conscience* New York: Simon and Schuster 1984 pp 225-6

[9] P. Gourevitch *We wish to inform you that tomorrow we will be killed with our families* pb London: Picador 2000 pp 270-1

[10] *Loc. cit.*

[11] F. Azeze *Unheard Voices* Addis Ababa: Addis Ababa University Press 1998 p 200

[12] Concern newsletter spring 1987

[13] M. Roseman *The Past in Hiding* London: Allen Lane 2000 p 99

[14] T. B. Macaulay 'Lord Clive' in *Historical Essays*

[15] P. Moon (ed.) *The Transfer of Power 1942–7* vol viii London: HMSO 1979 pp 293–304

[16] Quoted in J. Heitzman and R. L. Worden (eds) *Bangladesh: A Country Study* Washington: Federal Research Division 1989 p 29

[17] *The Irish Times* 7 June 1971

[18] J. Iman *Of Blood and Fire: The Untold Story of Bangladesh's War of Independence* translated by Mustafizur Rahman 2nd ed Dhaka: Dhaka University Press 1998. This passionate diary of the events of 1970 by a broadcaster and writer describes the effects of the army's aggressive government: a curfew, the constant harrassing of broadcasters and university teachers, the lists of banned books, and the replacement of Hundu street names with Muslim ones. Since her son was, quite rightly, suspected of being a member of the Freedom Fighters, the author's husband and second son were picked up and tortured for several days. The intense fear and hatred of the Biharis is a common theme of the diary.

[19] This was more demanding than it might sound: a typical canteen meal of the day was meat and two vegetables followed by a solid pudding of some sort, washed down with tea.

[20] In February 1971 Africa Concern restored relations with the Nigerian govern-

ment by an unusually formal letter of agreement between the Nigerian ambassador and chairman Vincent Grogan. However, it was not until the board meeting of 26 August 1971 that a board vote somewhat patronisingly declared that 'we should continue the practice of consulting with governments in countries which we are aiding or preparing to aid. We should also keep our Department of Foreign Affairs advised about large projects contemplated or in hand.'

²² A. Finucane *op. cit.*

Chapter 4

¹ M. Harris, overseas operations director of Oxfam 1970–84, quoted in M. Black *op. cit.* p xxii

² D. Levine *Wax and Gold* Chicago: Chicago University Press 1965 p 232

³ K. Doheny *No Hands but Yours: Memoirs of a Missionary* Dublin: Veritas 1997 pp 102–3

⁴ Azeze *op. cit.* pp 40–44.

⁵ A. Sen *Poverty and Famines—An Essay on Entitlement and Deprivation* pb Oxford: Oxford University Press 1982 chap. 7

⁶ R. Kapuscinski *The Emperor* pb London: Pan 1983 pp 151–162

⁷ UNHCR *Handbook for Emergencies* 2nd ed Geneva: UNHCR 2000 pp 28–30

⁸ W. Shawcross *The Quality of Mercy: Cambodia, Holocaust and Modern Conscience* New York: Simon and Schuster 1984 p 240

⁹ In his evidence to the UK Select Committee on Overseas Development in 1978 Aengus Finucane expressed himself as 'strongly opposed' to such ear-marking schemes. 'It certainly helps to foster greater awareness,' he conceded, 'but it also inhibits efficiency tremendously. The idea of fostering a particular child as a project is the extreme example of it. But I do not think that is a good idea. I am not in favour of it.'

Chapter 5

¹ Council minutes, February 1977

² See for instance the *Irish Independent* 5, 6 and 7 May 1976

³ During the period 1968–98 Africa Concern and Concern spent 10 per cent of its total income on 'non-field' activities, which includes all fundraising, administration and development education (see Appendix 2).

⁴ *Trócaire: The First Ten Years* Dublin: Trócaire 1983. Only two of the 26 Catholic dioceses did not take part in the Lenten Fast.

⁵ In his letter John O'Loughlin Kennedy asked rhetorically 'Did Schweitzer set out to make a "significant impact"—did Shanahan?' These were interesting role models. Albert Schweitzer, who died in 1965, was a German theologian who famously established a leper colony in Gabon. The colony was subsequently criticised for its primitive medical arrangements. Bishop Shanahan was the pioneering Holy Ghost missionary in Nigeria between 1902 and 1931.

⁶ After many years with Concern Margaret O'Keefe joined UNHCR.

[7] Concern newsletter autumn 1980

[8] Paddy Maguinness tells a story of how he was about to receive a substantial donation around this time. Just before signing the cheque, the donor explained how glad he was to be giving the money to Concern, and not that dreadful Trócaire crowd which had just had such a bad fraud!

[9] However, for Anne O'Mahony, who volunteered at this time, the publicity was a blessing in disguise, for at least everyone knew exactly what Concern was!

[10] Concern newsletter summer 1983

Chapter 6

[1] Michael Buerk's opening to Mohamed Amin's first film on the 1984 Ethiopian famine. Quoted in P. Harrison and R. Palmer *News out of Africa* London: Hilary Shipman 1986 p 122

[2] T. Kelly *Terina: Diary of a Hostage in Ethiopia* Dublin: Wolfhound Press 1984 p 15

[3] Given the carefully preserved folk memory of the Irish famine of 1845–9 it is curious to discover that 'even among the elderly there was little mention of earlier famines. The Great Famine of 1888–92 was a distant memory. However an old woman from Lasta and two old men from Dese recalled their fathers speaking about it.' A. Pankhurst *Resettlement and Famine in Ethiopia: The Villagers' Experience* Manchester: Manchester Univeristy Press 1992 p 29

[4] Azeze *op. cit.* pp 184, 173

[5] Pankhurst *op. cit.* p 28

[6] K. Jansson, M. Harris and A. Penrose *The Ethiopian Famine* London: Zed Books 1987 pp 133–5

[7] B. Geldof *Is That It?* London: Penguin 1986 pp 269–70

[8] A Band Aid background information paper issued in February 1987 reported that the UK had donated $40 million, the US $25 million and 'Eire' $8.5 million.

[9] Bruno Bettelheim 'Eichmann: the system, the victims' in *Surviving the Holocaust* London: Fontana 1986 p 135

[10] D. Purcell and P. Langan *Ethiopia: The Dark Hunger* Dublin: Magill 1984 p 86

[11] Inter-agency rivalry was common in every environment. Because they were always housed together, and usually went out together, Concern staff were sometimes regarded as stand-offish by other agencies.

[12] Purcell and Langan *op. cit.* p 8

[13] The oral poets shrewdly noted the obvious response 'Even children and old women/Have claimed they are suckling mothers'. In some areas the very act of weighing the child was regarded as humiliating: 'Oh Famine, I saw how mean you could be/My children were weighed like grain/ But they did not benefit/If they had I would have been spared the indignity of begging.' Azeze *op. cit.* pp 203–4

[14] Purcell and Langan *op. cit.* pp 41–2

[15] *Ibid.* p 83

[16] In conversation with the author, December 2001

[17] Azeze *op. cit.* p 200. Another verse comments on how strange it was to see the

white women wearing sandals, the traditional footwear of priests.

[18] R. McClean *A Cross Shared: Ethiopia–Derry* Ballyshannon: Donegal Democrat p 15

[19] *Ibid.* p 16

[20] *Ibid.* pp 52–3

[21] *Ibid.* McClean's recipe for a successful camp is worth recording: 'The first priority is clean water. Second is good sanitation. Third is proper food. Fourth is adequate shelter. Only fifth comes medicine and medical expertise, because if you don't have the first four priorities your patients will die from a variety of diseases, despite your best medicines.' (p 57)

[22] *Ibid.* pp 54, 59

[23] Quoted in Pankhurst *op. cit.* p 15. For his detailed study of the villagers' experience of the resettlement programme Dr Pankhurst picked one of the areas, Ketto, in which Concern worked.

[24] Pankhurst *op. cit.* p 17

[25] Azeze *op. cit.* pp 190–1

[26] Geldof *op. cit.* pp 424–5

[27] Pankhurst *op. cit.* p 121

[29] Concern newsletter August 1980

[31] Pankhurst *op. cit.* p 270

[32] She was also subjected to some indoctrination in respect of Concern's role in the resettlement camps. Many in Tigray believed that part of the motivation for the resettlement programme was to remove potential trouble-makers from rebellious areas.

Chapter 7

[1] Finucane *op. cit.*

[2] R. Bonner 'A Reporter at Large—Famine' in *The New Yorker* 13 March 1989 pp 85-101

[3] Scenes of trainloads of starving people arriving in all the modern banality of a railway station inevitably reminded Western onlookers of the Jews arriving at the camps of the Final Solution. As the newsletter put it: 'The cause may be different, the location far away, but the intensity of the suffering is still obscene.'

[4] Concern newsletter winter 1988

[5] To put this into a local perspective—at this time the greater Dublin area had a population of just over one million people, of whom between 25 and 30 died every day.

[6] Bonner *op. cit.* pp 96-7

[7] P. Harrison and R. Palmer *News out of Africa* London: Hilary Shipman 1986 p 100

[8] B. Parsons, H. Byrne and A. El Tom 'An Evaluation of Concern's Programme in Sudan' unpublished March/April 1989

[9] C. Elliott 'The Work of Concern in Bangladesh: An Evaluation' unpublished

1986.

[10] Before the civil war Raymond Kennedy had run classes in Nigeria for new parish priests explaining about such things, which of course had formed no part of the seminary curriculum.

[11] Volunteers on the whole have always tended to be practical and extrovert rather than intellectual; so when the 1988 evaluation of the Sudan programme noted 'the absence of any books or publications on the Sudan or on or in Arabic in any of the houses where volunteers lived', this would not have surprised anyone familiar with other fields.

[12] The authorities' suspicions were no doubt accelerated by the constant stream of media people who found near Muglad a convenient airstrip. As the only Westerners on the spot Concern staff were regularly expected to drop everything and brief whoever arrived on the latest horror stories from the camps, as well as much else besides.

[13] The very poorest are usually so poor that there is simply nothing on to which a development programme could fasten. Government pressure nowadays tends to push development projects into somewhat more favoured areas, as does the donor pressure for both absorption and sustainability.

Chapter 8

[1] P. Gourevitch *We wish to inform you that tomorrow we will be killed with our families* pb London: Picador 2000 p 292

[2] WHO *Small Arms and Global Health Geneva: World Health Organisation* 2001 p 2. This paper was the WHO's contribution to the UN Conference on Illicit Trade in Small Arms and Light Weapons.

[3] The 1911 *Encyclopaedia Britannica*, under the heading 'Torture' reported that the article was of historic interest only, since states no longer engaged in such practices (review of biography of Helen Bamber, *Times Literary Supplement* 15 April 1999).

[4] These events are vividly described in M. Dobbs *Down with Big Brother: The Fall of the Soviet Union* London: Bloomsbury 1997

[5] F. Stewart, V. FitzGerald and associates *War and Under-development Vol 1 The Economic and Social Consequences of Conflict* Oxford: Oxford University Press 2001 pp 2–3

[6] E. Mysliwiec *Punishing the Poor: The International Isolation of Kampuchea* Oxford: Oxfam 1988 p 5

[7] D. P. Chandler *Brother Number One: A political biography of Pol Pot* Oxford: Westview 1992 p 123

[8] UNHCR *The State of the World's Refugees: Fifty Years of Humanitarian Action* Oxford: UNHCR 2000 p 82

[9] *Op. cit.* pp 81–2

[10] Concern special newsletter December 1979

[11] Quoted in W. Shawcross *The Quality of Mercy: Cambodian Holocaust and Modern Conscience* New York Simon and Schuster 1984 p 178

[12] S. Peterson *Me Against My Brother: At War in Somalia, Sudan and Rwanda* London: Routledge 2000 pp 13–15

[13] *Op. cit.* p 38

[14] *Op. cit.* p 52

[15] M. Robinson *A Voice for Somalia* Dublin: O'Brien Press 1992 pp 16–17

[16] J. Borton et al *The International Response to Conflict and Genocide: Lessons from the Rwanda Experience Study III* Copenhagen: Steering Committee of the Joint Evaluation of Emergency Assistance to Rwanda 1996 Chapter 4 part 1

[17] J. Drumtra *Life After Death: Suspicion and Reintegation in Post-Genocide Rwanda* New York: US Committee for Refugees 1998

[18] This was not the first prison Concern had built. Similar circumstances in one of the camps on the Cambodian border had led to a similar response. In 1986 Aengus Finucane sent a note to the finance department: 'Please make 25,000 Birr available from our contingency fund for a community health centre in Addis. The health centre is in an Addis prison which houses political prisoners. An average of 450 prisoners a day are treated. It is a very sensitive matter and the project is not one which can receive any publicity.'

Chapter 9

[1] T. Zeldin *An Intimate History of Humanity* pb ed London: Mandarin 1995 p 253

[2] R. Brauman 'The Médicins sans Frontières experience' in K. Cahill (ed) *A Framework for Survival* New York: BasicBooks 1993 pp 202–20

[3] Zeldin *op. cit.* chapter 14

[4] Based on Alex Rondos 'Compromising to Achieve' in J. B. Schneewind (ed) *Giving: Western Ideas of Philanthropy* Indianopolis: Indianapolis University Press 1996 pp 199–200

[5] *Business and Finance* June 1991

[6] When they got there they discovered that although they were well paid by local standards, they were earning less than their international counterparts. The explanation for this was that they were merely on secondment from their home job, which was being kept for them, unlike that of the international expatriates. Although this was common agency practice, there was some grumbling, often stimulated by equality-minded expatriates.

[7] And it was of course true that a tiny number of local staff have been discovered to have exploited Conern's seemingly unending wealth. The vulnerability of locals to pressure is a universal concern—for instance, in Ireland gardaí do not serve in their local area.

Chapter 10

[1] *To The Bitter End: The Diaries of Victor Klemperer 1942–45* Translated by Martin Chalmers London: Weidenfeld & Nicolson 1999 p 12

[2] Nicholas Stockton of Oxfam, quoted in T. Vaux *The Selfish Altruist* London: Earthscan 2001 p 77

Index

Addis, Willa 180
Afghanistan 205
Africa Concern 20, 21, 23, 26, 29, 33, 39, 79
—aid delivery 21–3, 26–7
—founded 15, 24
—other activities 24-5, 29, 33, 34-5, 79
—subscriptions to 15, 21, 24
—religious status of 37
Agency for Personal Service Overseas (APSO) 84–5, 160
Allied Irish Banks 39
aid programmes (*see also* NGOs)
—funding of 31, 188
—dilemmas of: 140, 188, 203; exit strategy 31, 188; exit, voice or loyalty 60, 140–1, 156
—loss of respect for 172
—management of 69–70, 183–4; limits to expenditure on administration 84
al Bashir, Ahmad 160
Al–Mahdi, Sadiq 151, 160
Amin, Lovely 210
Amin, Mohamed 128, 130, 156
Andrews, David 173, 174
Andrews, Todd 26
Angola 163, 192, 204, 206
Ansari, Imran 203
Arnold, Tom 212
Asfaw, Tiruwork 68, 133

Band Aid 129, 140, 141, 187
Bangladesh 35–6, 38, 40, 45–64, 77, 81, 88–9, 93, 95, 146, 188, 195, 206, 210
—*char* people of 46
—floods 46, 150–1, 192, 195
—freedom fighters 50: Sher–e–Bangla hospital 61–2
—programme sites: Dhaka 51, 57, 95; Demra 57, 95; Chittagong 57; Dimla 203; Dinajpur 57; Khulna 58; Mirpur 57; Mymensingh 58; Saidpur 52–3, 57
—population of 46
—progamme evaluation 157–160
—tubewells 155
—vagrants' homes 58–60
Barnes, Joe 50, 168
Barrett, Joan 50
Barre, Siad 170
Begg, David 7, 199, 200–3, 205, 212
Belgian International Air Services (BIAS) 27
Bettelheim, Bruno 44, 129
Biafra 2, 11–28 *passim,* 32
—genocide fears 12, 14, 16, 28
—Uli airport 18, 22–3, 27
Biggs, Rev. Ivan 16, 39
Biharis 41, 47, 49, 52–3
Bird, Charlie 63
Bono 136
BRAC 63, 158, 169, 195
Bread for the World 63
British Overseas Development Administration 147
Broderick, Ann 142
Brosnan, Fr Michael 78
Browne, Joan Helena 50
Browne, Vincent, 63

Buerk, Michael 128, 130, 156
Bunworth, Ciúnas 93, 129
Burke, Liam 63
Burundi 4, 5, 6, 157, 176, 192, 206
—Bujumbura 4
—Ministries of 5–6
—Concern programmes in 6–7
Butler, Fr Billy 22
Butler, Jill 148
Byrne, Brendan 37
Byrne, Hugh 160, 189
Byrne, Fr Kevin 171
Byrne, Fr Tony 22
Byrnes, Mary 50

Caffrey, Ethna 61
CAFOD 63, 129
Cambodia 2, 165, 170, 188, 192, 206, 210, 212
—Khmer Rouge 166, 210
—refugees from 161–70
camps, prison and refugee 41–5
—concentration: Cuba 42, Boer 42, Gulag 42, German 41, 42–3, 44
—impact on local economy 43, 44
—medical problems 134
—psychology of inmates 44–5
—refugee and IDP: Salt Lake, Calcutta 43, 50; Thailand 43–4, 167–70; Weedpatch (USA) 42; Wollo (Ethiopia) 44; Zaire (Congo) 44
CARE 129
Caritas Internationalis 16, 22, 25
Casey, Bishop Eamon 71
Casey, Irene 51–2
Chambers, Monica 61
Chaudhury, Rab 51
Chechnya 172
Chompala, Sr Theodora 67

Christmas Fast 72–3, 190–1, 147
—origins of 20–1
Coen, Mary 142
Cold War, impact of 124, 163–5, 170
—proxy wars 124, 151
colonialism 9
Columbanus, Knights of 16, 19, 37
Columcille, The 1, 24, 33–6, 39, 144
Comhlámh 148
Common Market (*see* European Union)
Concern 39, 84, 129
—emergency/development roles 29, 63–4, 70–1, 79, 84–5, 95–6, 154–5, 161, 197, 204–5
—field directors 63–4, 70–1, 73
—field/head office relations 38, 63–4, 83–4, 88, 188
—fundraising activities 71–3, 80, 84, 147, 190, 191
—Handcrafts 80
—houses, in the field 55, 126
—income and expenditure 81, 87, 88, 91, 92, 97, 147, 189–90, 193, 196–7
—Northern Ireland office 147, 190–1
—offices: Lower Grand Canal Street 39, Lower Camden Street 39, Northumberland Road 15, Pembroke Road 39
—organisation: Council 80–1; Executive Committee 88; members 80; office 83, 196
—philosophy 60, 140, 145–6, 154–5, 181, 185, 187, 203
—small projects 40, 82
—staff: local 53, 158–60, 194; head office 72, 81, 83, 185, 202–3;
—strategic review 204–5

—USA, and 83, 92, 97, 193, 197–8
—volunteers: 40, 148, 174, 184;
    attitudes of 53–7, 187; criticised
    84, 158–9; health and safety of
    54 ; kidnapped 125–6, 151–2
Congo 178, 179, 206
Connolly, Séamus 79, 83
Conroy, Moira 125, 130, 131
Considine, Mary 171
Convery, Sheila 146
CORR 63
Corristine, John and Margaret, 76
Courtney, Mick 23
Coyle, Bernie 90
Coyne, Mary 90
Cracknell, Basil 189
Crane, Patrick 20
Crowe, Paul 79, 150
Crudge, Dolores 69
Cuba 41
Cummins, Anne 55

Dalzell, Howard 141, 196
de Paul, St Vincent 184
Delville, Max 6
Devlin, Dorothy 58
Dimbleby, Jonathan 66, 67, 179
—film 'The Unknown Famine'
    67–9
Dinka 160
Doheny, Fr Kevin
—in Biafra 13, 22
—heads CRDA in Ethiopia 66, 68
Doheny, Fr Michael 79, 83, 190,
    197
—Chief Executive 90–1
—films of 72, 147
—influence of 62
—writings quoted 37–8, 52, 61–2,
    77–8, 169
Doherty, Paddy 135

Doyle, Dolores 50

East Pakistan (*see* Bangladesh)
El Tom, Abdullah 157, 160
Elliott, Prof. Charles 195
—evaluation of Bangladesh
    programme 158–60
Ennis, Anita 171
Eritrea 76, 125, 127, 149
—nationalists 75, 125, 144
Ethiopia 65–70, 124–43, 164, 206
European Union 5, 85, 187, 193,
    205
European Community Humanitar-
    ian Office (ECHO) 189

Fahey, Paddy 69
Fanning, Michael 134
Food and Agriculture Organisation
    (UN) 186
Farrelly, Fintan 93, 125, 126
Fay, Áine 212
Fingleton, Michael 34, 36, 37, 93,
    94
Finucane, Fr Aengus 23, 93, 129,
    145, 168, 173, 176
—in Bangladesh 53–64 *passim*, 88–
    9
—chief executive 94–7, 148–9
—ideas of 53, 71, 154, 158, 160,
    184–5, 194
—retirement 193–9
Finucane, Fr Jack 4, 7–8, 28, 171,
    176, 180, 188
—in Bangladesh 93
—in Ethiopia 70, 73–6, 126, 128,
    137–9, 142, 149, 160
FitzGerald, Garret 21
Fitzgerald, Maurice 31, 33, 36, 37
Fitzpatrick, Mags 54
Forsyth, Frederick 17, 22

Fryer, Pat 90

Garang, John 151
Geldof, Bob 128–9, 139
Gilsenan, Eileen 172
Goal 175, 190, 192
Gorta 84
Grameen Bank 158, 195
Grogan, Vincent 16, 25, 33, 38, 71
Guckian, Mary 16, 86
Gunther, John 9

Hailait, Laurent 6
Haile Selassie 66–8, 124–5, 137
Haiti 207
Hamilton, Richard 6
Hamlin fistula clinic 75, 76
Harrington, Essie 80
Hederman, Carmencita 144
Hennessy, Cathy 153
Hepburn, Audrey 172
HIV/AIDS 186, 192, 209
Holahan, Michael 90
Holocaust, images of 14, 133, 140,
    180
Holy Ghost Congregation 11, 12,
    13, 14, 74, 159, 194
—difficulties of, after the collapse
    of Biafra 32–3
—welfare formation 54–5, 74
Honduras 207
Houphouet–Boigny, Félix 17
Howell, P. J. 93, 146, 212
Humphreys, Mary 57, 79, 83

India 49–50
—Calcutta 50
International Committee of the
    Red Cross (ICRC) 23, 131, 172
Intervention Humanitaire
    Africaine 7

Iran 40
Iraq 192, 195
Ireland
—External Affairs and Concern
    26, 35
—social and economic change in
    85–6, 200
—government of 25
—Hierarchy of 15, 26, 30, 84
—secularisation in 83, 187
Irish Missionary Union 84
Irish Red Cross 29, 84
—hospital in St Lô 30–1
Irish Times, The 13, 48
Israel 135

Jackson, Bill 85
Jagoe, Val 16
Jamaica 40
Jenden, Penny 140
Johnson, Bishop William 92
Johnson, Eanna 212
Johnstone, Johnnie 148
Joint Biafra Famine Appeal 16, 18,
    27, 29
—Send One Ship campaign 18–20
Joint Church Aid 18, 23, 26, 27, 32,
    157

Kampuchea (*see* Cambodia)
Karamajong, famine 95
Keane, Neil 55
Keating, Eamon 196
Keating, Paul 22
Kelly, Bríd 136
Kelly, Terina 125–6
Kennedy, John O'Loughlin 9, 15,
    29, 37, 80, 85, 93
—executive director Africa
    Concern 21, 33, 34–9
Kennedy, Kay O'Loughlin 9, 15,

21, 29, 36, 37, 86, 146
Kennedy, Fr Raymond 9, 11, 14, 15,
 24, 25, 33, 85
—executive director Concern 37,
 39, 53, 55, 63, 68–9, 71, 73, 76,
 78, 82–3, 212
—general manager Africa Concern
 24–7, 35
—resignation 89–90
—in Inda/Bangladesh 38, 50
Kent, Mgr Bruce 90
Kenya 173, 174
Kierans, Peter 212
Kilcullen, Justin 167
Kilkenny, John 176
Kinahan, Sally-Anne 205
Kinsella, Susan 51–2
Korbach, SS 21
Korea 207
Korem 132
Kouchner, Bernard 184

Lalibela 65, 66, 127
Lane, Liz 54
Langan, Pat 131
Laos 167, 192, 207
Lehane, Fr Aidan 94–5
Liberia 207
Little, John 150
Little Sisters of the Assumption 39,
 146
Logical Framework matrix 188–9
Lovett, Marguerite 50
Lucey, Elaine 146

MacSorley, Dominic 44, 149, 170,
 177, 179, 180
Maguinness, Paddy 96, 147, 190,
 196
Maldah people of Bangladesh 57
Malhuret, Claude 140, 184

Markpress PR Agency 16
McAleese, Mary 212
McClean, Dr Ray 131–6
McCormack, Seán 16
McDonagh, Mike 153, 173, 175
McDonnell, Theresa 150–1, 189
McGrath, Paddy 20
McKee, Kate 50, 55
McLoughlin, Anne 125–6
McQuaid, John Charles 11
Médecins sans Frontières (MSF) 6,
 7, 140, 156, 175, 183–4
Mengistu, Colonel 125, 143
Menschen fur Menschen 141
Mensen in Nood 24
Mill, John Stuart 10
Miller, Auriol 5, 6
Miller, John 168
Miller, Phil 179
Missionary Annals 10, 28
Mobin, Mohammed 160, 188, 195
Moore, Judge Kingsmill 16, 36
Moriarty, Kay 50
Morley, Rosary 90
Mozambique 149, 192, 207, 209
Mullin, Harry 22
Murphy, Mary 7

Nevin, Donal 16
NGOs 5, 6, 179, 189, 204
—local 158, 160, 195, 197, 203, 205,
 211
—relations with local powers 144,
 154, 172
Nigeria 9, 11, 159, 194
Nolan, Liam 69
Nuer 160
Nyerere, Julius 17, 149

Ó Murchú, Dónal 82
O'Boyle, Phena 212

O'Brien, Sr Elizabeth 51, 53, 56–7
O'Brien, Philip 93, 160
O'Connor, Patrick 191
Office of Foreign Disaster
    Assistance 156
O'Higgins, Tom 212
Ojukwu, Colonel 25
O'Leary, Sheelagh 58
O'Loughlin, Maura 50
O'Mahony, Anne 133, 168, 181
O'Mahony, Margaret 173
O'Morchoe, David 95
Oromo 71, 143
O'Shea, Kathleen 50
O'Sullivan, Fr Donal 17
O'Sullivan, Patrick 50
O'Toole, Fr Jimmy 79
Oxfam 63, 84, 129, 178, 202, 205

Pakistan 35, 47, 195
—1971 famine appeal 36, 49
Parsons, Brendan 160
Patten, Chris 147
Pearce, Brian 69
Peru 40
Peterson, Scott 172
Place, Valerie 176
Pol Pot 166, 170
Port Harcourt 12, 16, 18
Prendergast, Fr Joe 22
Purcell, Deirdre 45, 63

Quinn, Fiona 142

Rahman, Sheikh Mujibur 48, 63,
    131–2
Reagan, Ronald 138
Reynolds, Eileen 90
Robinson, President Mary
—visits Baidoa 173–5
Rohingyas 89

Rwanda 176–82, 196–7, 204, 208
—Hutu–Tutsi relations 157, 176–7

Salt Lake, Calcutta 43, 50
São Tomé 21, 22, 23, 24
Sargent, Peter 6
Save the Children Fund 125, 126,
    129, 180
Scally, Suzanne 77
Searight, Joy 50
Secours Catholique 63
Secours Populaire Français 141
Sen, Amartya 140
Shirina, Augustine 150
Shorr, Irwin 53
Siad Barre 170
Sierra Leone 82, 163, 186, 204, 208
Simpson, Vivian, MP 16
Somalia 124, 149, 154, 164, 165,
    170–6, 208
—Baidoa 171–2, 173–4, 175
—Mogadishu 175, 176
South Africa 42
Spain, Kevin 171
SPLA 152
Srimangal 51, 53, 56
St Vincent de Paul Society 34
Staunton, Seán 50
Sudan 44, 151–4
—evaluation report 157, 160–2
—programmes: Khartoum 153,
    154, 167; Omdurman 152
Svea Atlantic 144, 145

Tanzania 92, 93, 149, 192, 208, 209
Tarbett, Alex 91–6
Teresa, Mother 37, 38, 62, 184
television, impact of 17, 128, 141,
    156, 179, 196
Thailand 93, 94, 149, 165, 167, 192
Thatcher, Margaret 138

Tindill, Dennis 84
Trócaire 63, 71, 72, 84, 91, 190, 201
—Lenten Campaign 72

Uganda 93, 192, 208
Uli airport 18, 22, 23
UNHCR 94, 167–8, 174
UNICEF 161, 172, 192
USAID 139, 161, 188
USSR 124, 163, 164

Vatican II 37
Viatores Christi 15
Vietnam 165, 167
volunteers (*see* Concern volunteers)
VSO 148

Walsh, Siobhán 198
war, as cause of underdevelopment
    163–5
War on Want 129
Whelan, Bishop Joseph 28, 33
Williams, Alan 39, 71, 72
World Council of Churches 22
World Food Programme (WFP)
    161, 208
World Vision 139, 155
World Wildlife Fund 185

Yemen Arab Republic 40, 68, 77–
    80, 93

Zaire (*see* Congo)